ANACHRONOPOLIS

THE TRAVELER

STAN LEE

MARK WAID

TOM PEYER

CHAD HARDIN

VOLUME TWO

Ross Richie - Chief Executive Officer

Matt Gagnon - Editor-in-Chief

Adam Fortier - VP-New Business

Wes Harris - VP-Publishing

Lance Kreiter - VP-Licensing & Merchandising

Chip Mosher - Sales & Marketing Director

Bryce Carlson - Managing Editor

Ian Brill - Editor

Dafna Pleban - Editor

Christopher Burns - Editor

Shannon Watters - Assistant Editor

Eric Harburn - Assistant Editor

Adam Staffaroni - Assistant Editor

Brian Latimer - Lead Graphic Designer

Stephanie Gonzaga - Graphic Designer

Phil Barbaro - Operations

Ivan Salazar - Marketing Manager

Devin Funches - Sales & Marketing Assistant

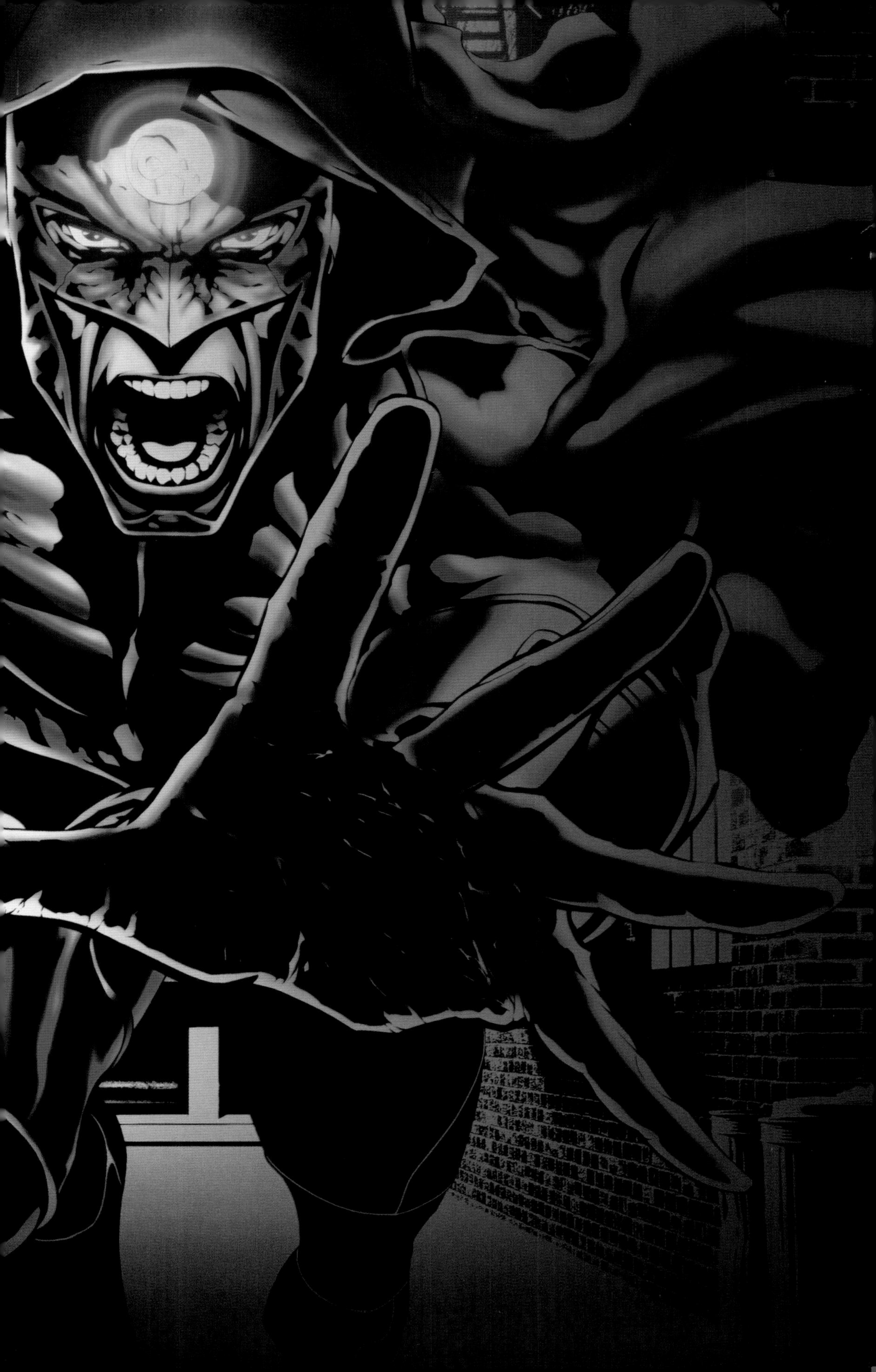

GRAND POOBAH
STAN LEE

WRITTEN BY
MARK WAID & TOM PEYER

ART BY
CHAD HARDIN

COLORS BY
CHRIS BECKETT

LETTERS BY
ED DUKESHIRE

COVER
SCOTT CLARK

GRAPHIC DESIGNER
BRIAN LATIMER
WITH DANIELLE KELLER

EDITOR
DAFNA PLEBAN

MANAGING EDITOR
BRYCE CARLSON

EDITOR-IN-CHIEF
MATT GAGNON

PUBLISHER
ROSS RICHIE

SPECIAL THANKS
GILL CHAMPION

BOOM! STUDIOS

Stan Lee's POW! ENTERTAINMENT

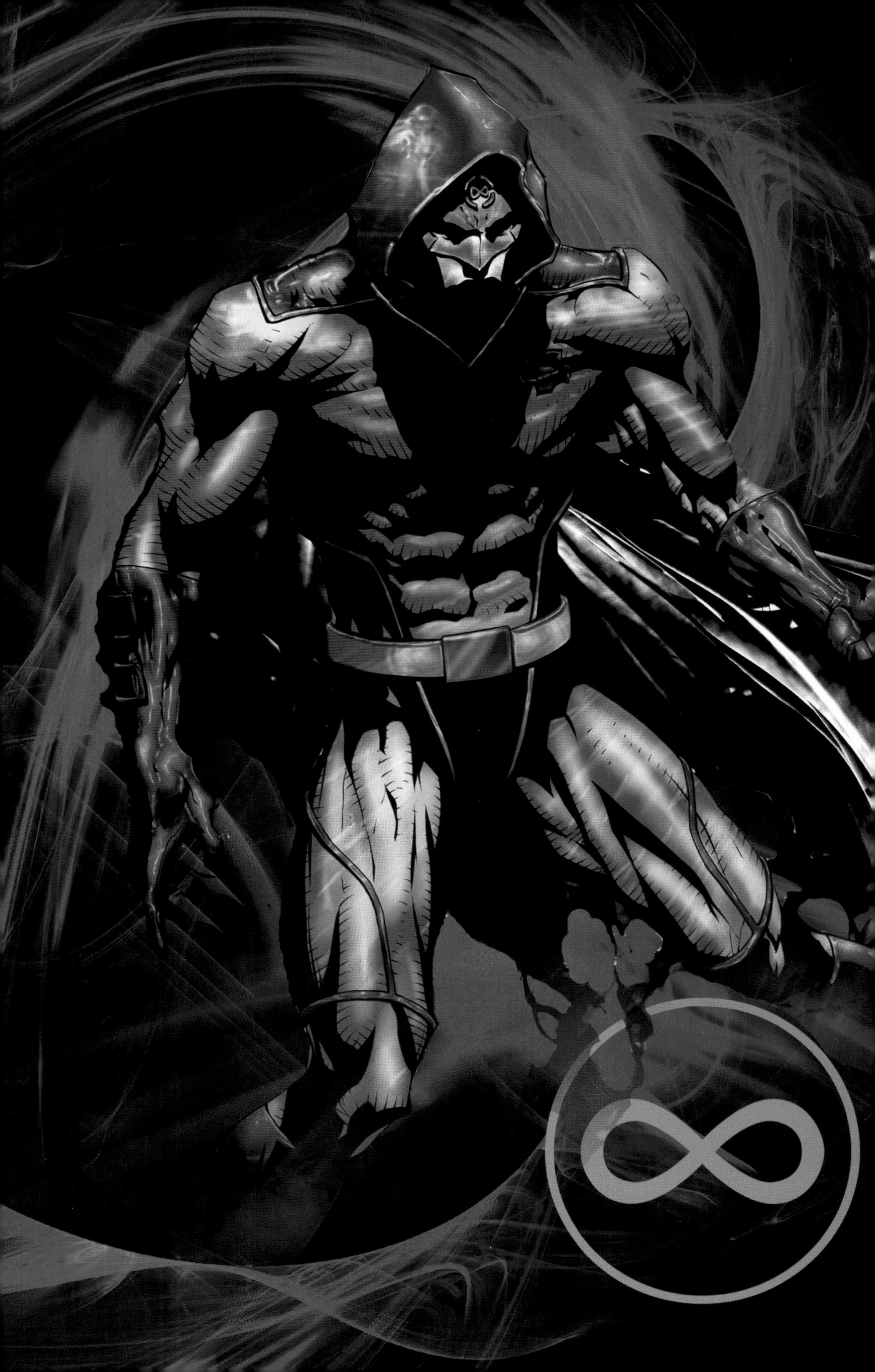

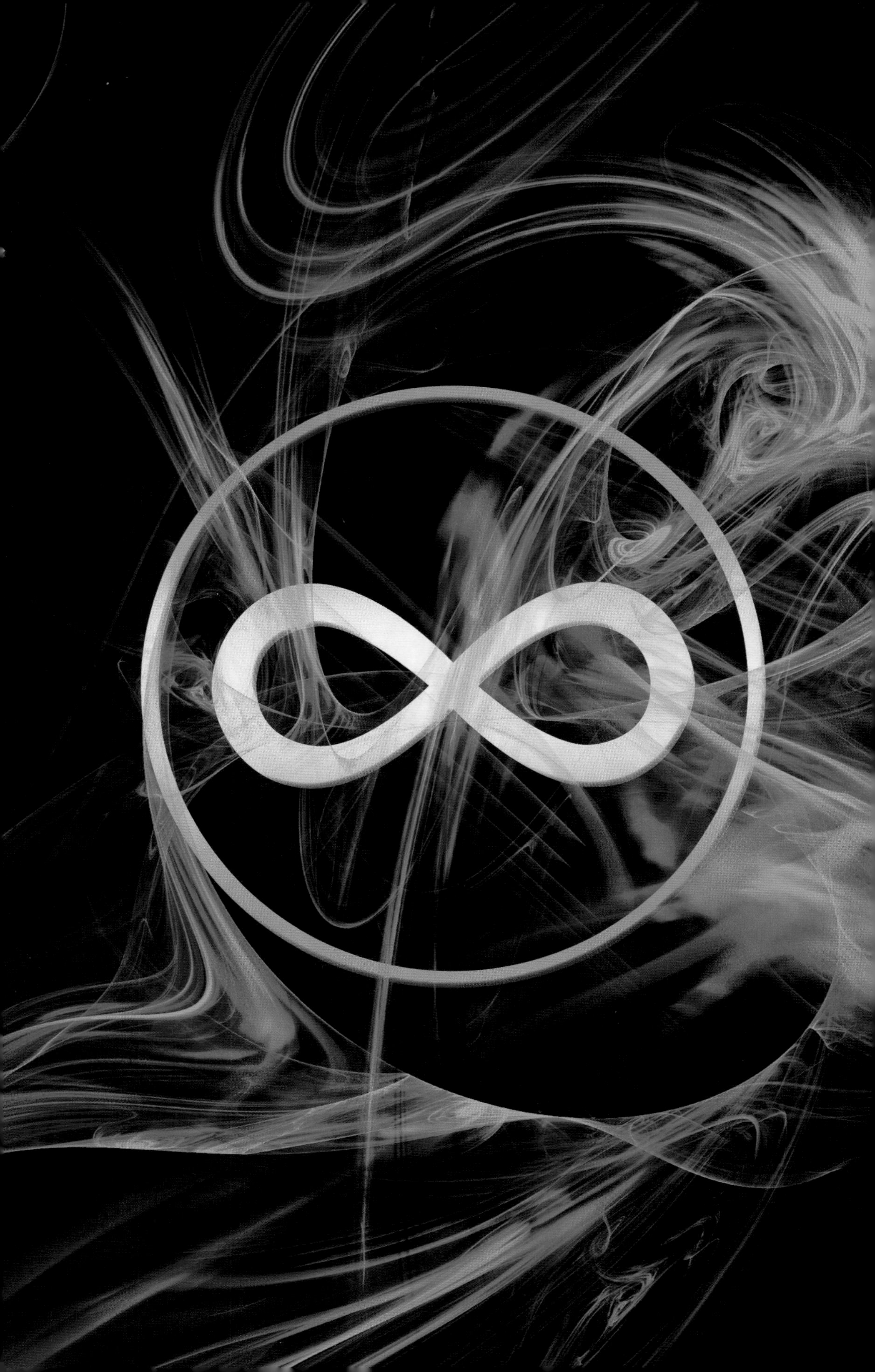

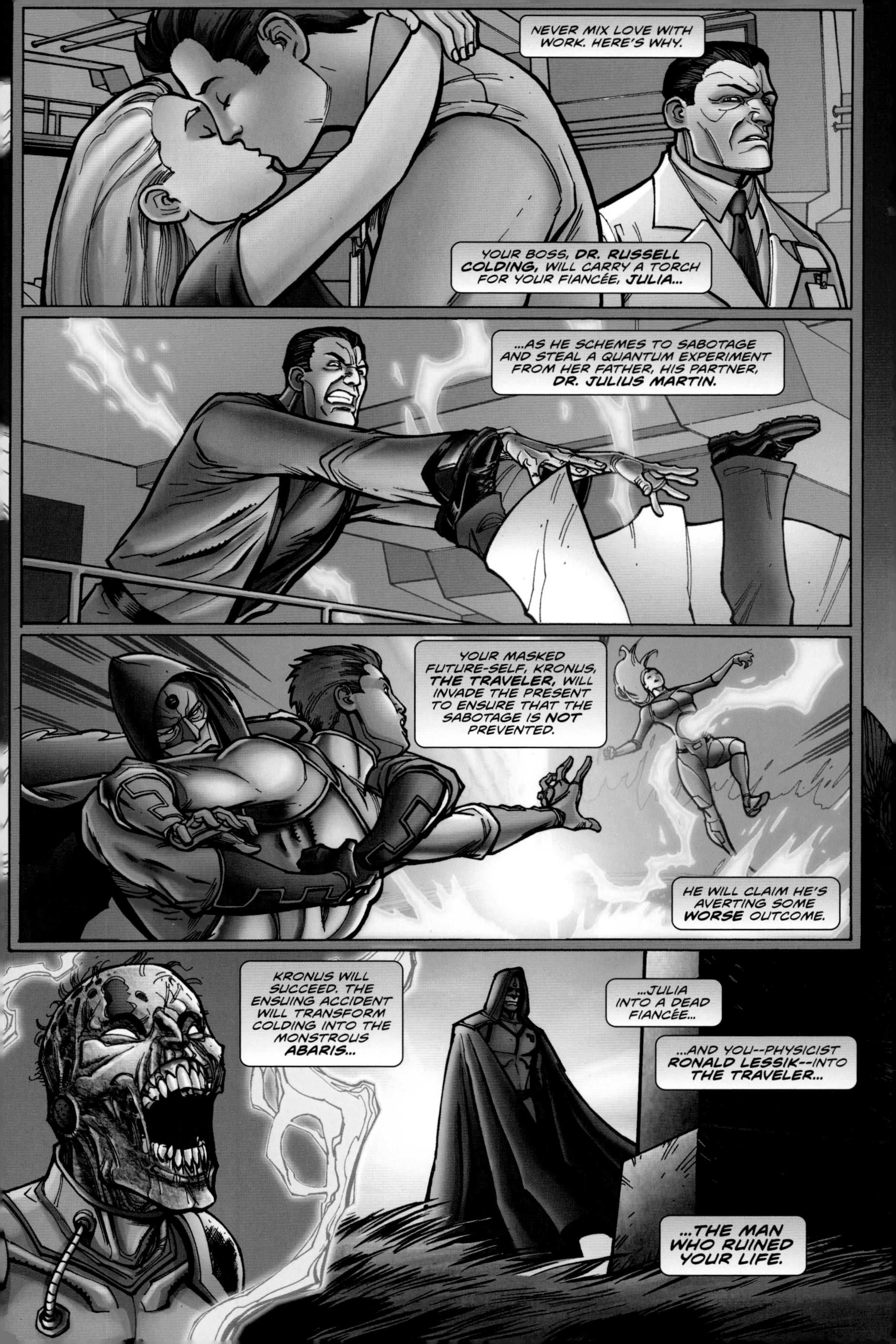
NEVER MIX LOVE WITH WORK. HERE'S WHY.
YOUR BOSS, DR. RUSSELL COLDING, WILL CARRY A TORCH FOR YOUR FIANCÉE, JULIA...
...AS HE SCHEMES TO SABOTAGE AND STEAL A QUANTUM EXPERIMENT FROM HER FATHER, HIS PARTNER, DR. JULIUS MARTIN.
YOUR MASKED FUTURE-SELF, KRONUS, THE TRAVELER, WILL INVADE THE PRESENT TO ENSURE THAT THE SABOTAGE IS NOT PREVENTED.
HE WILL CLAIM HE'S AVERTING SOME WORSE OUTCOME.
KRONUS WILL SUCCEED. THE ENSUING ACCIDENT WILL TRANSFORM COLDING INTO THE MONSTROUS ABARIS...
...JULIA INTO A DEAD FIANCÉE...
...AND YOU--PHYSICIST RONALD LESSIK--INTO THE TRAVELER...
...THE MAN WHO RUINED YOUR LIFE.

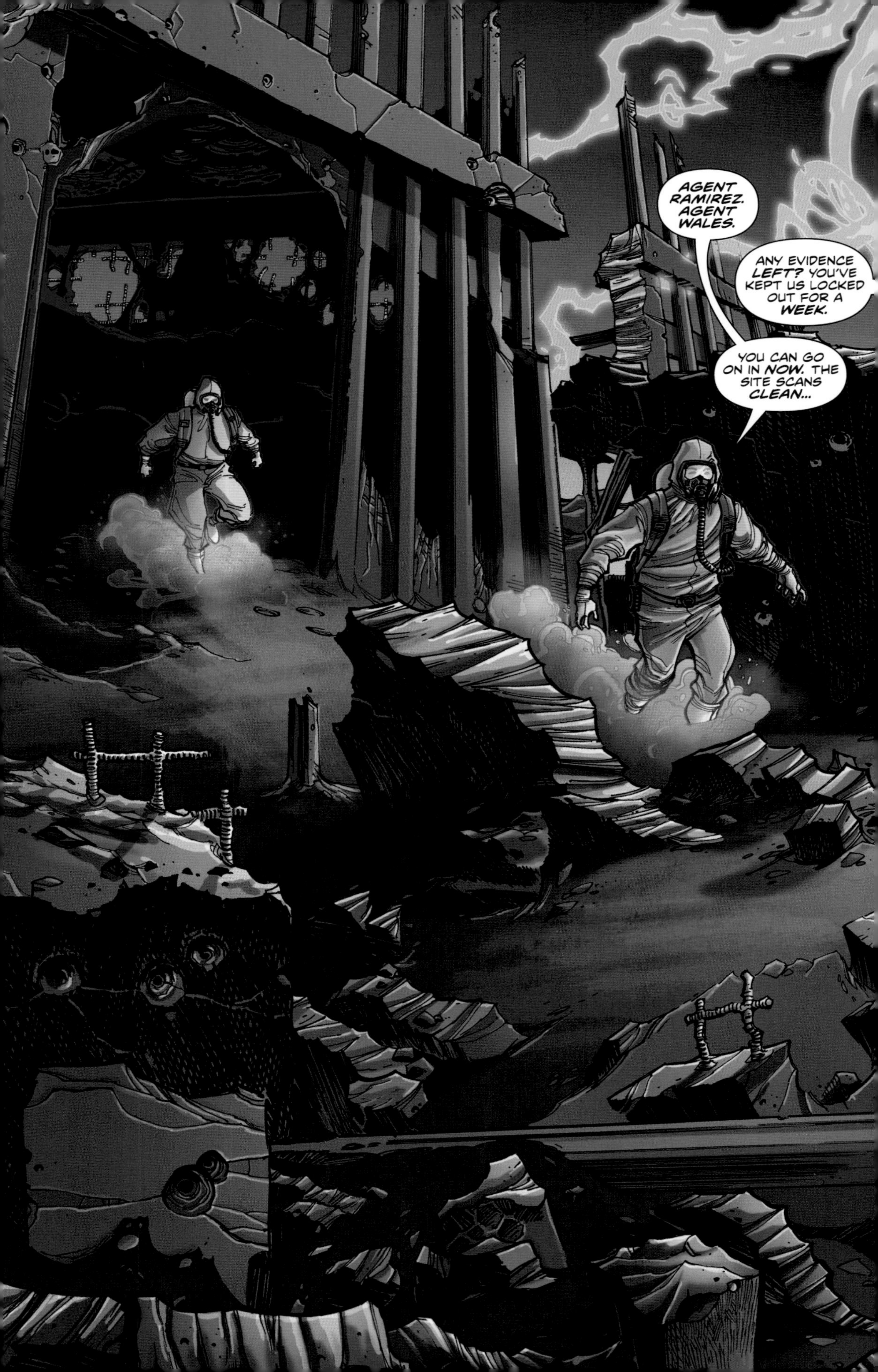
AGENT RAMIREZ. AGENT WALES.
ANY EVIDENCE LEFT? YOU'VE KEPT US LOCKED OUT FOR A WEEK.
YOU CAN GO ON IN NOW. THE SITE SCANS CLEAN...

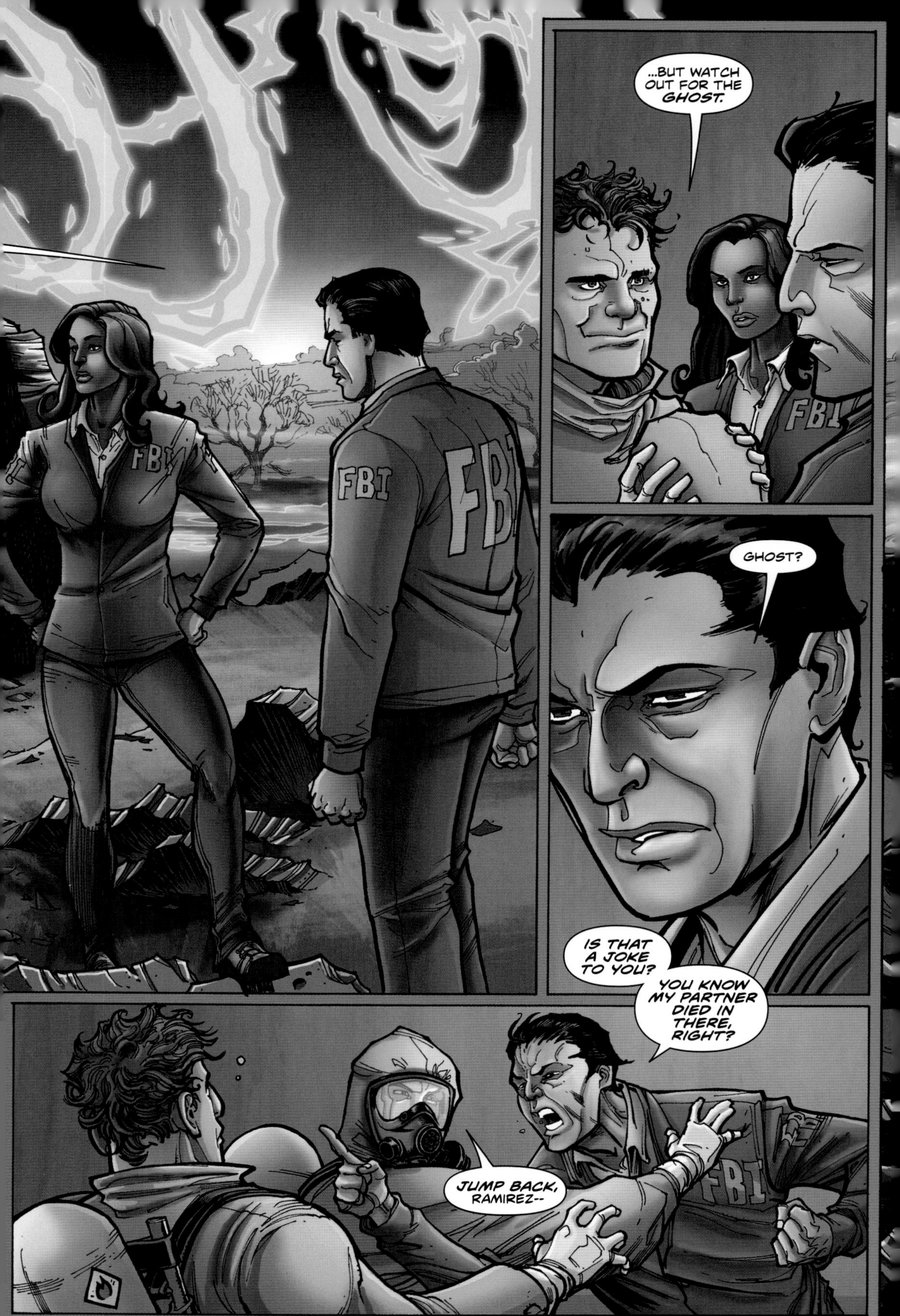
...BUT WATCH OUT FOR THE GHOST.
GHOST?
IS THAT A JOKE TO YOU?
YOU KNOW MY PARTNER DIED IN THERE, RIGHT?
JUMP BACK, RAMIREZ--

--THAT'S NOT WHAT HE MEANT, AND WE *DIDN'T* KNOW.

WE *BOTH* KEPT CATCHING A GLIMPSE OF SOME CREEPY APPARITION, AND THEN IT WOULD FADE. MASK, HOOD, CLOAK...YOUNG MALE.

THE TRAVELER.

THE ONE WHO *CAUSED* THIS.

HOW DO WE *PROVE* IT?

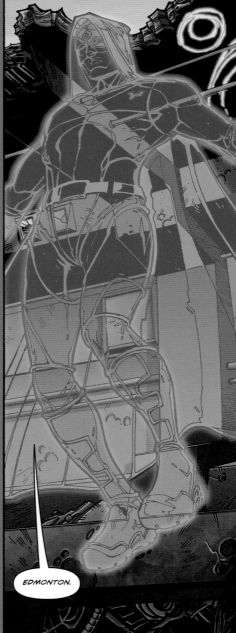

ONE OF THE VICTIMS, JULIA'S *FIANCÉ.* THE *GEEK.* ROLAND.

RONALD.

I WENT *OUT* WITH THEM ONCE. HE BROUGHT THIS FRIEND, A *PHYSICIST* LIKE *HIM.* ALL THEY TALKED ABOUT WAS *PARTICLES.*

HE'D RECOGNIZE A CLUE THAT'D GO OVER OUR HEADS. OVER OUR *LAB TECHS'* HEADS. OVER *STEPHEN HAWKING'S* HEAD.

WORTH A TRY. YOU GET A *NAME?*

NATE. I THINK. NATHAN--

EDMONTON.

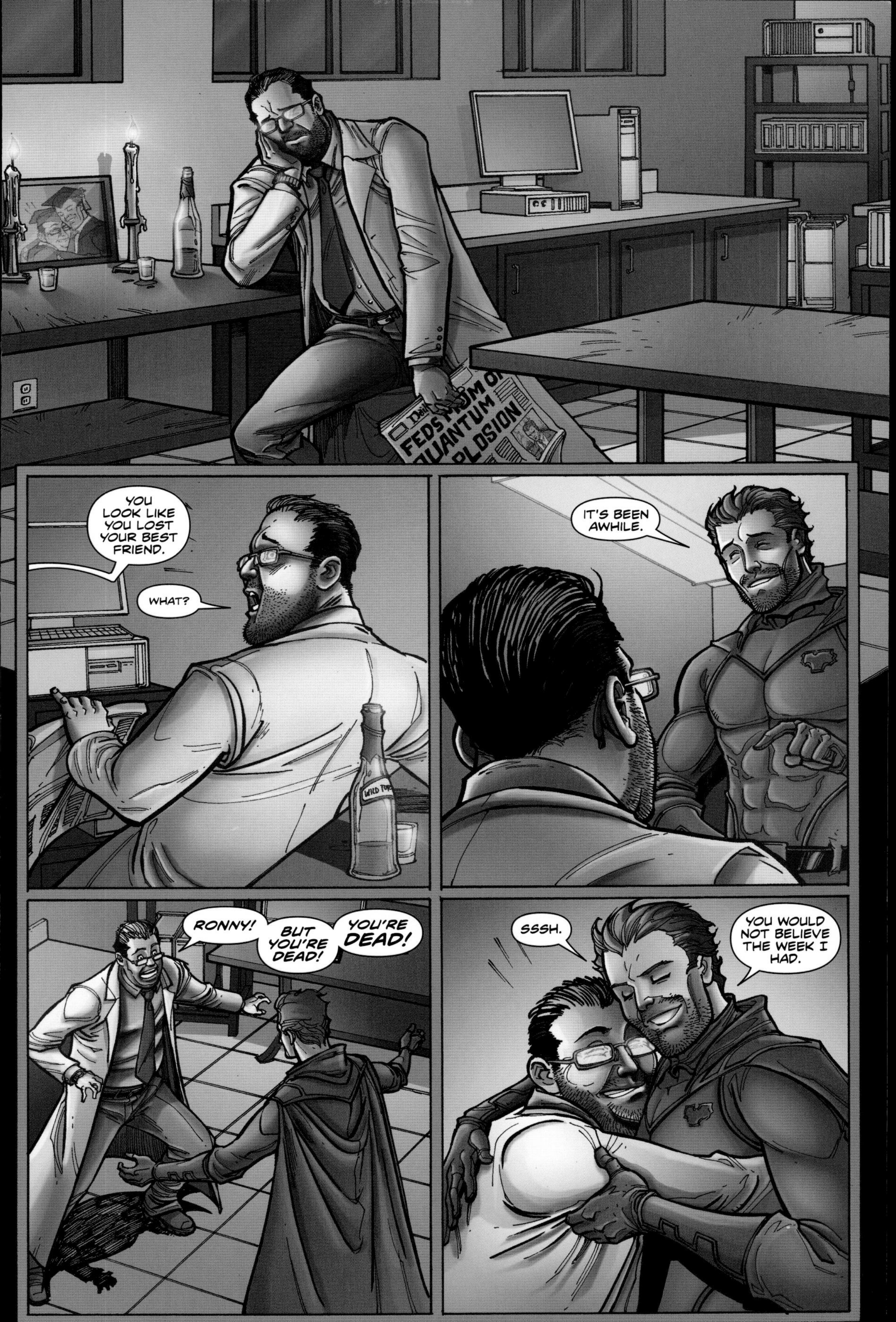
FEDS
YOU LOOK LIKE YOU LOST YOUR BEST FRIEND.
WHAT?
IT'S BEEN AWHILE.
RONNY!
BUT YOU'RE DEAD!
YOU'RE DEAD!
SSSH.
YOU WOULD NOT BELIEVE THE WEEK I HAD.

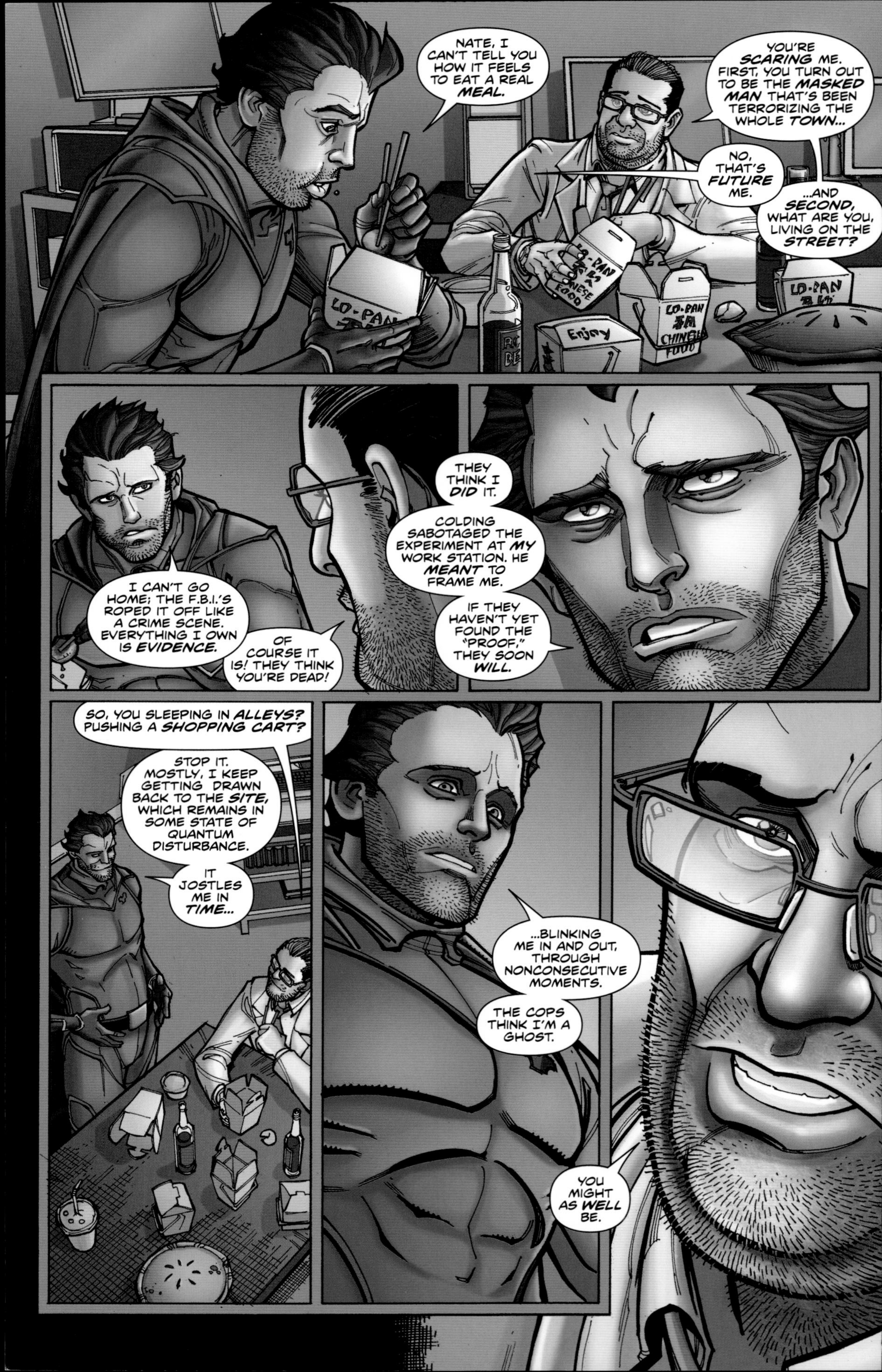
NATE, I CAN'T TELL YOU HOW IT FEELS TO EAT A REAL MEAL.
YOU'RE SCARING ME. FIRST, YOU TURN OUT TO BE THE MASKED MAN THAT'S BEEN TERRORIZING THE WHOLE TOWN...
NO, THAT'S FUTURE ME.
...AND SECOND, WHAT ARE YOU, LIVING ON THE STREET?
LO-PAN
Enjoy
CHINESE FOOD
I CAN'T GO HOME; THE F.B.I.'S ROPED IT OFF LIKE A CRIME SCENE. EVERYTHING I OWN IS EVIDENCE.
OF COURSE IT IS! THEY THINK YOU'RE DEAD!
THEY THINK I DID IT.
COLDING SABOTAGED THE EXPERIMENT AT MY WORK STATION. HE MEANT TO FRAME ME.
IF THEY HAVEN'T YET FOUND THE "PROOF," THEY SOON WILL.
SO, YOU SLEEPING IN ALLEYS? PUSHING A SHOPPING CART?
STOP IT. MOSTLY, I KEEP GETTING DRAWN BACK TO THE SITE, WHICH REMAINS IN SOME STATE OF QUANTUM DISTURBANCE.
IT JOSTLES ME IN TIME...
...BLINKING ME IN AND OUT, THROUGH NONCONSECUTIVE MOMENTS.
THE COPS THINK I'M A GHOST.
YOU MIGHT AS WELL BE.

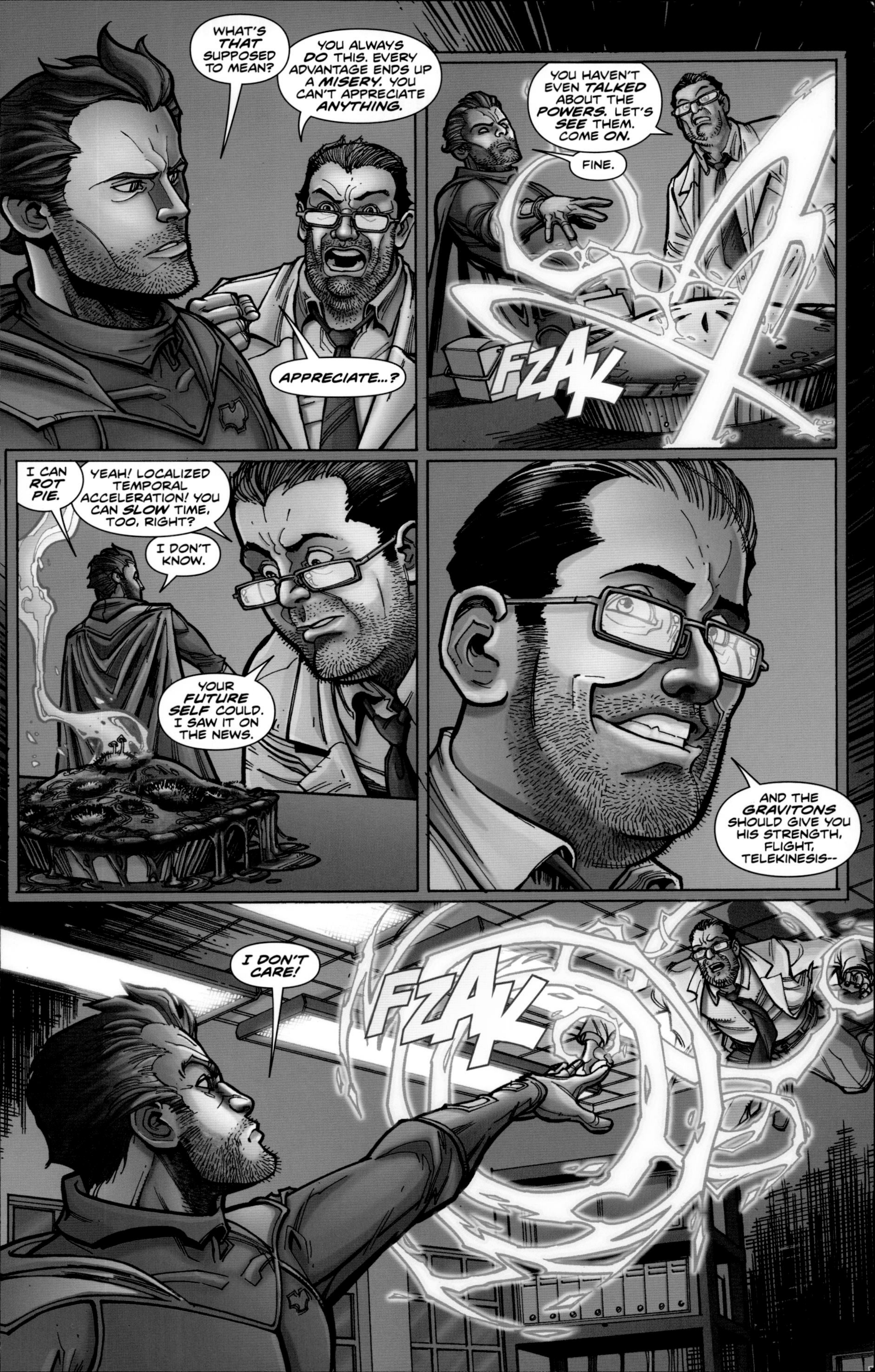
WHAT'S THAT SUPPOSED TO MEAN?
YOU ALWAYS DO THIS. EVERY ADVANTAGE ENDS UP A MISERY. YOU CAN'T APPRECIATE ANYTHING.
APPRECIATE...?
YOU HAVEN'T EVEN TALKED ABOUT THE POWERS. LET'S SEE THEM. COME ON.
FINE.
FZAK
I CAN ROT PIE.
YEAH! LOCALIZED TEMPORAL ACCELERATION! YOU CAN SLOW TIME, TOO, RIGHT?
I DON'T KNOW.
YOUR FUTURE SELF COULD. I SAW IT ON THE NEWS.
AND THE GRAVITONS SHOULD GIVE YOU HIS STRENGTH, FLIGHT, TELEKINESIS--
I DON'T CARE!
FZAK

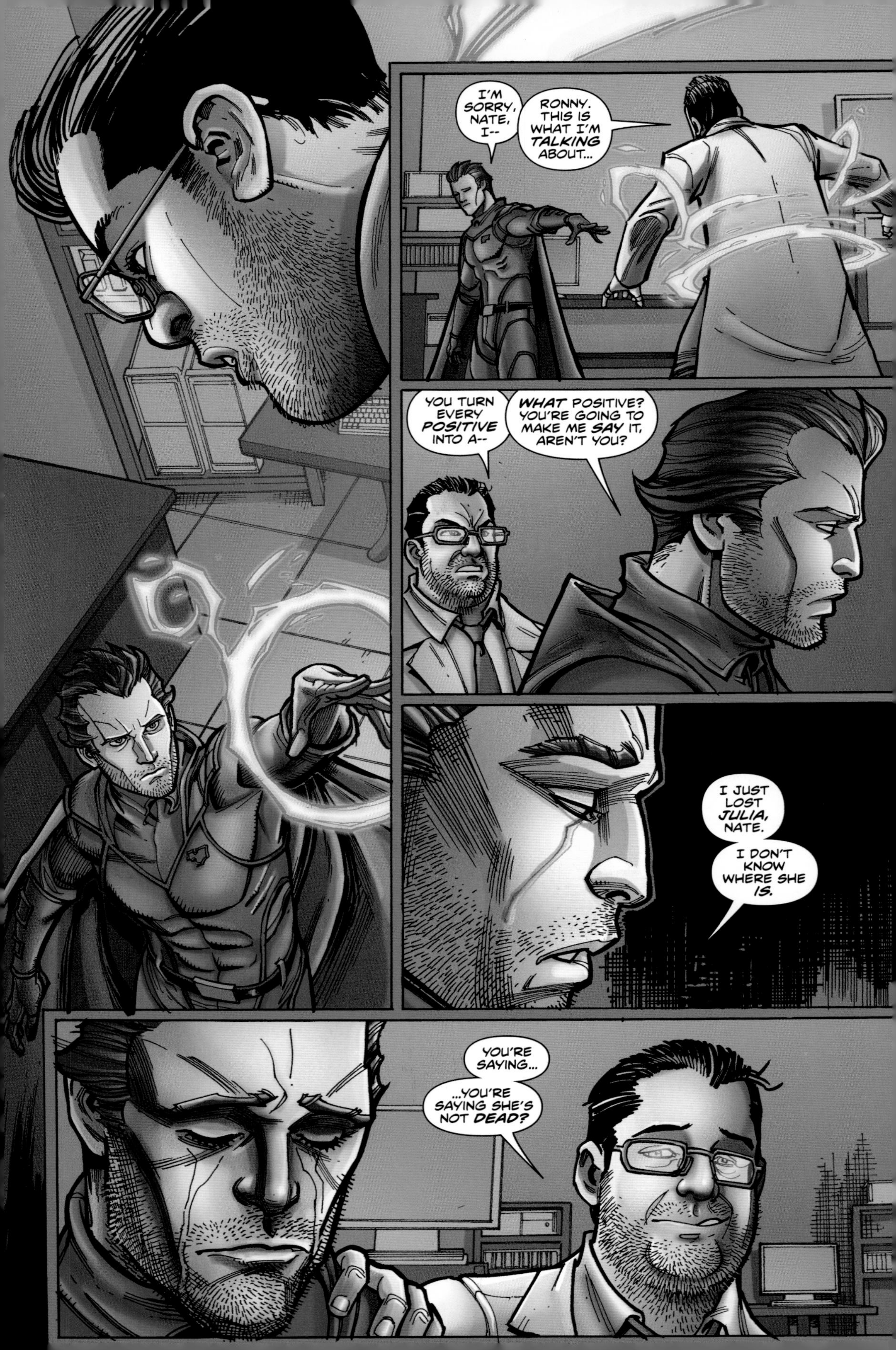
I'M SORRY, NATE, I--
RONNY. THIS IS WHAT I'M TALKING ABOUT...
YOU TURN EVERY POSITIVE INTO A--
WHAT POSITIVE? YOU'RE GOING TO MAKE ME SAY IT, AREN'T YOU?
I JUST LOST JULIA, NATE.
I DON'T KNOW WHERE SHE IS.
YOU'RE SAYING...
...YOU'RE SAYING SHE'S NOT DEAD?

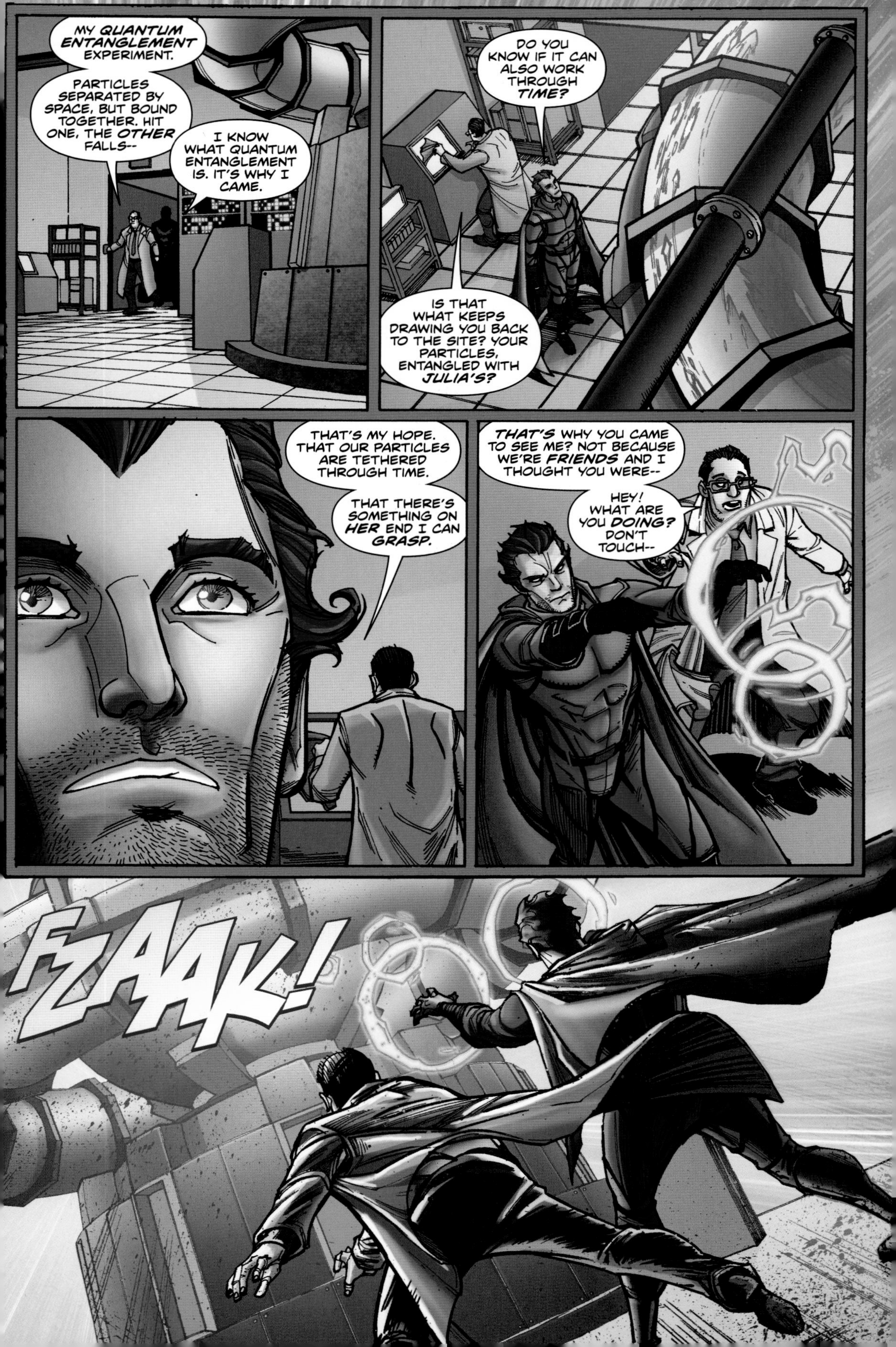
MY QUANTUM ENTANGLEMENT EXPERIMENT.
PARTICLES SEPARATED BY SPACE, BUT BOUND TOGETHER. HIT ONE, THE OTHER FALLS--
I KNOW WHAT QUANTUM ENTANGLEMENT IS. IT'S WHY I CAME.
DO YOU KNOW IF IT CAN ALSO WORK THROUGH TIME?
IS THAT WHAT KEEPS DRAWING YOU BACK TO THE SITE? YOUR PARTICLES, ENTANGLED WITH JULIA'S?
THAT'S MY HOPE. THAT OUR PARTICLES ARE TETHERED THROUGH TIME.
THAT THERE'S SOMETHING ON HER END I CAN GRASP.
THAT'S WHY YOU CAME TO SEE ME? NOT BECAUSE WE'RE FRIENDS AND I THOUGHT YOU WERE--
HEY! WHAT ARE YOU DOING? DON'T TOUCH--
FZAAK!

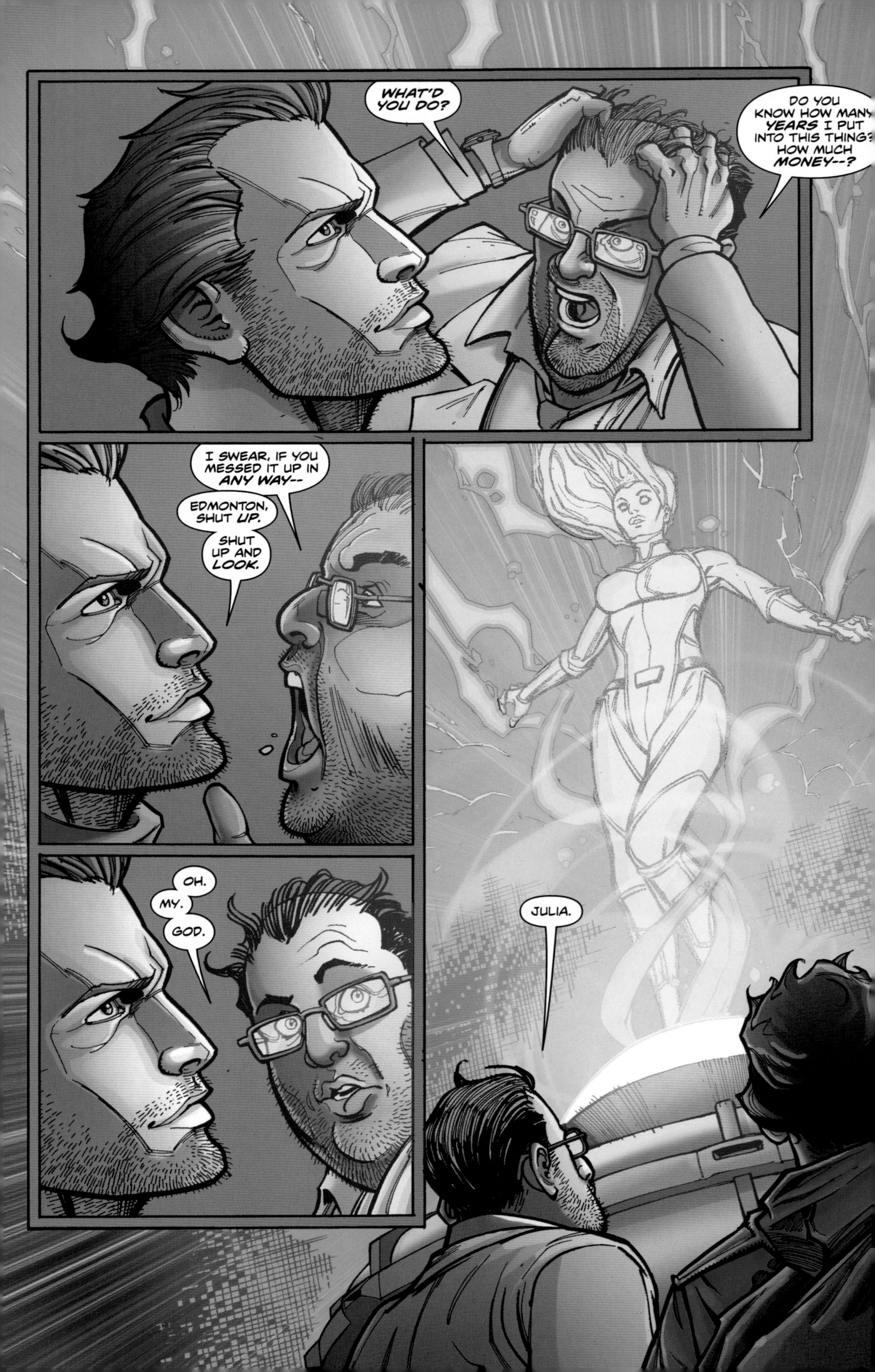
WHAT'D YOU DO?
DO YOU KNOW HOW MANY YEARS I PUT INTO THIS THING? HOW MUCH MONEY--?
I SWEAR, IF YOU MESSED IT UP IN ANY WAY--
EDMONTON, SHUT UP.
SHUT UP AND LOOK.
OH.
MY.
GOD.
JULIA.

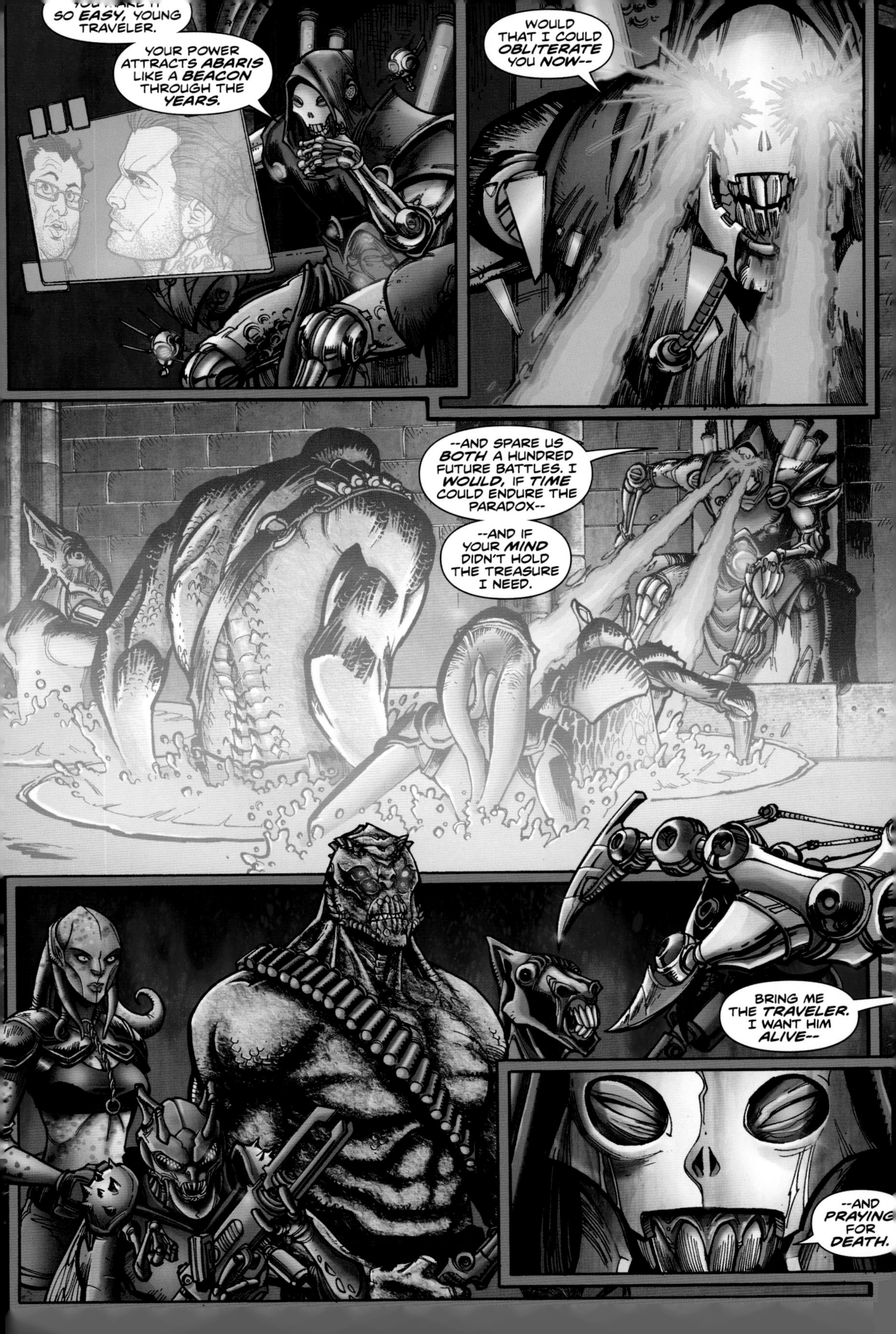
SO EASY, YOUNG TRAVELER.
YOUR POWER ATTRACTS ABARIS LIKE A BEACON THROUGH THE YEARS.
WOULD THAT I COULD OBLITERATE YOU NOW--
--AND SPARE US BOTH A HUNDRED FUTURE BATTLES. I WOULD, IF TIME COULD ENDURE THE PARADOX--
--AND IF YOUR MIND DIDN'T HOLD THE TREASURE I NEED.
BRING ME THE TRAVELER. I WANT HIM ALIVE--
--AND PRAYING FOR DEATH.

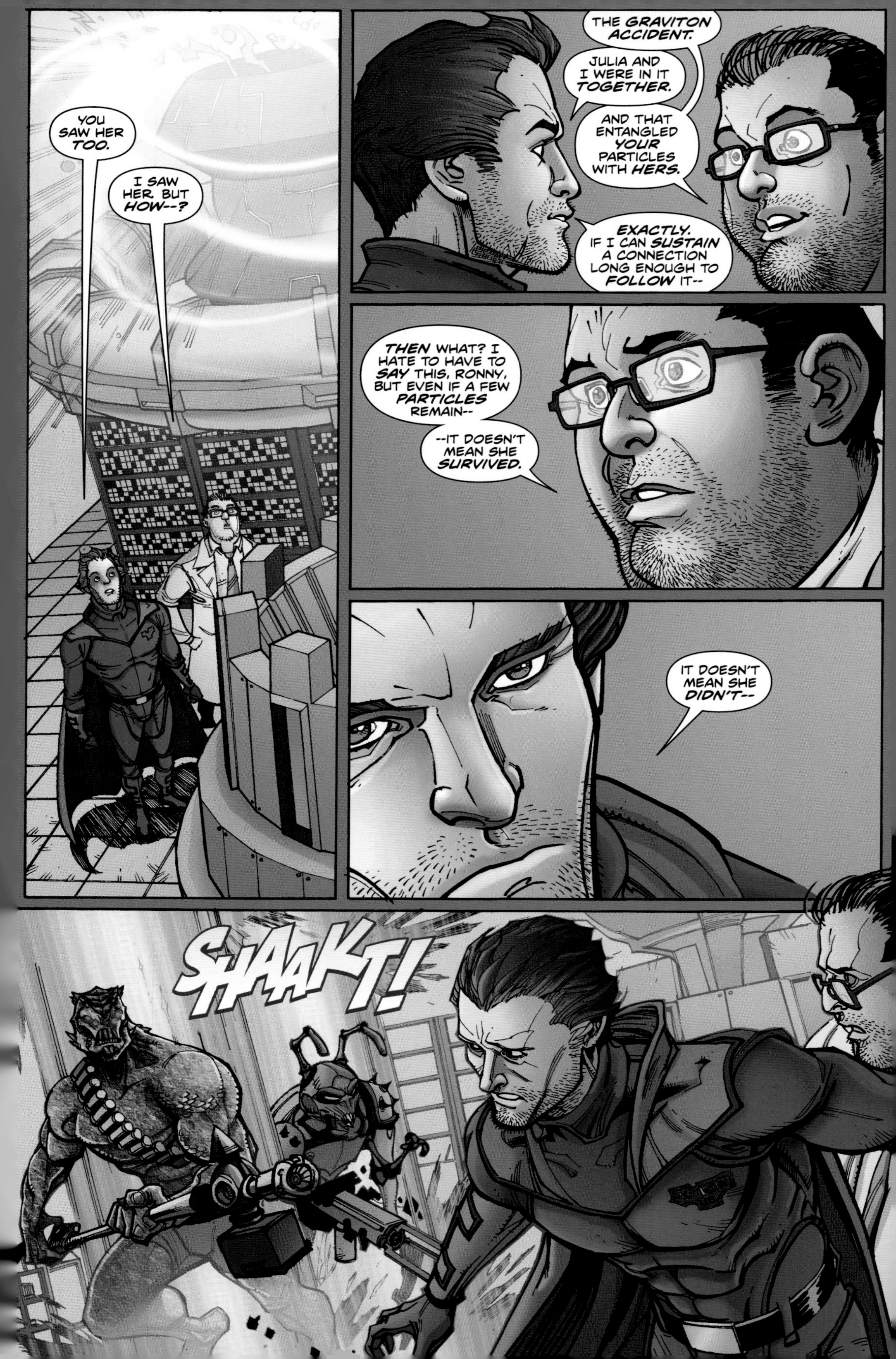

YOU SAW HER *TOO.*
I SAW HER. BUT *HOW--?*
THE *GRAVITON ACCIDENT.*
JULIA AND I WERE IN IT *TOGETHER.*
AND THAT ENTANGLED *YOUR* PARTICLES WITH *HERS.*
EXACTLY. IF I CAN *SUSTAIN* A CONNECTION LONG ENOUGH TO *FOLLOW* IT--
THEN WHAT? I HATE TO HAVE TO *SAY* THIS, RONNY, BUT EVEN IF A FEW *PARTICLES* REMAIN--
--IT DOESN'T MEAN SHE *SURVIVED.*
IT DOESN'T MEAN SHE *DIDN'T--*
SHAAKT!

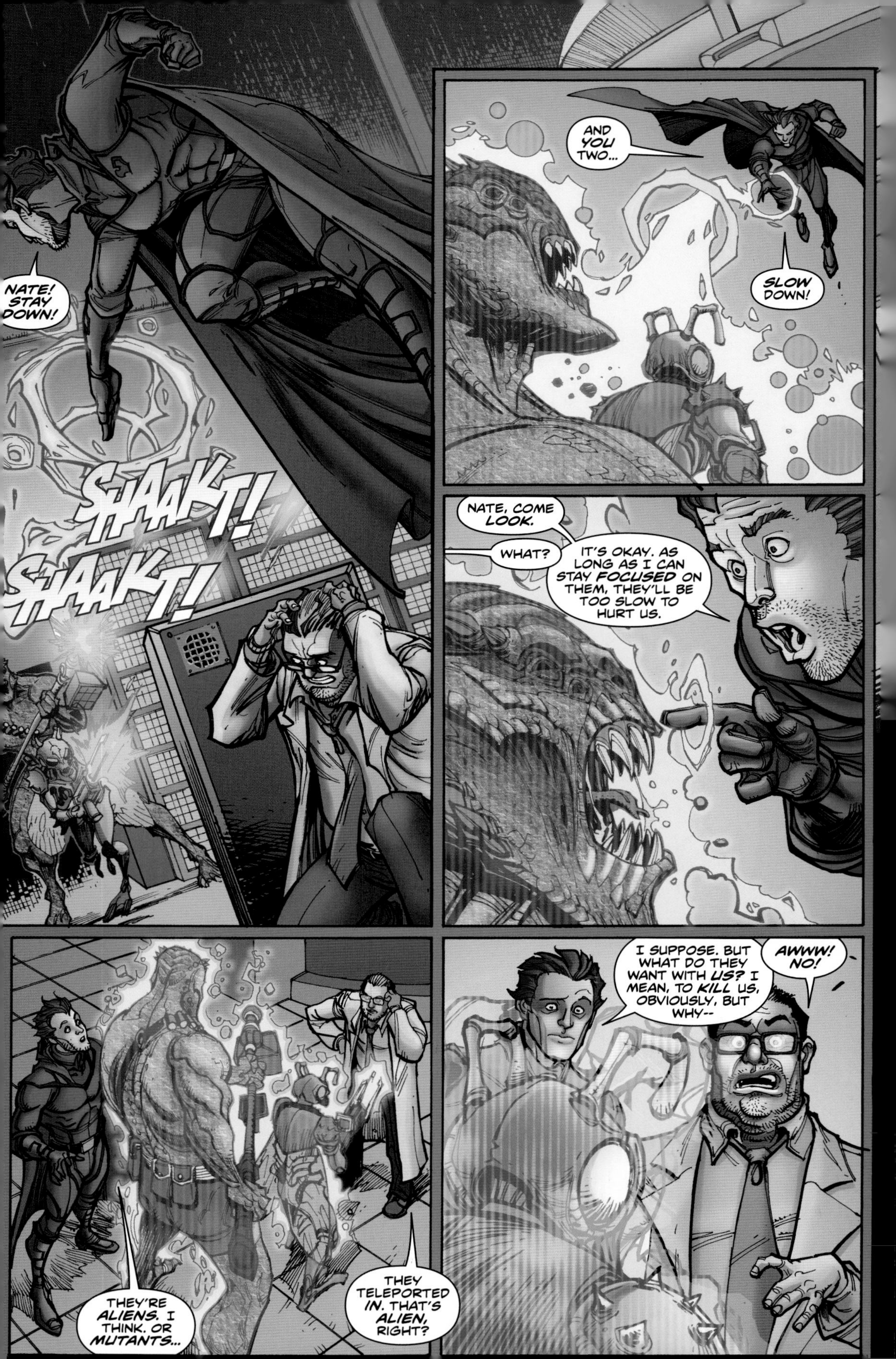
NATE! STAY DOWN!
SHAAKT! SHAAKT!
AND YOU TWO...
SLOW DOWN!
NATE, COME LOOK.
WHAT?
IT'S OKAY. AS LONG AS I CAN STAY FOCUSED ON THEM, THEY'LL BE TOO SLOW TO HURT US.
THEY'RE ALIENS. I THINK. OR MUTANTS...
THEY TELEPORTED IN. THAT'S ALIEN, RIGHT?
I SUPPOSE. BUT WHAT DO THEY WANT WITH US? I MEAN, TO KILL US, OBVIOUSLY, BUT WHY--
AWWW! NO!

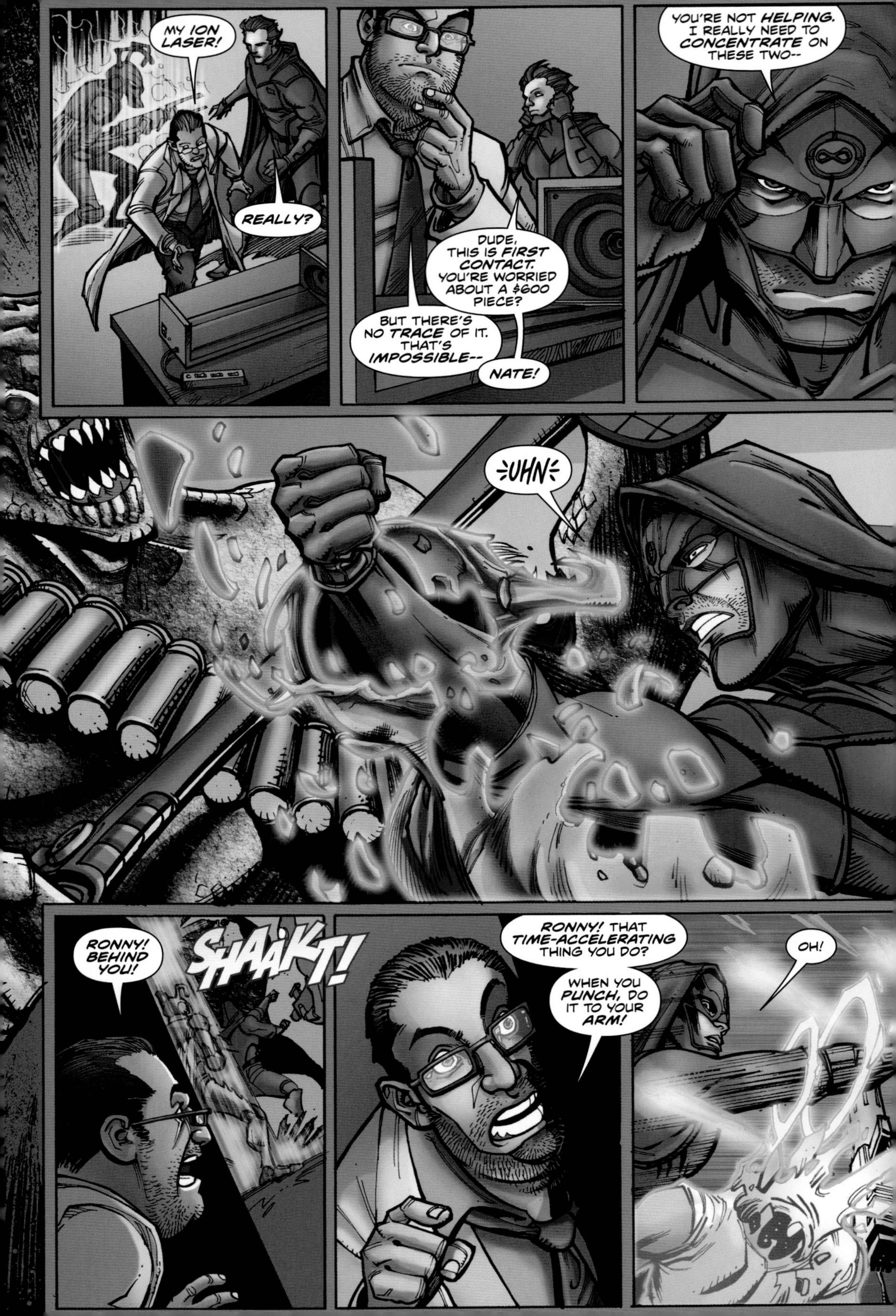
MY ION LASER!
REALLY?
BUT THERE'S NO TRACE OF IT. THAT'S IMPOSSIBLE--
DUDE, THIS IS FIRST CONTACT. YOU'RE WORRIED ABOUT A $600 PIECE?
NATE!
YOU'RE NOT HELPING. I REALLY NEED TO CONCENTRATE ON THESE TWO--
UHN
RONNY! BEHIND YOU!
SHAAKT!
RONNY! THAT TIME-ACCELERATING THING YOU DO?
WHEN YOU PUNCH, DO IT TO YOUR ARM!
OH!

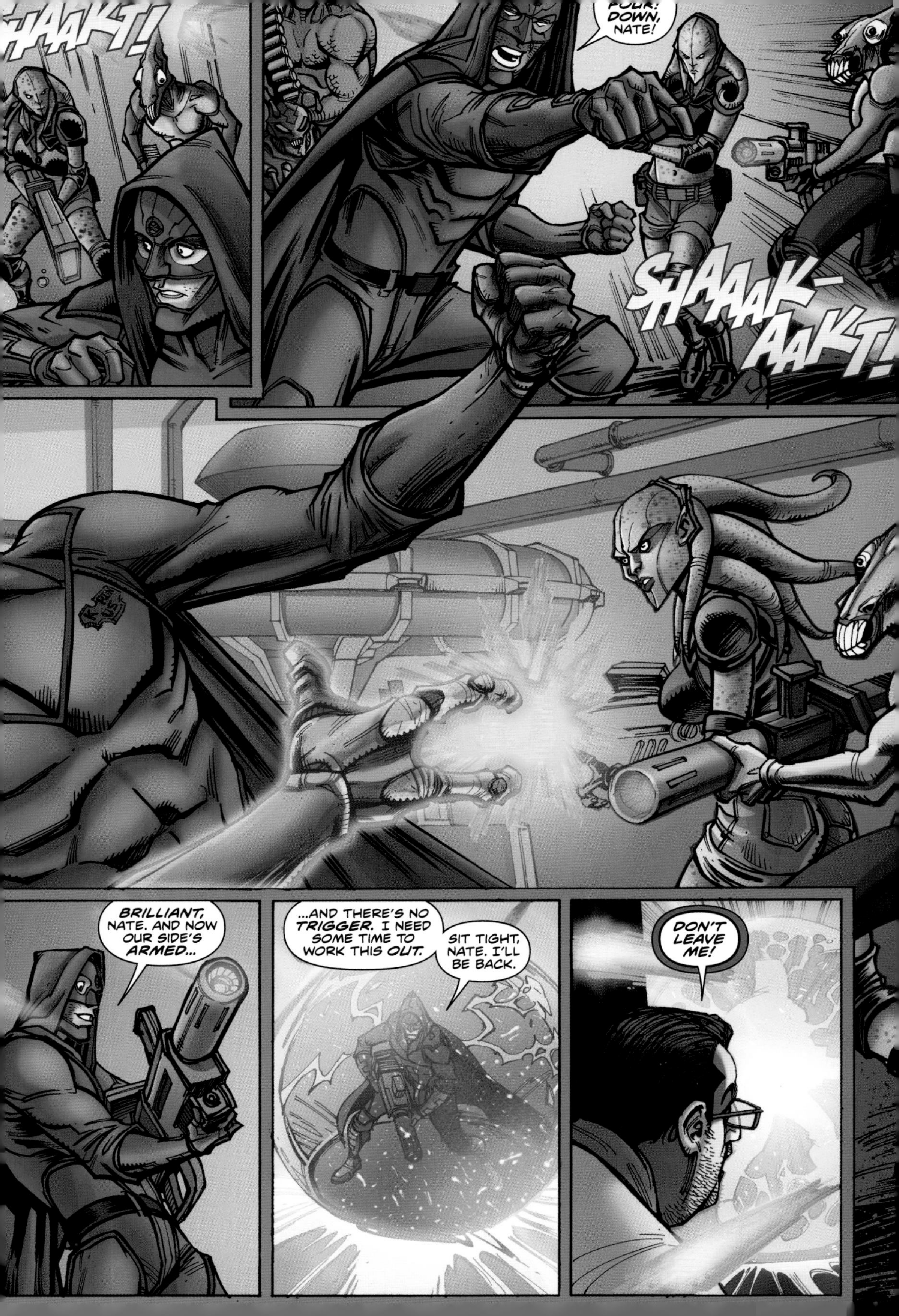
SHAAKT!
DOWN, NATE!
SHAAAK-AAKT!
BRILLIANT, NATE. AND NOW OUR SIDE'S ARMED...
...AND THERE'S NO TRIGGER. I NEED SOME TIME TO WORK THIS OUT.
SIT TIGHT, NATE. I'LL BE BACK.
DON'T LEAVE ME!

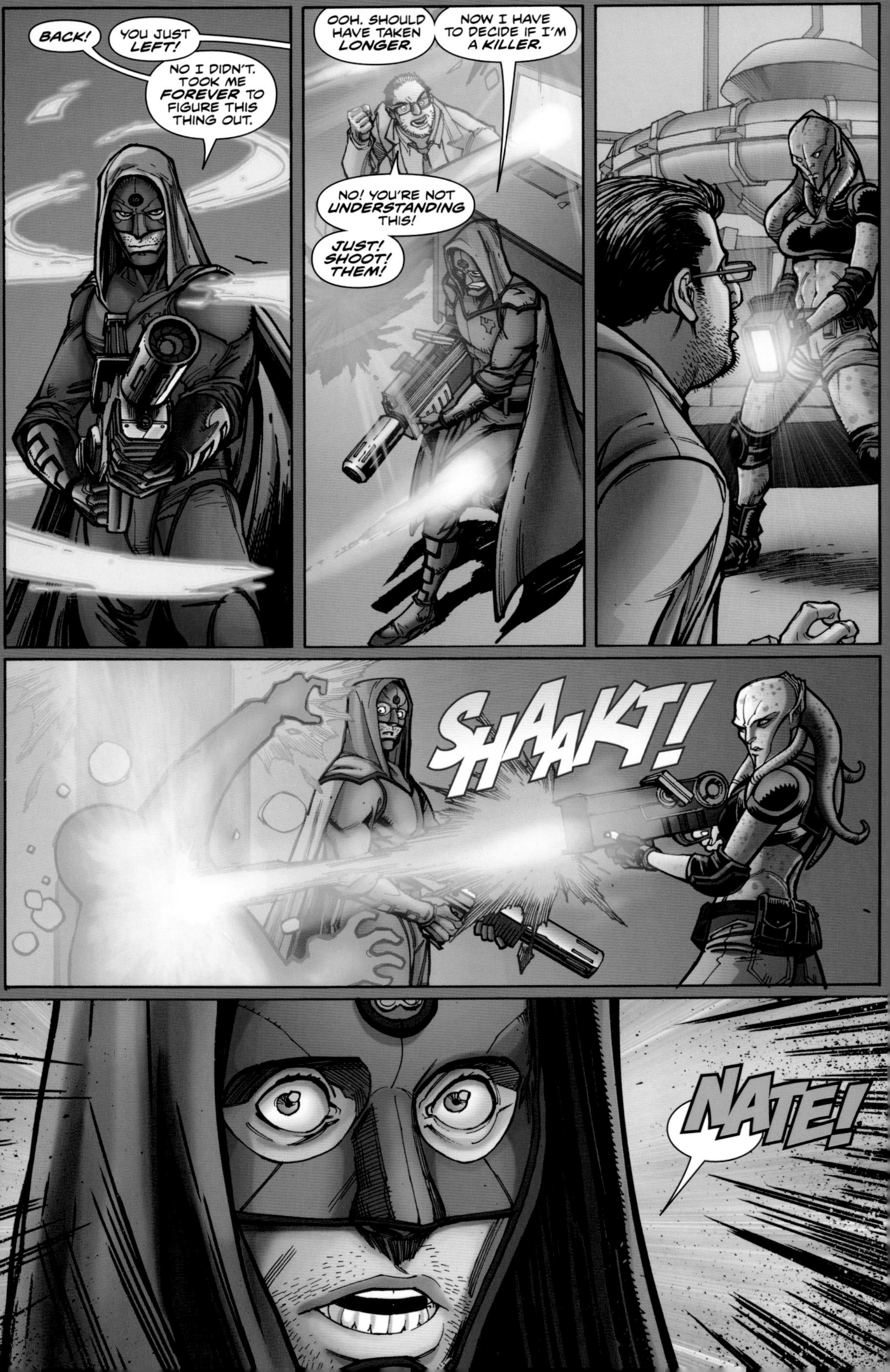
BACK!
YOU JUST LEFT!
NO I DIDN'T. TOOK ME FOREVER TO FIGURE THIS THING OUT.
OOH. SHOULD HAVE TAKEN LONGER.
NOW I HAVE TO DECIDE IF I'M A KILLER.
NO! YOU'RE NOT UNDERSTANDING THIS!
JUST! SHOOT! THEM!
SHAAKT!
NATE!

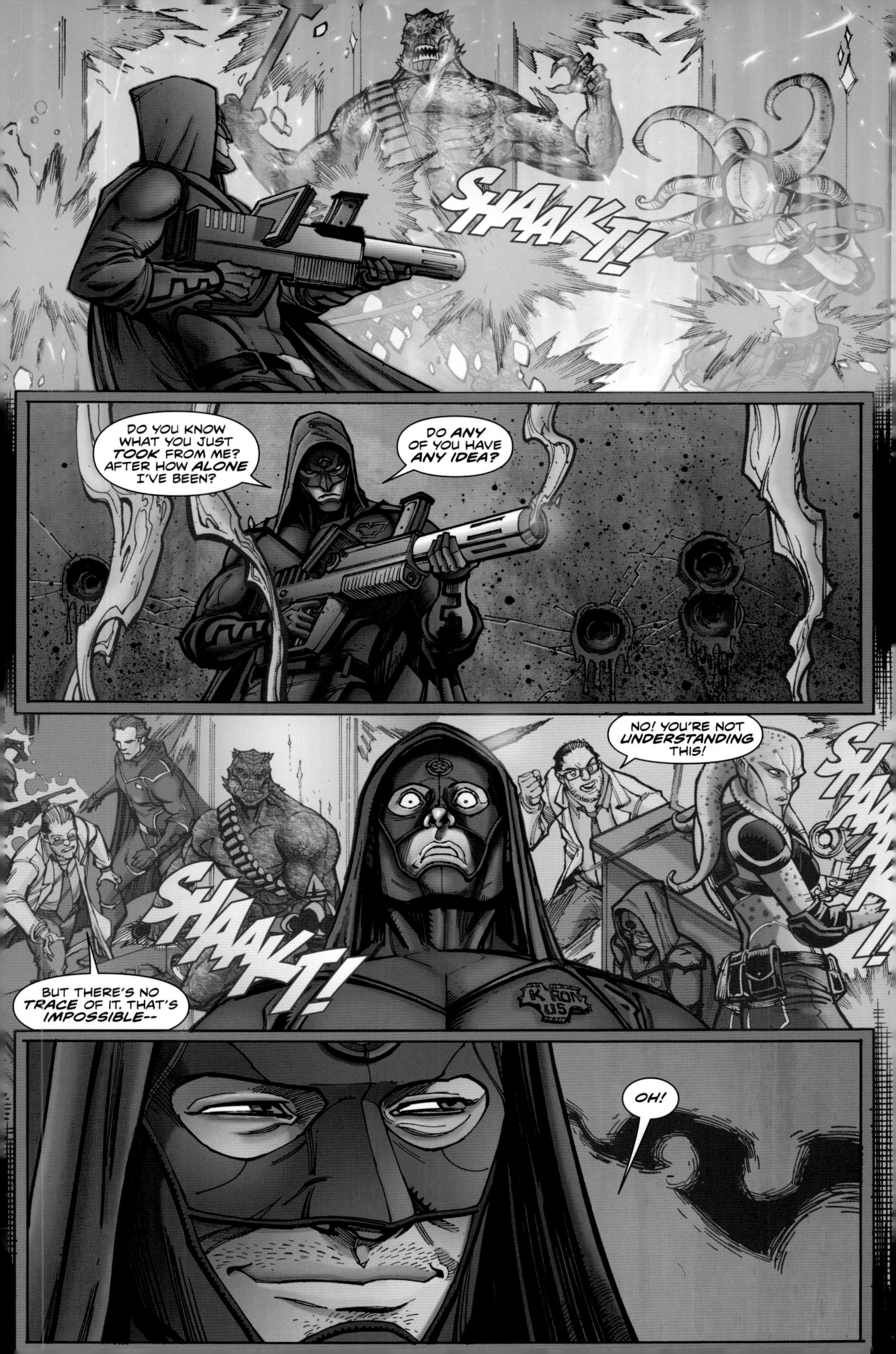
SHAAKT!!
DO YOU KNOW WHAT YOU JUST TOOK FROM ME? AFTER HOW ALONE I'VE BEEN?
DO ANY OF YOU HAVE ANY IDEA?
NO! YOU'RE NOT UNDERSTANDING THIS!
SHAAKT!
BUT THERE'S NO TRACE OF IT. THAT'S IMPOSSIBLE--
OH!

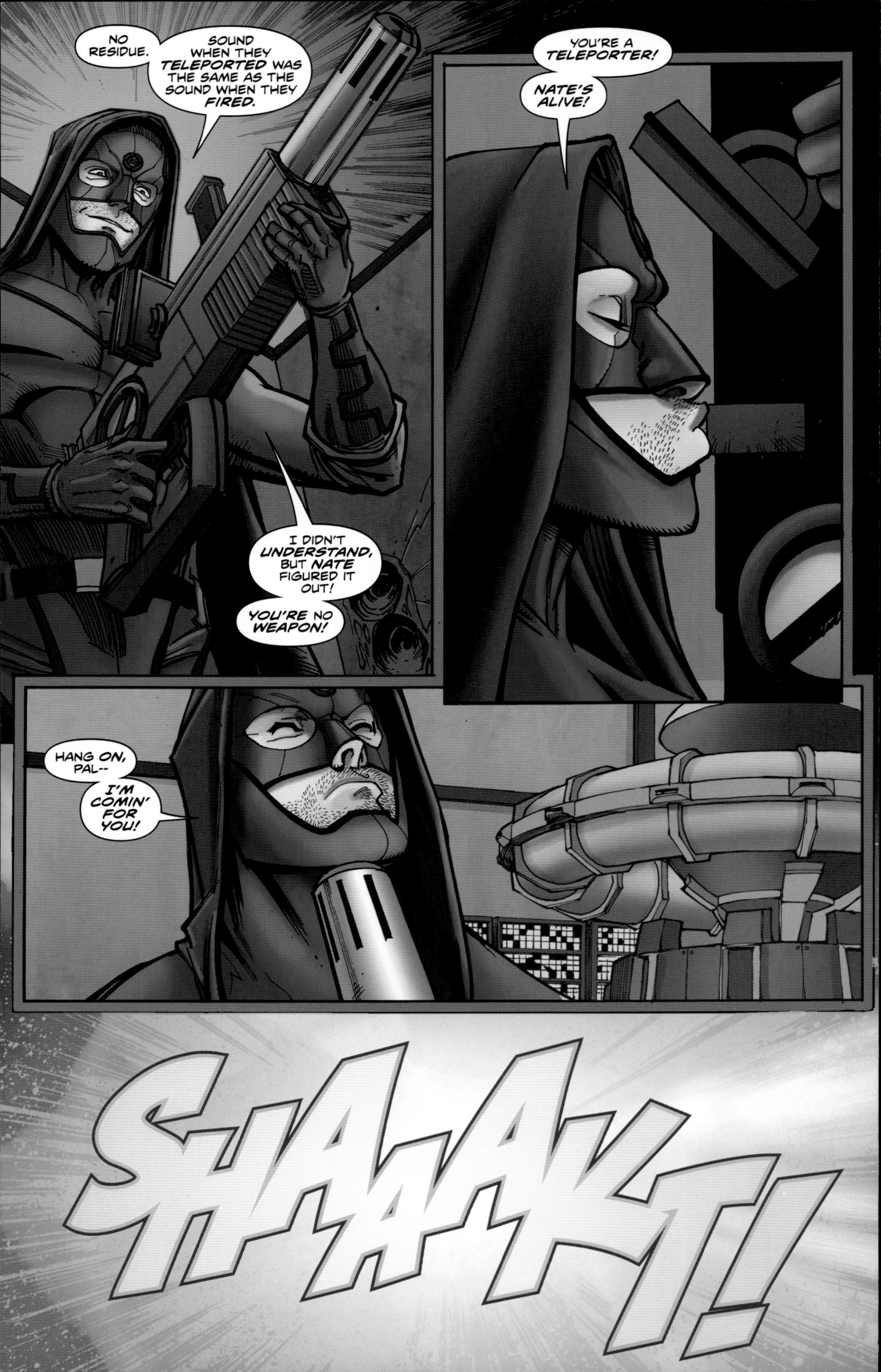
NO RESIDUE.
SOUND WHEN THEY TELEPORTED WAS THE SAME AS THE SOUND WHEN THEY FIRED.
YOU'RE A TELEPORTER!
NATE'S ALIVE!
I DIDN'T UNDERSTAND, BUT NATE FIGURED IT OUT!
YOU'RE NO WEAPON!
HANG ON, PAL--
I'M COMIN' FOR YOU!
SHAAKT!

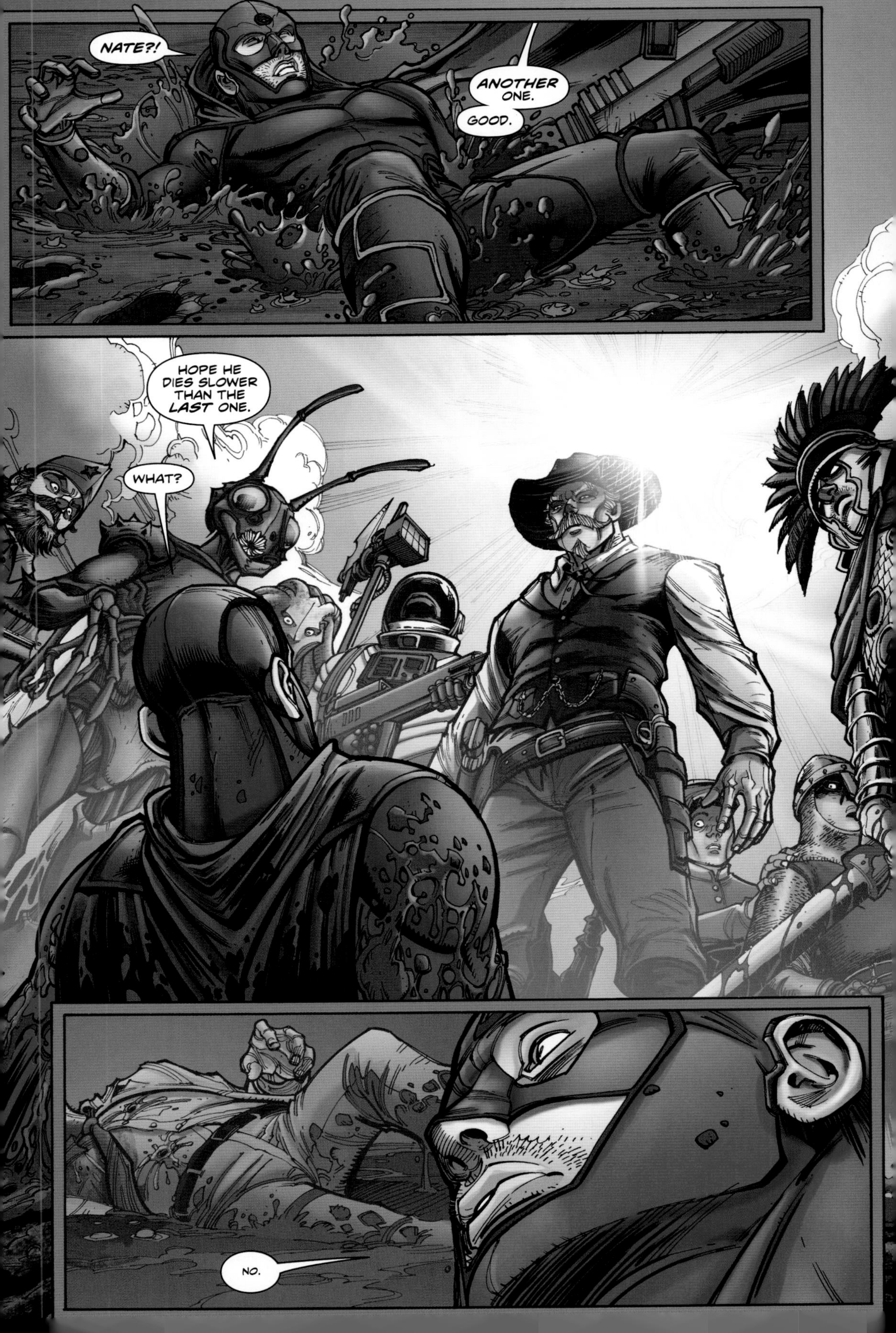
NATE?!
ANOTHER ONE.
GOOD.
HOPE HE DIES SLOWER THAN THE *LAST* ONE.
WHAT?
NO.

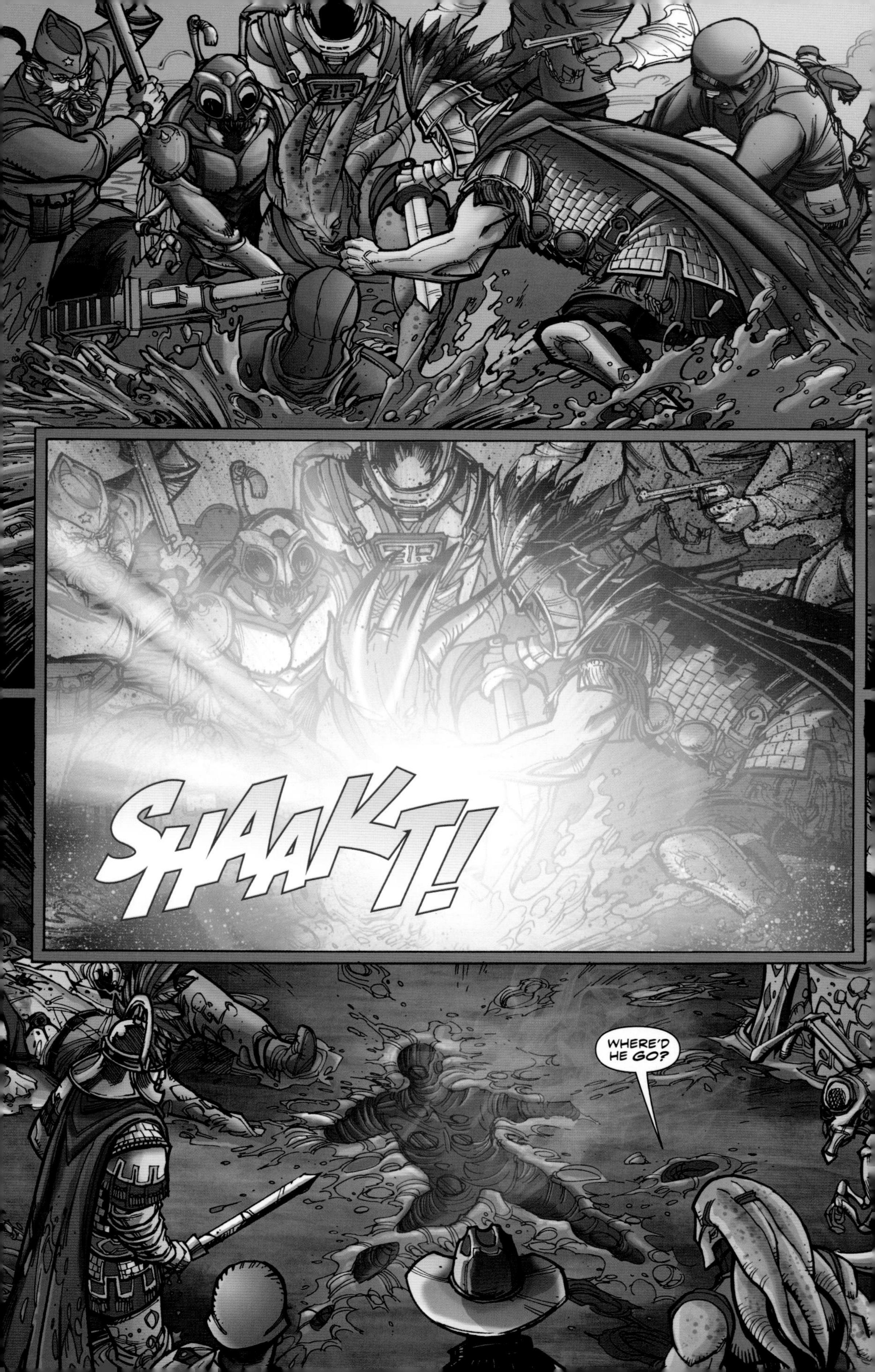
SHAAKT!
WHERE'D HE GO?

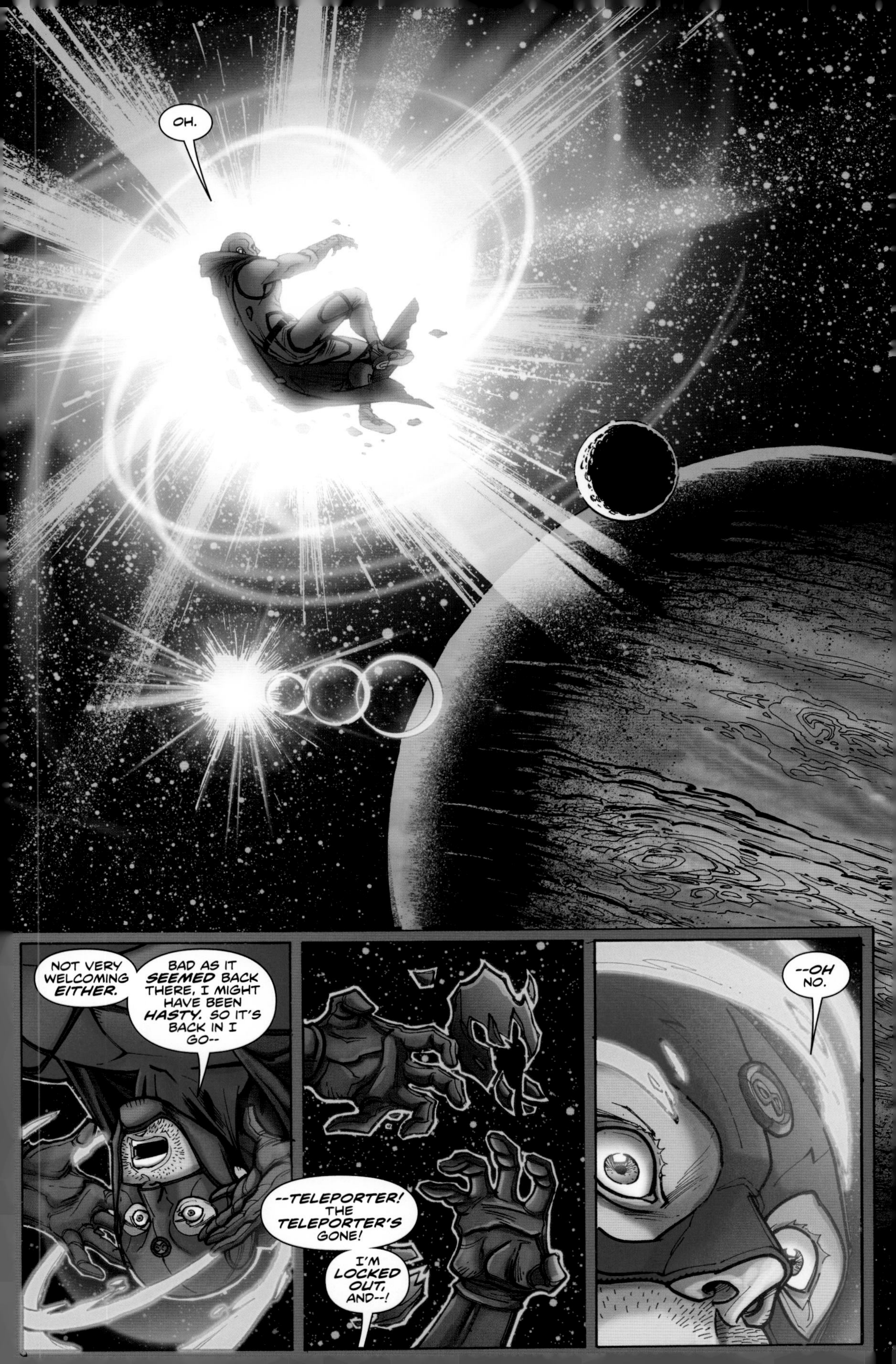
OH.
NOT VERY WELCOMING EITHER.
BAD AS IT SEEMED BACK THERE, I MIGHT HAVE BEEN HASTY. SO IT'S BACK IN I GO--
--TELEPORTER! THE TELEPORTER'S GONE!
I'M LOCKED OUT, AND--!
--OH NO.

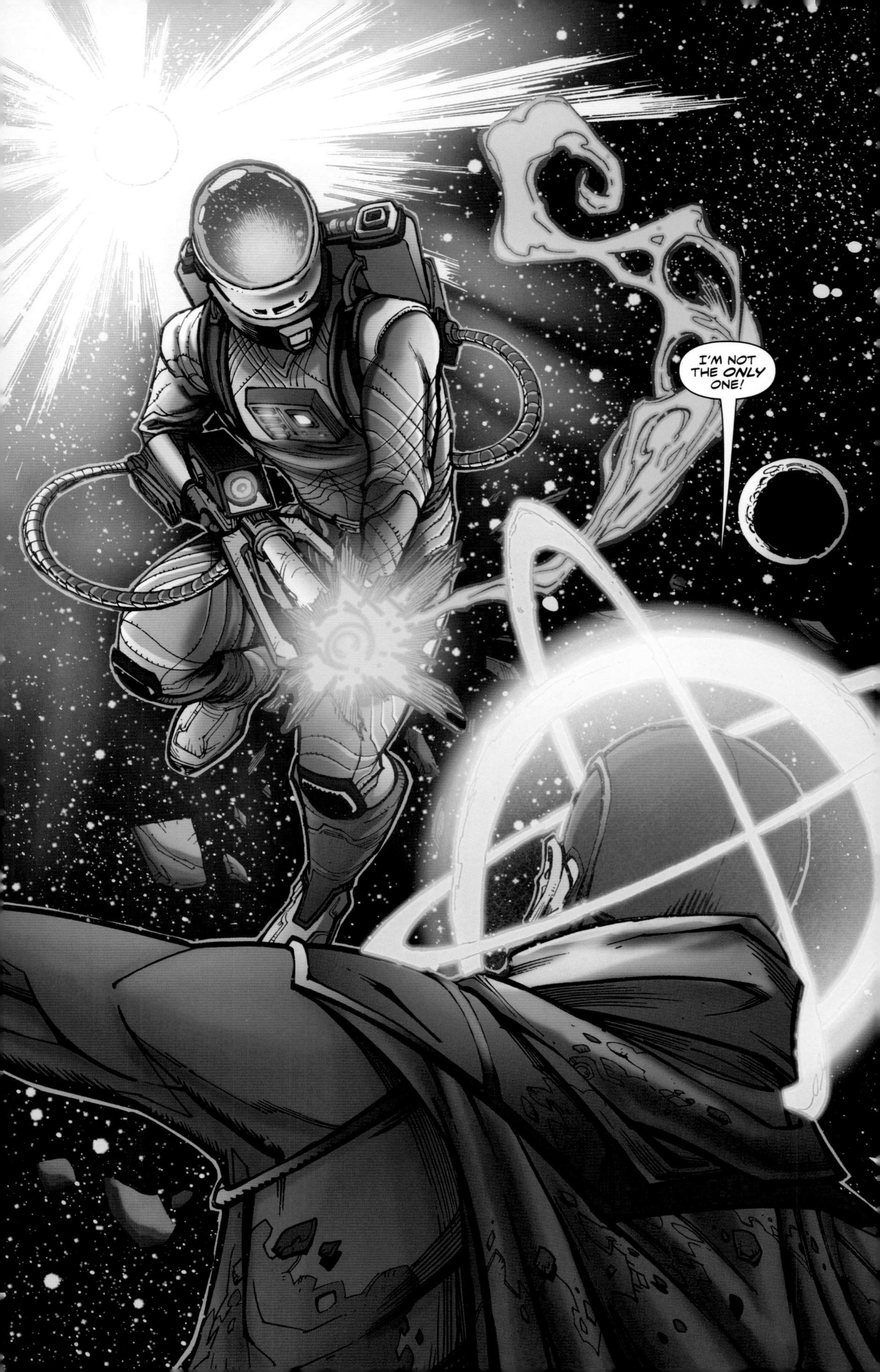
I'M NOT THE ONLY ONE!

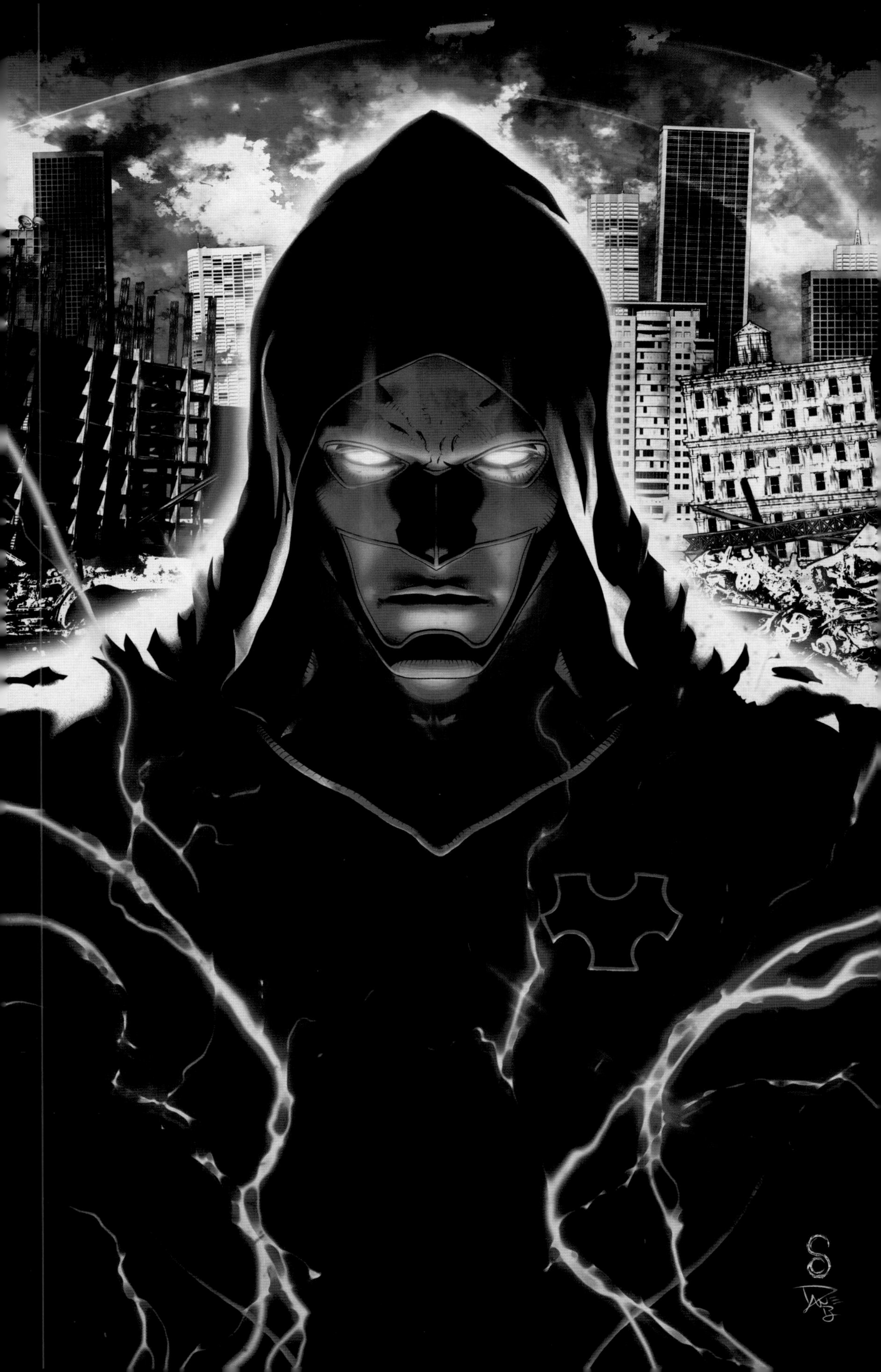

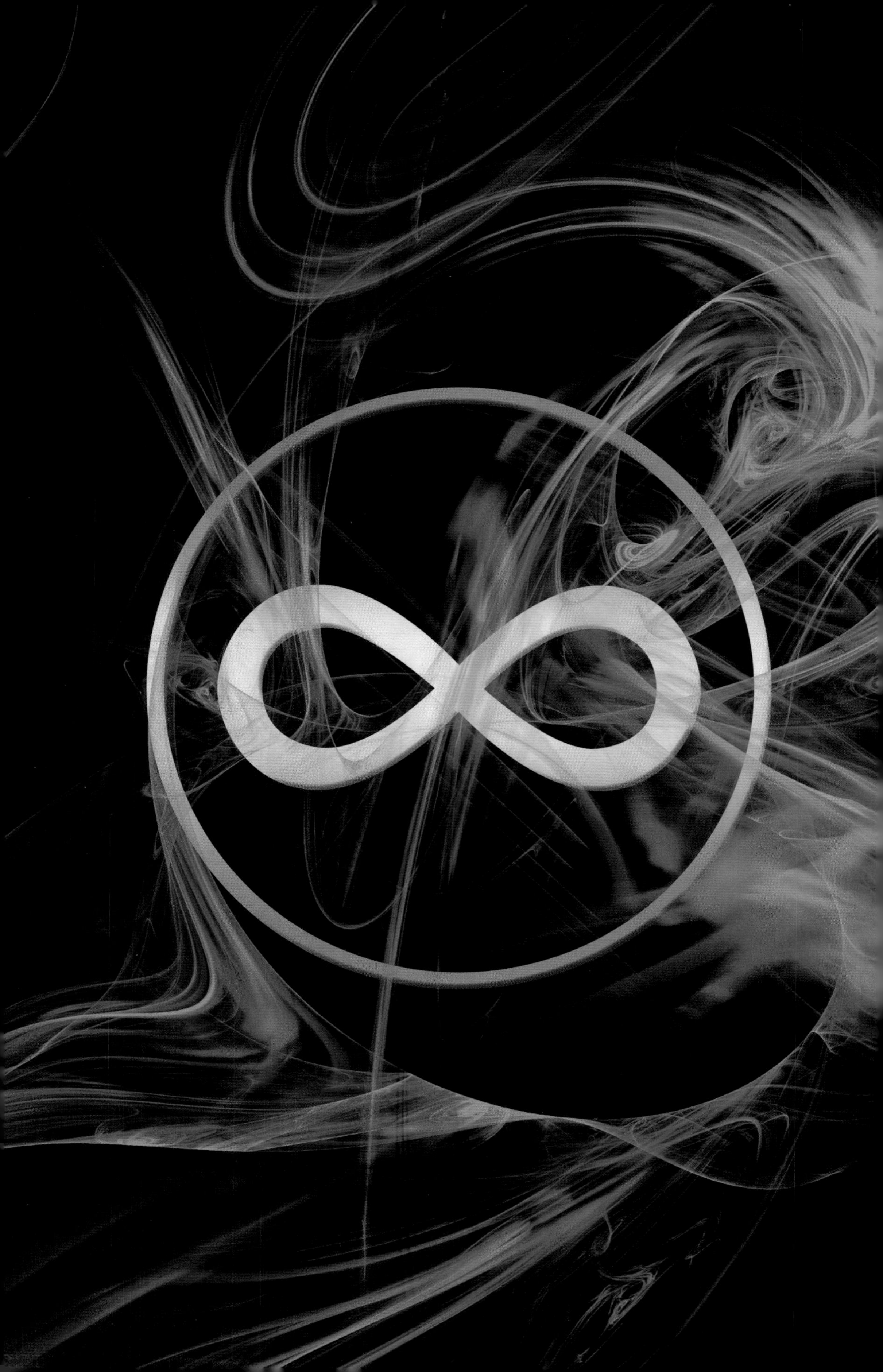

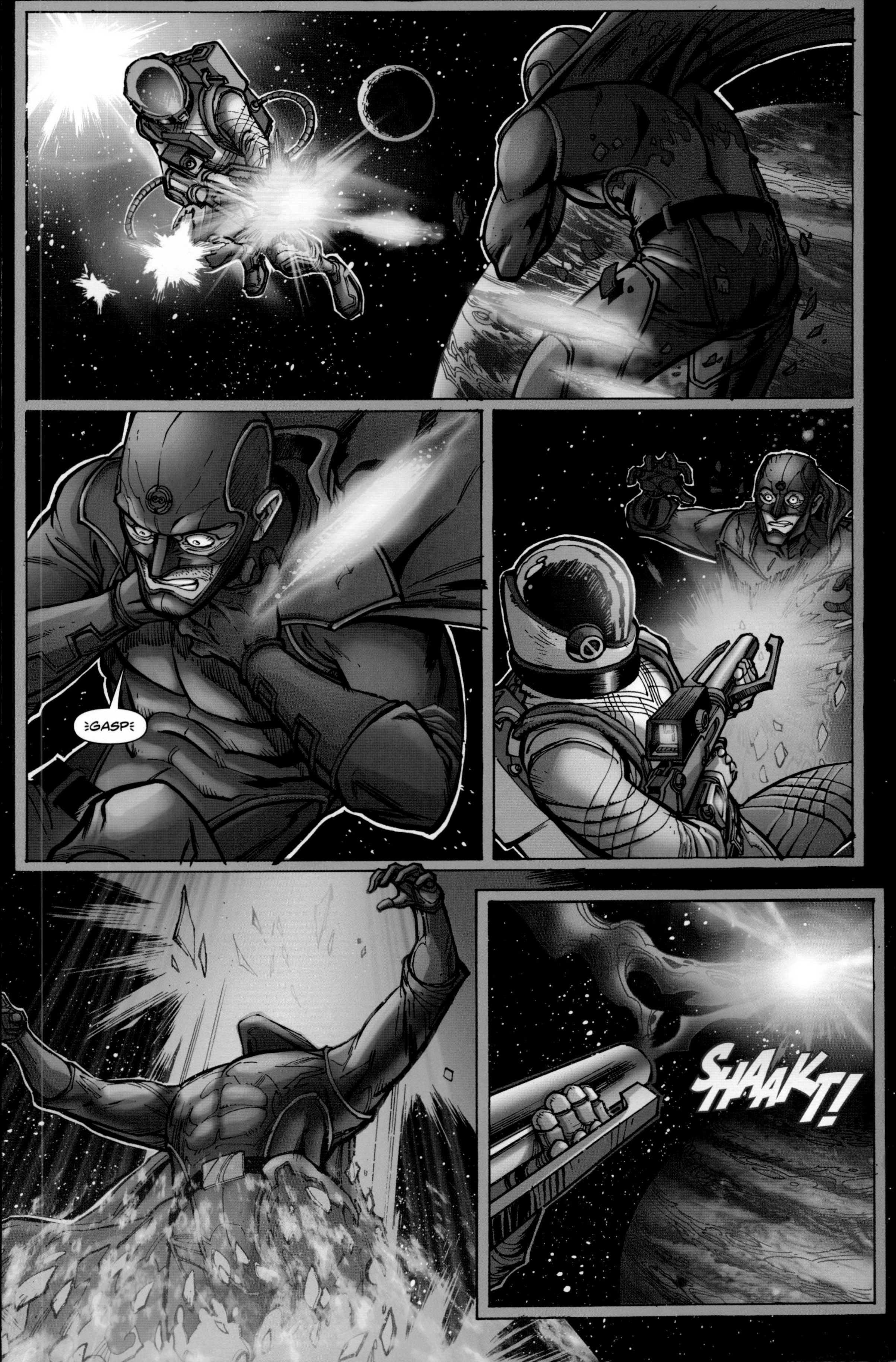
GASP
SHAAKT!

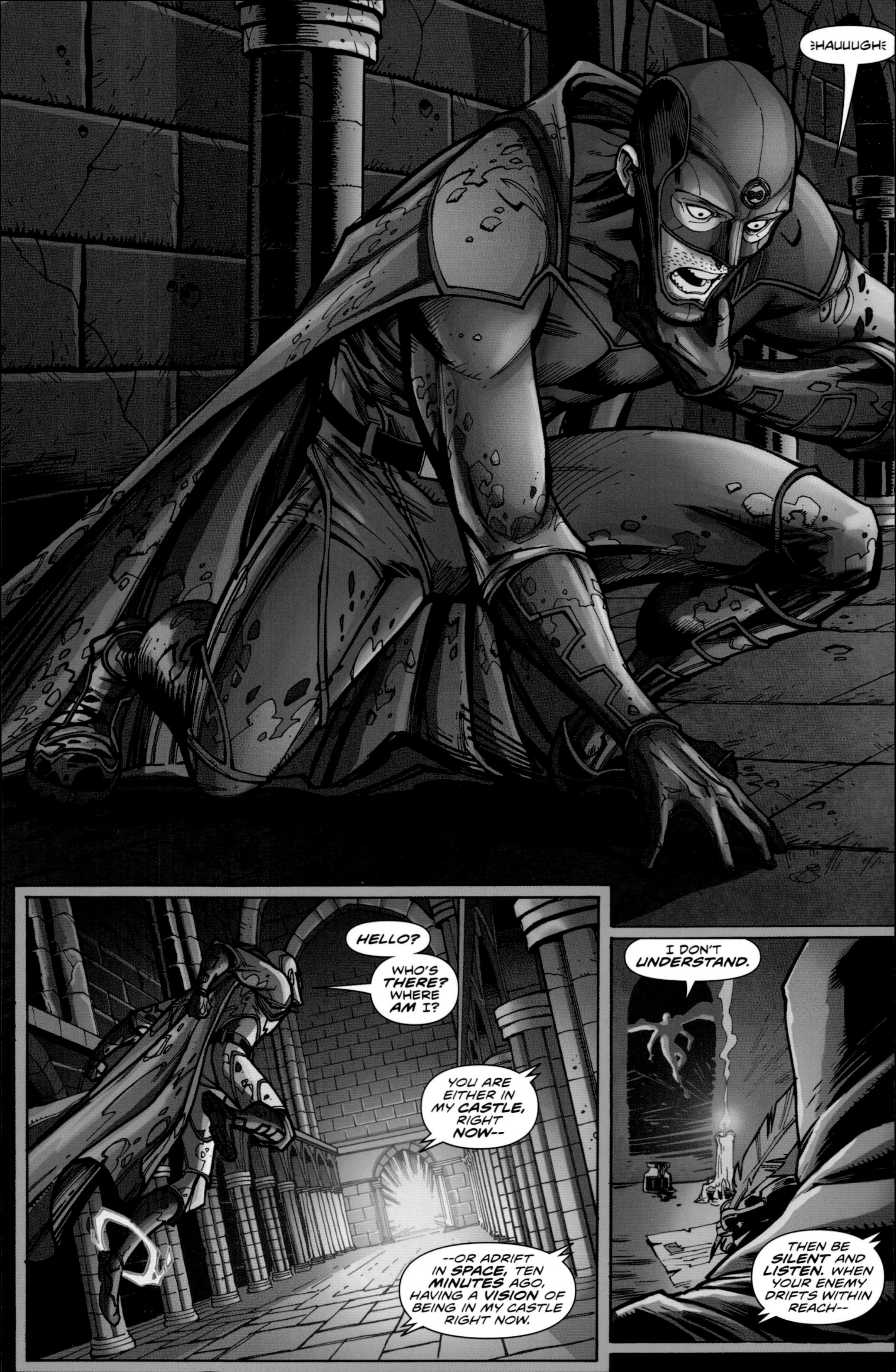
HAUUUGH
HELLO?
WHO'S THERE? WHERE AM I?
YOU ARE EITHER IN MY CASTLE, RIGHT NOW--
--OR ADRIFT IN SPACE, TEN MINUTES AGO, HAVING A VISION OF BEING IN MY CASTLE RIGHT NOW.
I DON'T UNDERSTAND.
THEN BE SILENT AND LISTEN. WHEN YOUR ENEMY DRIFTS WITHIN REACH--

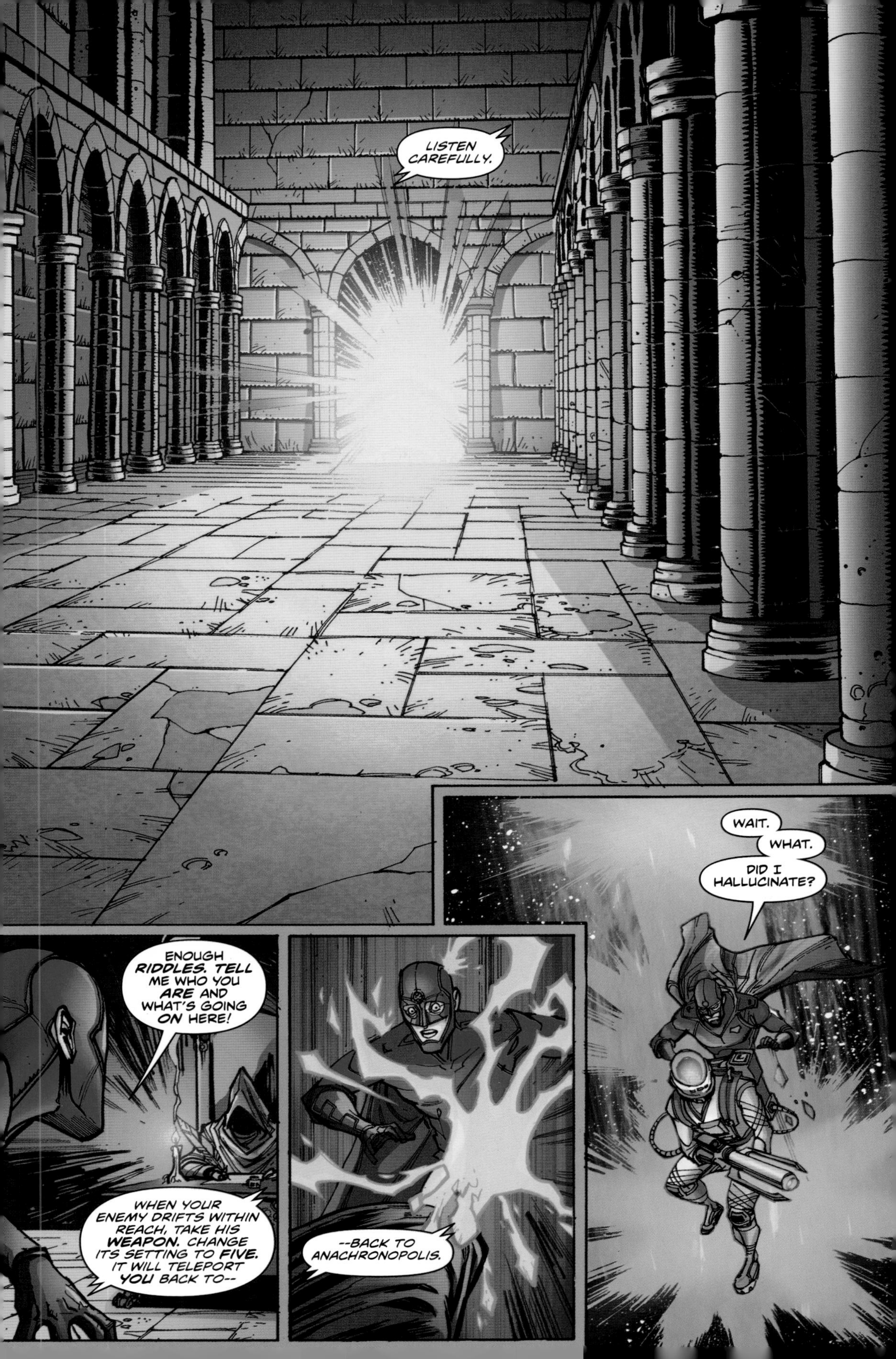
LISTEN CAREFULLY.
WAIT.
WHAT.
DID I HALLUCINATE?
ENOUGH RIDDLES. TELL ME WHO YOU ARE AND WHAT'S GOING ON HERE!
WHEN YOUR ENEMY DRIFTS WITHIN REACH, TAKE HIS WEAPON. CHANGE ITS SETTING TO FIVE. IT WILL TELEPORT YOU BACK TO--
--BACK TO ANACHRONOPOLIS.

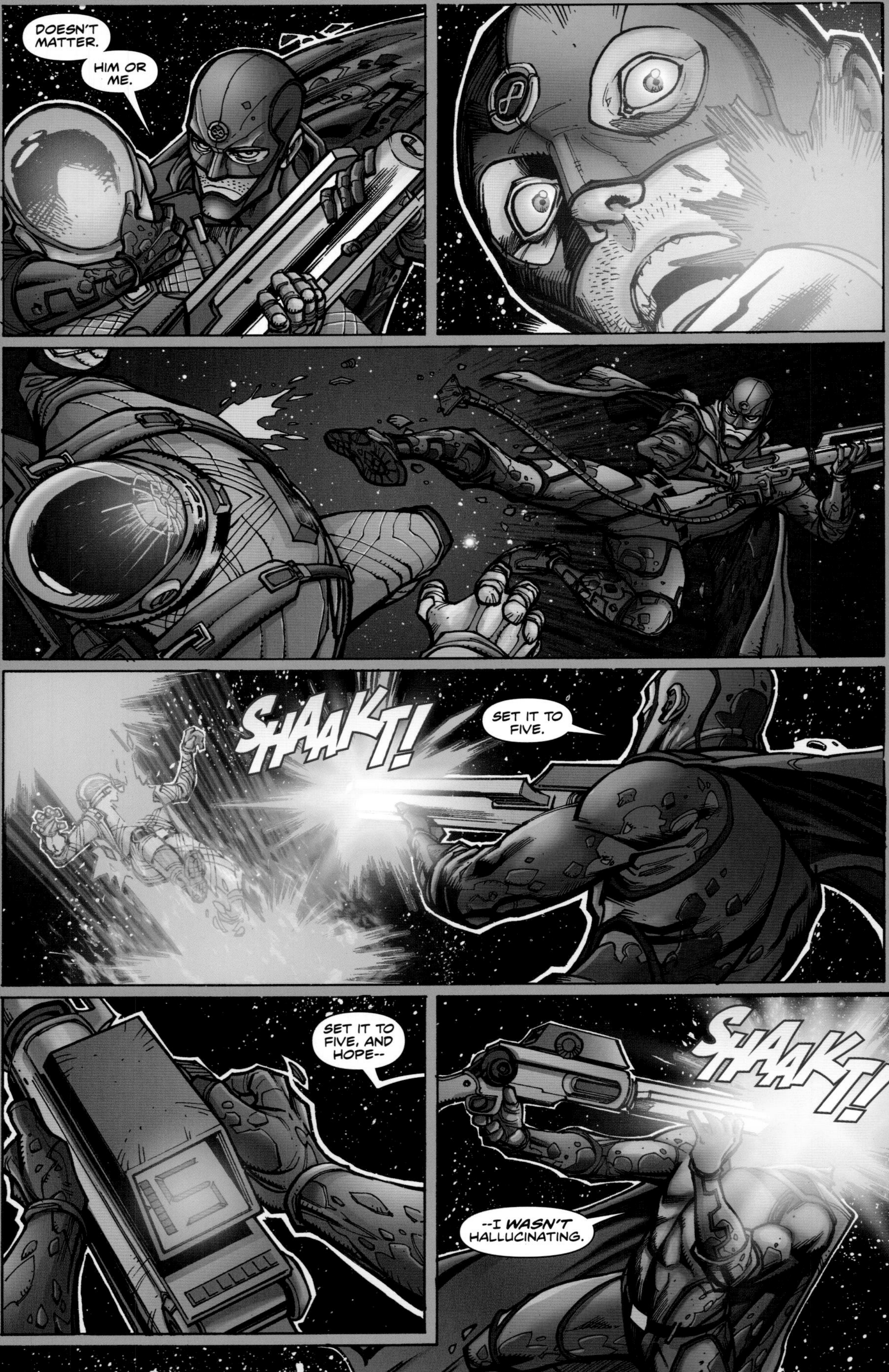
DOESN'T MATTER.
HIM OR ME.
SHAAKT!
SET IT TO FIVE.
SET IT TO FIVE, AND HOPE--
SHAAKT!
--I WASN'T HALLUCINATING.

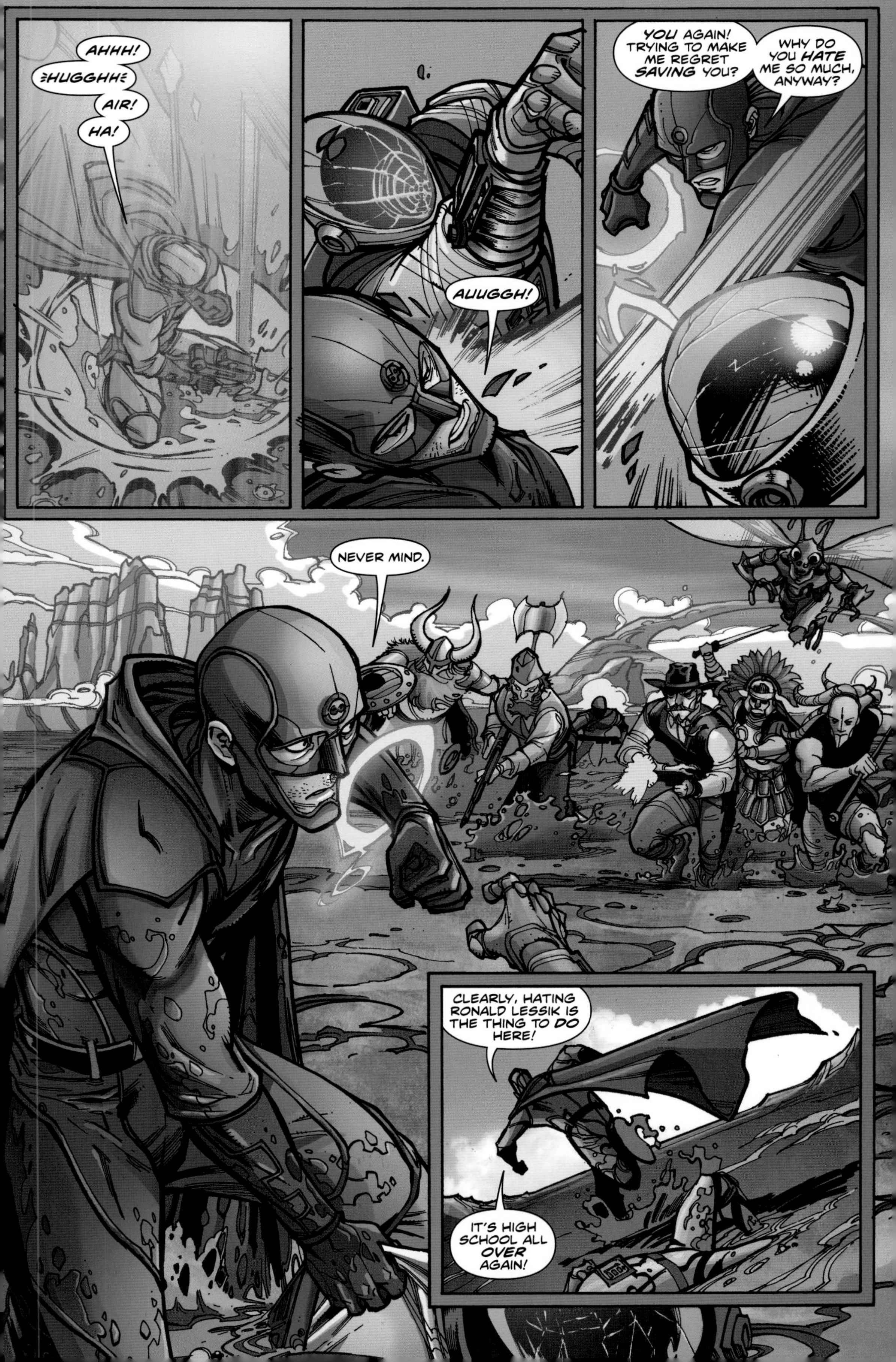
AHHH!
HUGGHH
AIR!
HA!
AUUGGH!
YOU AGAIN! TRYING TO MAKE ME REGRET SAVING YOU?
WHY DO YOU HATE ME SO MUCH, ANYWAY?
NEVER MIND.
CLEARLY, HATING RONALD LESSIK IS THE THING TO DO HERE!
IT'S HIGH SCHOOL ALL OVER AGAIN!

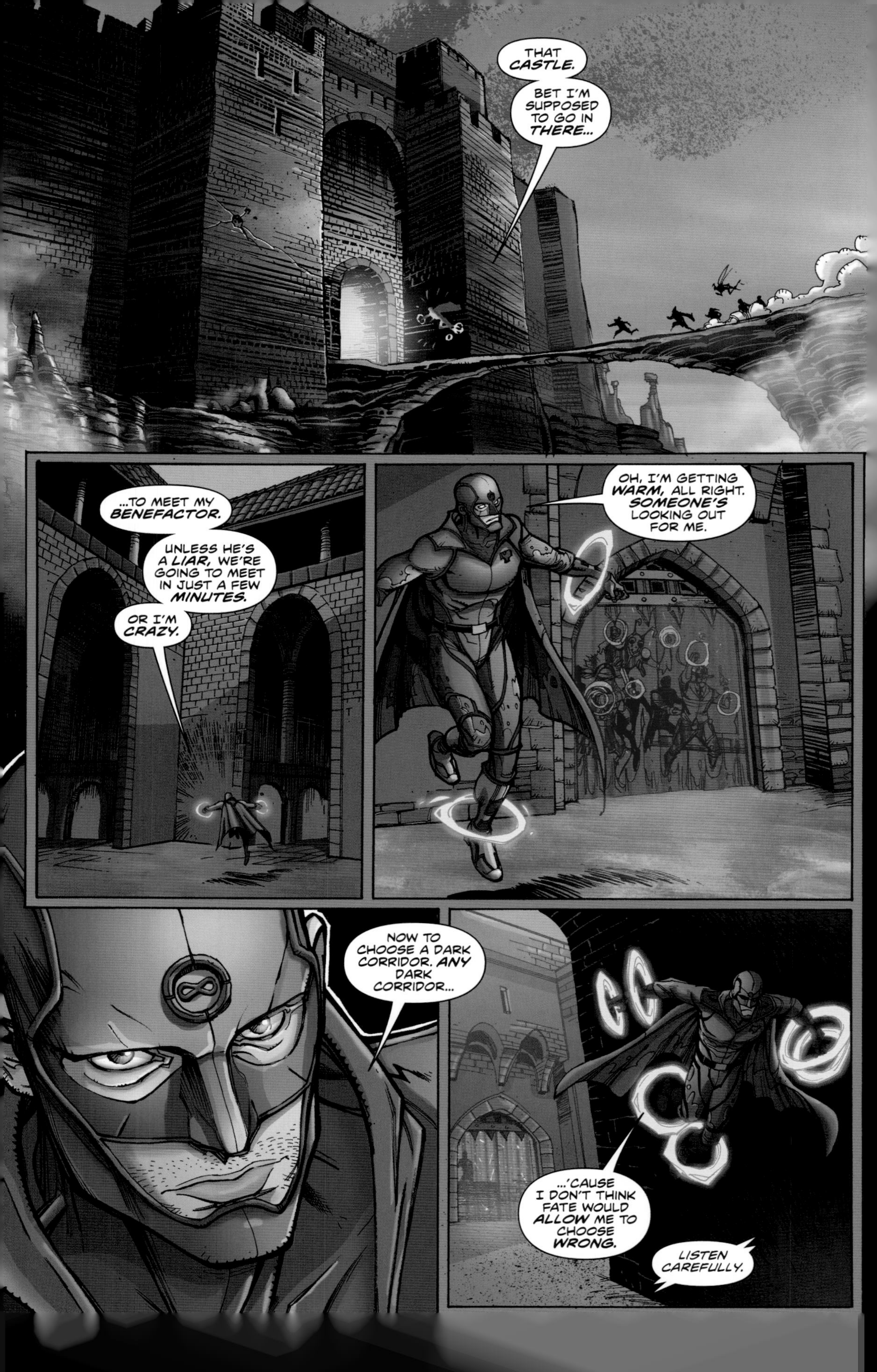
THAT CASTLE.
BET I'M SUPPOSED TO GO IN THERE...
...TO MEET MY BENEFACTOR.
UNLESS HE'S A LIAR, WE'RE GOING TO MEET IN JUST A FEW MINUTES.
OR I'M CRAZY.
OH, I'M GETTING WARM, ALL RIGHT. SOMEONE'S LOOKING OUT FOR ME.
NOW TO CHOOSE A DARK CORRIDOR. ANY DARK CORRIDOR...
...'CAUSE I DON'T THINK FATE WOULD ALLOW ME TO CHOOSE WRONG.
LISTEN CAREFULLY.

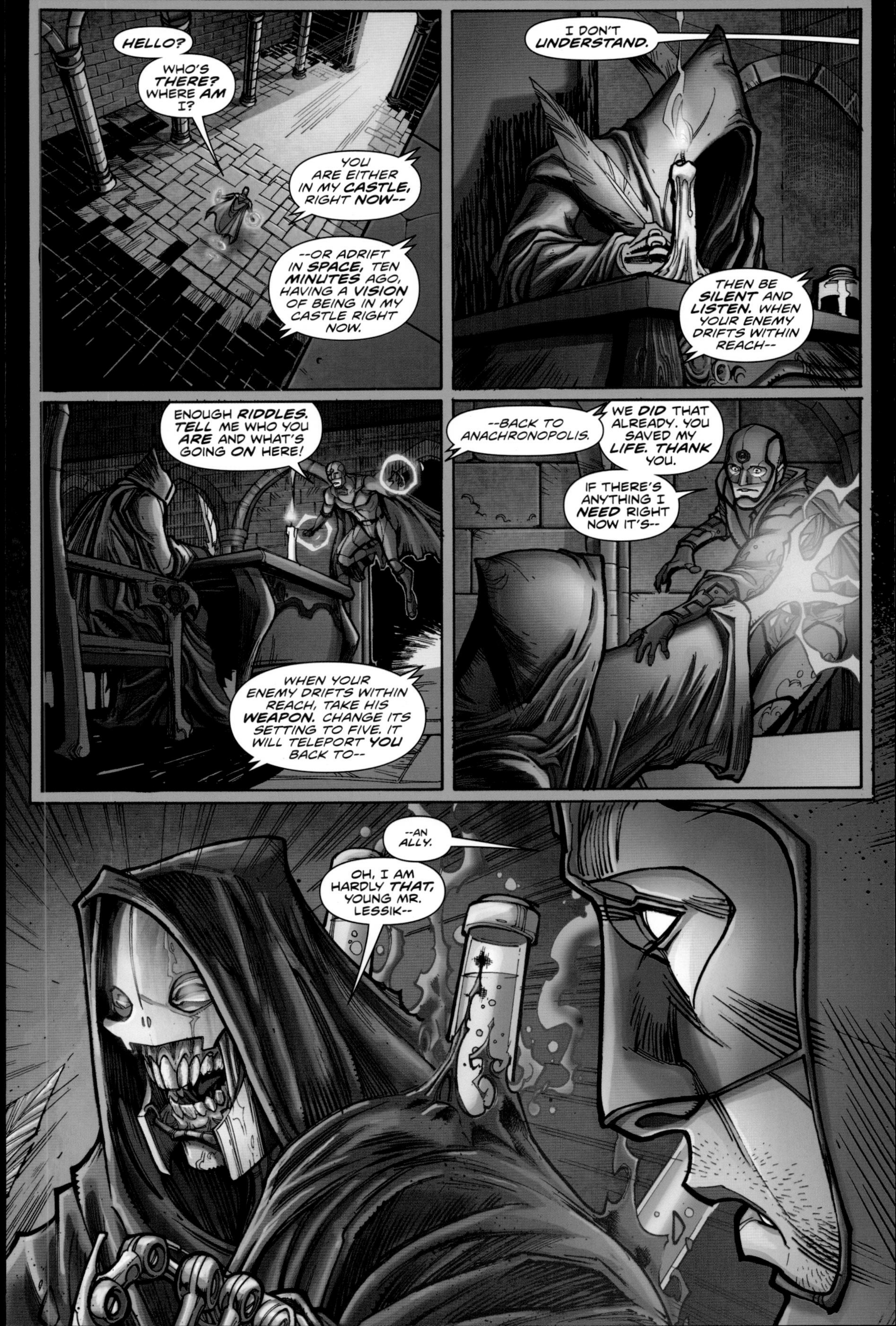
HELLO?
WHO'S THERE? WHERE AM I?
YOU ARE EITHER IN MY CASTLE, RIGHT NOW--
--OR ADRIFT IN SPACE, TEN MINUTES AGO, HAVING A VISION OF BEING IN MY CASTLE RIGHT NOW.
I DON'T UNDERSTAND.
THEN BE SILENT AND LISTEN. WHEN YOUR ENEMY DRIFTS WITHIN REACH--
ENOUGH RIDDLES. TELL ME WHO YOU ARE AND WHAT'S GOING ON HERE!
WHEN YOUR ENEMY DRIFTS WITHIN REACH, TAKE HIS WEAPON. CHANGE ITS SETTING TO FIVE. IT WILL TELEPORT YOU BACK TO--
--BACK TO ANACHRONOPOLIS.
WE DID THAT ALREADY. YOU SAVED MY LIFE. THANK YOU.
IF THERE'S ANYTHING I NEED RIGHT NOW IT'S--
--AN ALLY.
OH, I AM HARDLY THAT, YOUNG MR. LESSIK--

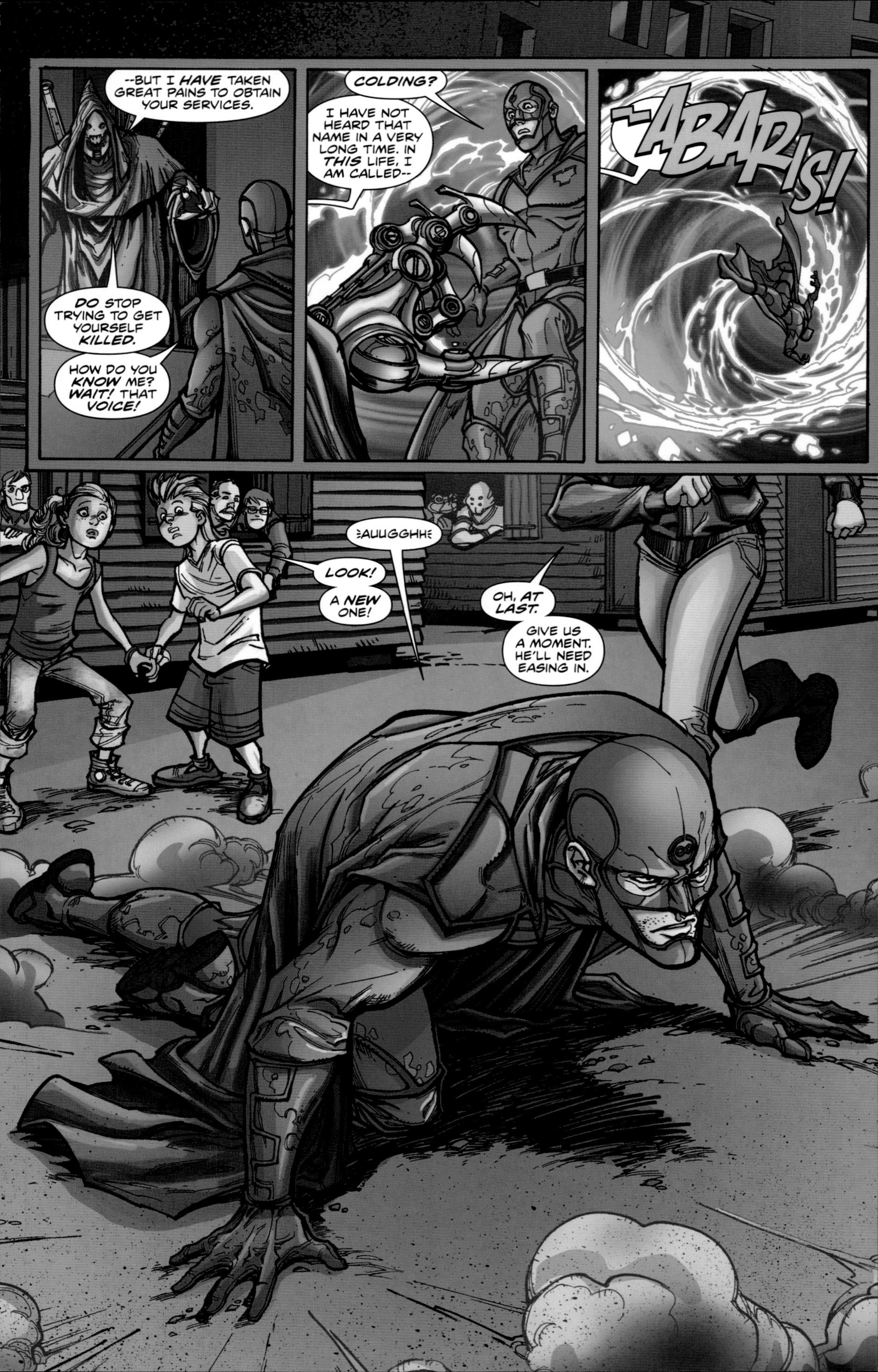
--BUT I HAVE TAKEN GREAT PAINS TO OBTAIN YOUR SERVICES.
DO STOP TRYING TO GET YOURSELF KILLED.
HOW DO YOU KNOW ME? WAIT! THAT VOICE!
COLDING?
I HAVE NOT HEARD THAT NAME IN A VERY LONG TIME. IN THIS LIFE, I AM CALLED--
--ABARIS!
AUUGGHH
LOOK!
A NEW ONE!
OH, AT LAST.
GIVE US A MOMENT. HE'LL NEED EASING IN.

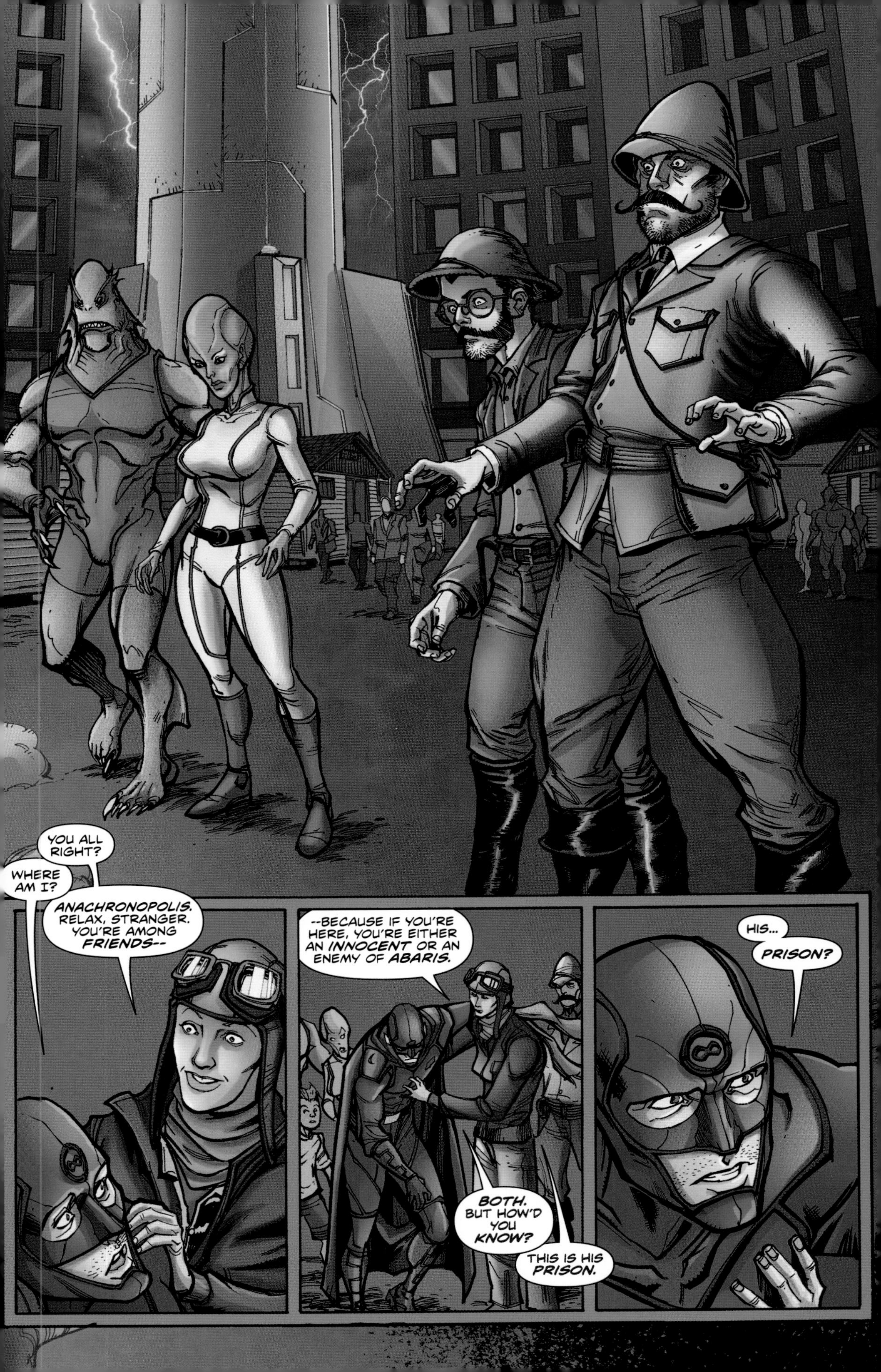
YOU ALL RIGHT?
WHERE AM I?
ANACHRONOPOLIS. RELAX, STRANGER. YOU'RE AMONG FRIENDS--
--BECAUSE IF YOU'RE HERE, YOU'RE EITHER AN INNOCENT OR AN ENEMY OF ABARIS.
BOTH. BUT HOW'D YOU KNOW?
THIS IS HIS PRISON.
HIS... PRISON?

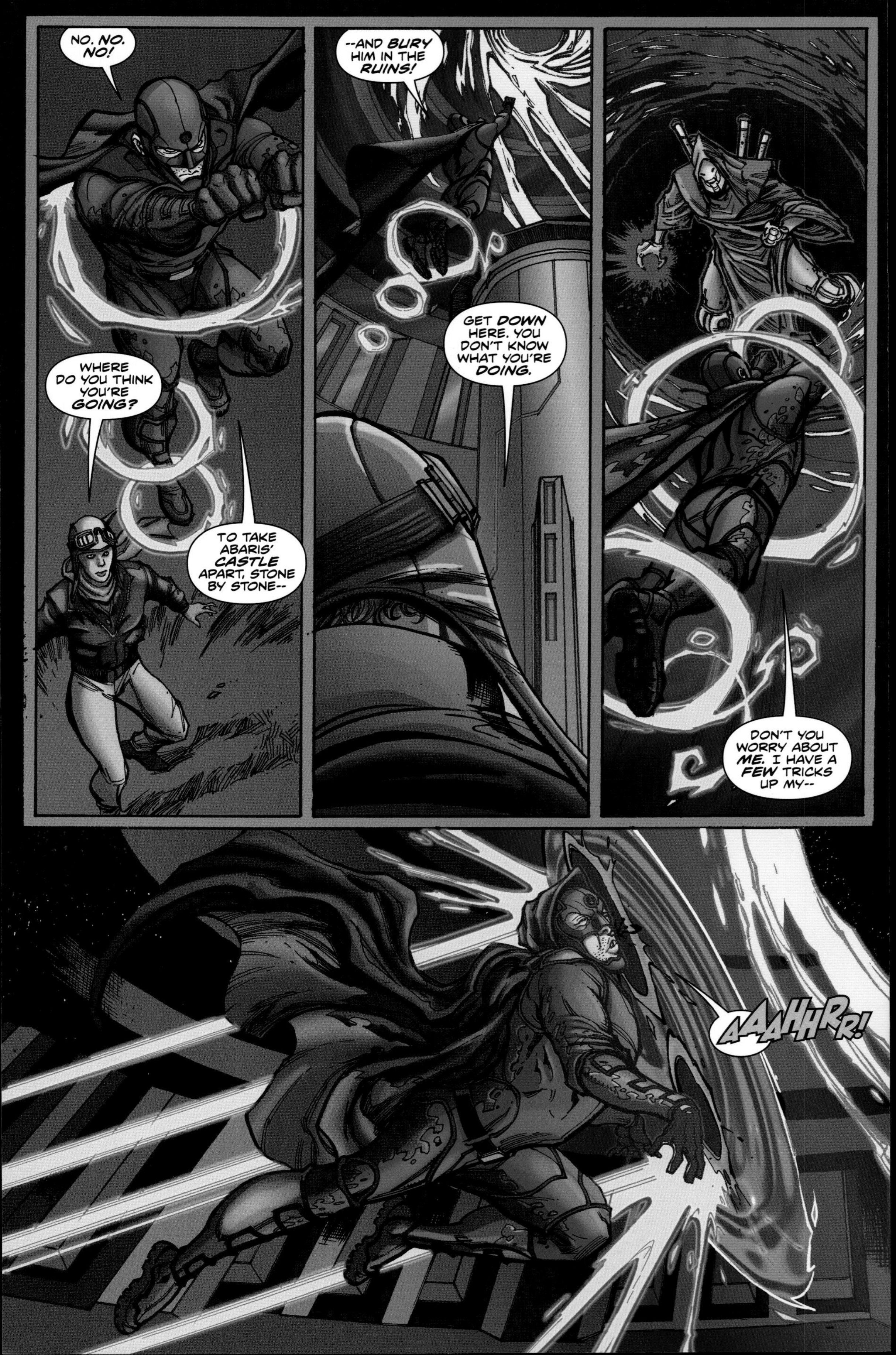
NO. NO. NO!
WHERE DO YOU THINK YOU'RE GOING?
TO TAKE ABARIS' CASTLE APART, STONE BY STONE--
--AND BURY HIM IN THE RUINS!
GET DOWN HERE. YOU DON'T KNOW WHAT YOU'RE DOING.
DON'T YOU WORRY ABOUT ME. I HAVE A FEW TRICKS UP MY--
AAAHHRR!

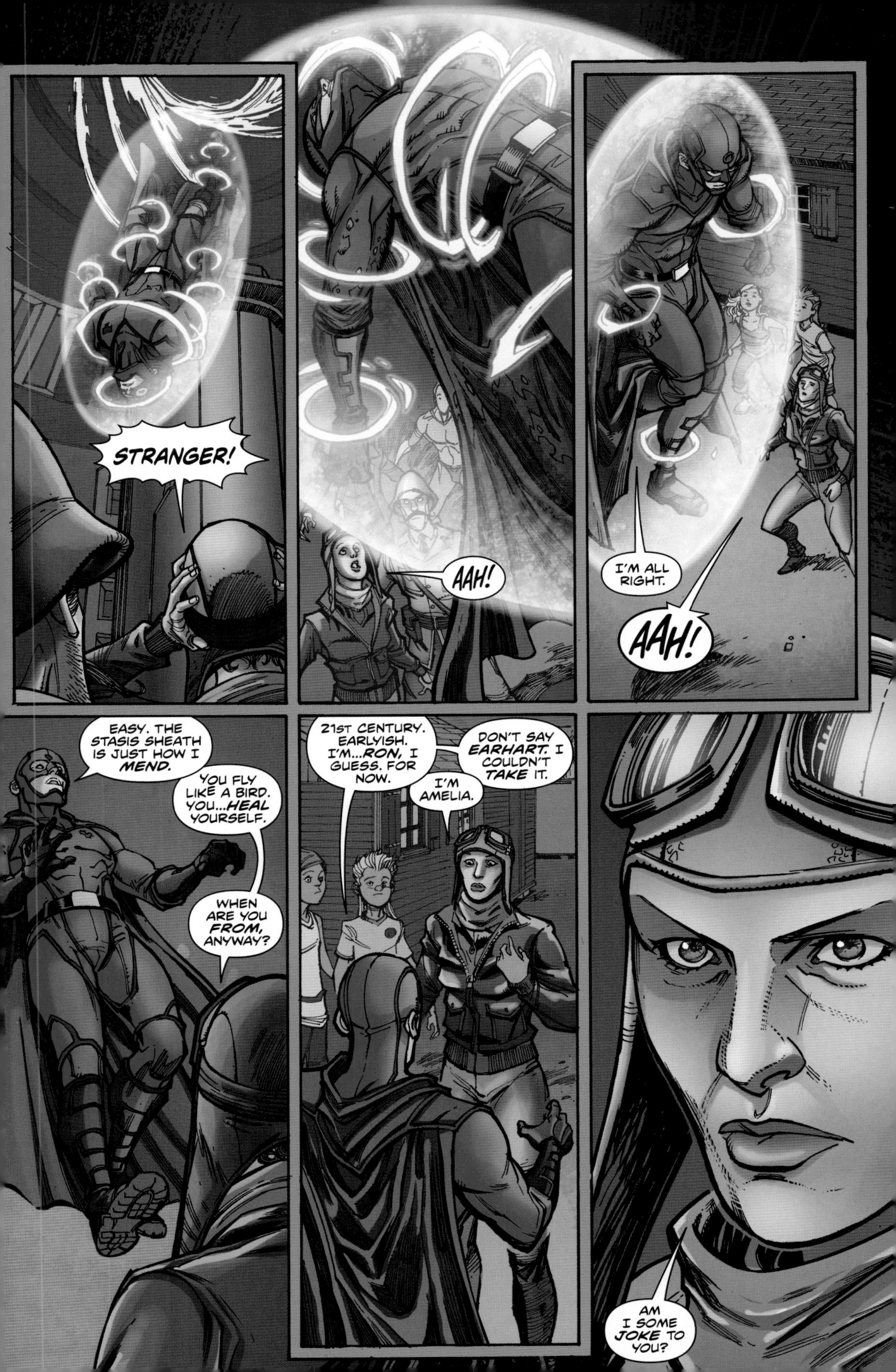

STRANGER!
AAH!
I'M ALL RIGHT.
AAH!
EASY. THE STASIS SHEATH IS JUST HOW I MEND.
YOU FLY LIKE A BIRD. YOU...HEAL YOURSELF.
WHEN ARE YOU FROM, ANYWAY?
21ST CENTURY. EARLYISH. I'M...RON, I GUESS. FOR NOW.
I'M AMELIA.
DON'T SAY EARHART. I COULDN'T TAKE IT.
AM I SOME JOKE TO YOU?

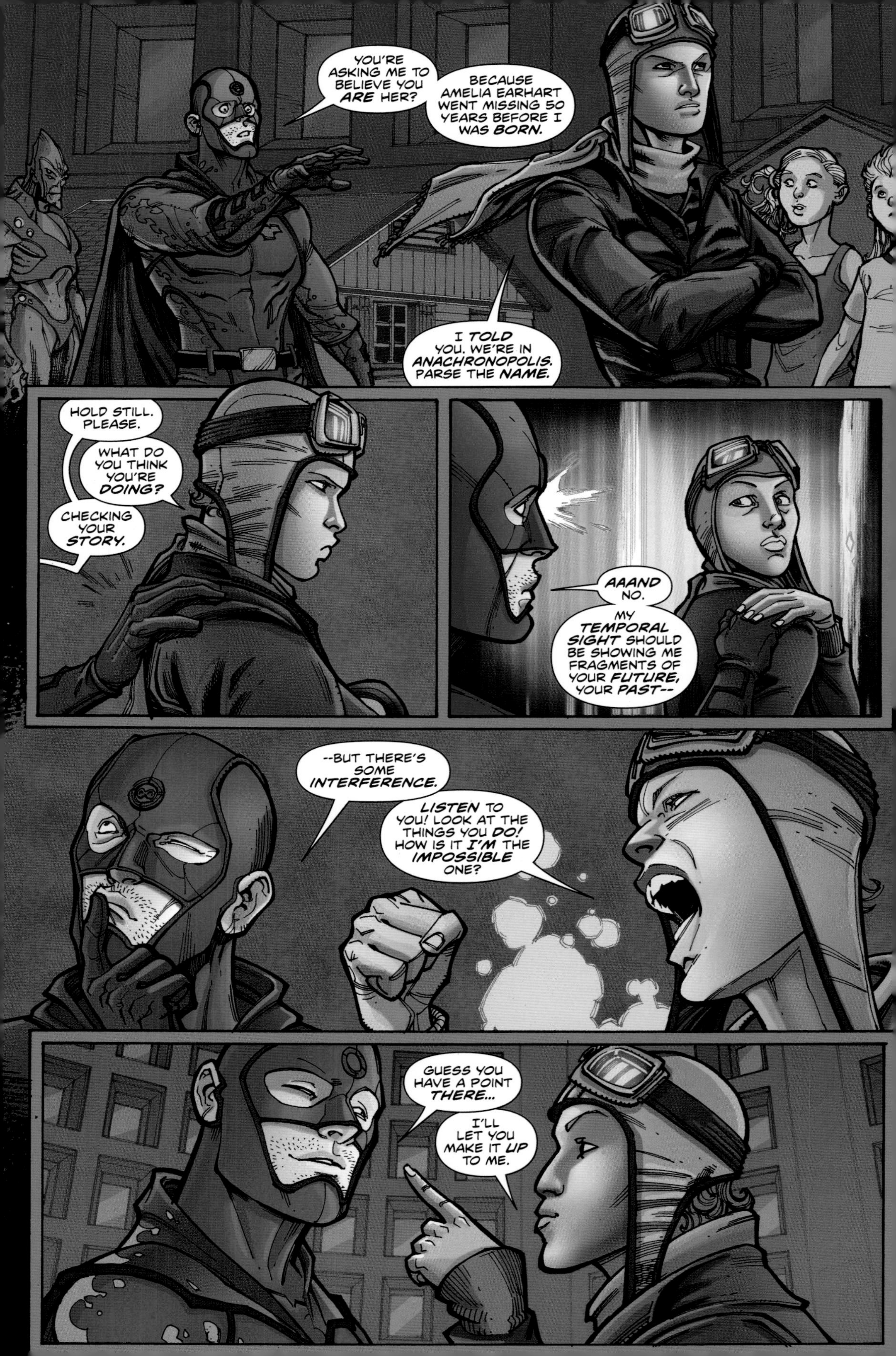
YOU'RE ASKING ME TO BELIEVE YOU ARE HER?
BECAUSE AMELIA EARHART WENT MISSING 50 YEARS BEFORE I WAS BORN.
I TOLD YOU. WE'RE IN ANACHRONOPOLIS. PARSE THE NAME.
HOLD STILL. PLEASE.
WHAT DO YOU THINK YOU'RE DOING?
CHECKING YOUR STORY.
AAAND NO.
MY TEMPORAL SIGHT SHOULD BE SHOWING ME FRAGMENTS OF YOUR FUTURE, YOUR PAST--
--BUT THERE'S SOME INTERFERENCE.
LISTEN TO YOU! LOOK AT THE THINGS YOU DO! HOW IS IT I'M THE IMPOSSIBLE ONE?
GUESS YOU HAVE A POINT THERE...
I'LL LET YOU MAKE IT UP TO ME.

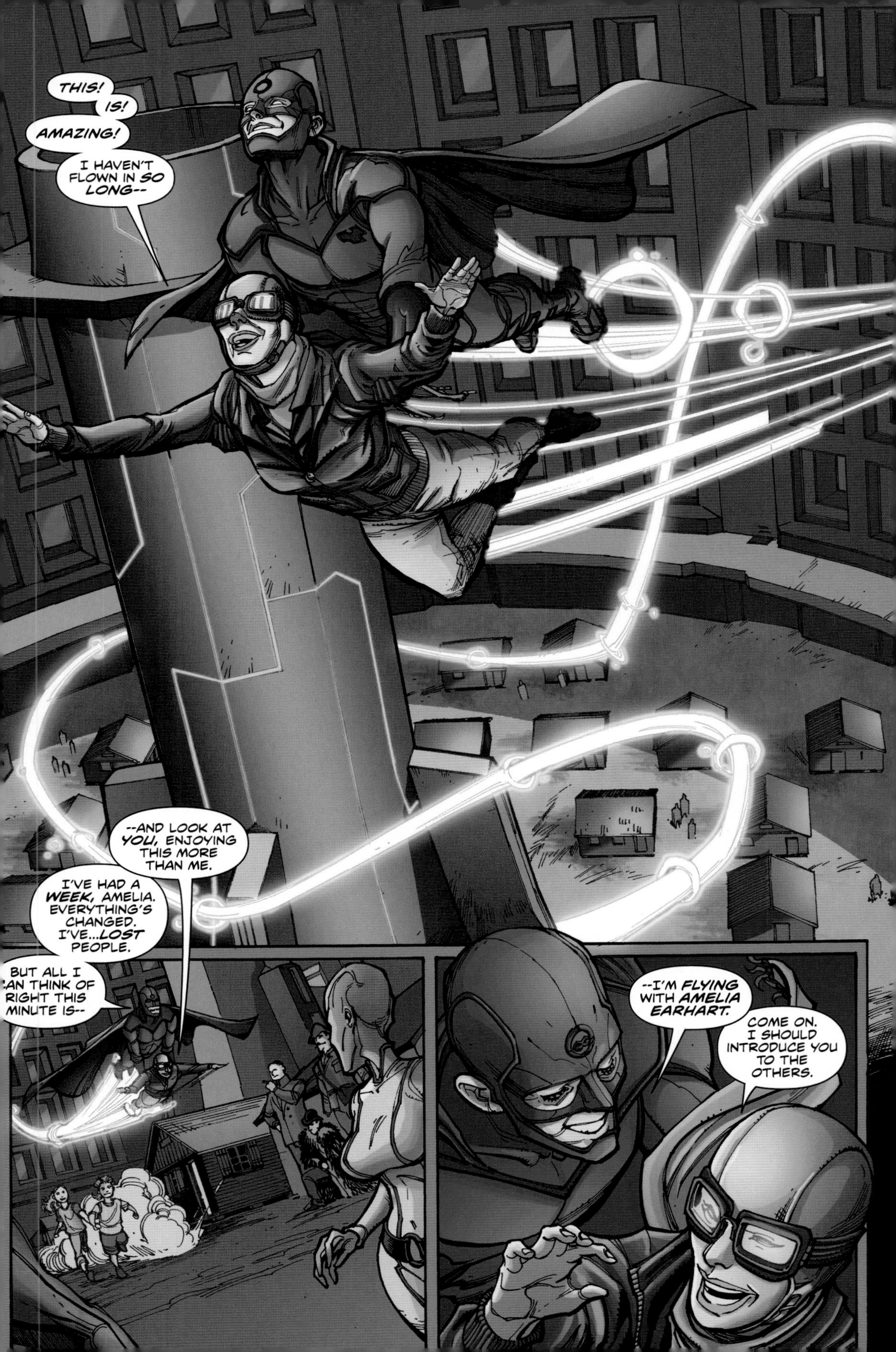
THIS!
IS!
AMAZING!
I HAVEN'T FLOWN IN SO LONG--
--AND LOOK AT YOU, ENJOYING THIS MORE THAN ME.
I'VE HAD A WEEK, AMELIA. EVERYTHING'S CHANGED. I'VE...LOST PEOPLE.
BUT ALL I CAN THINK OF RIGHT THIS MINUTE IS--
--I'M FLYING WITH AMELIA EARHART.
COME ON. I SHOULD INTRODUCE YOU TO THE OTHERS.

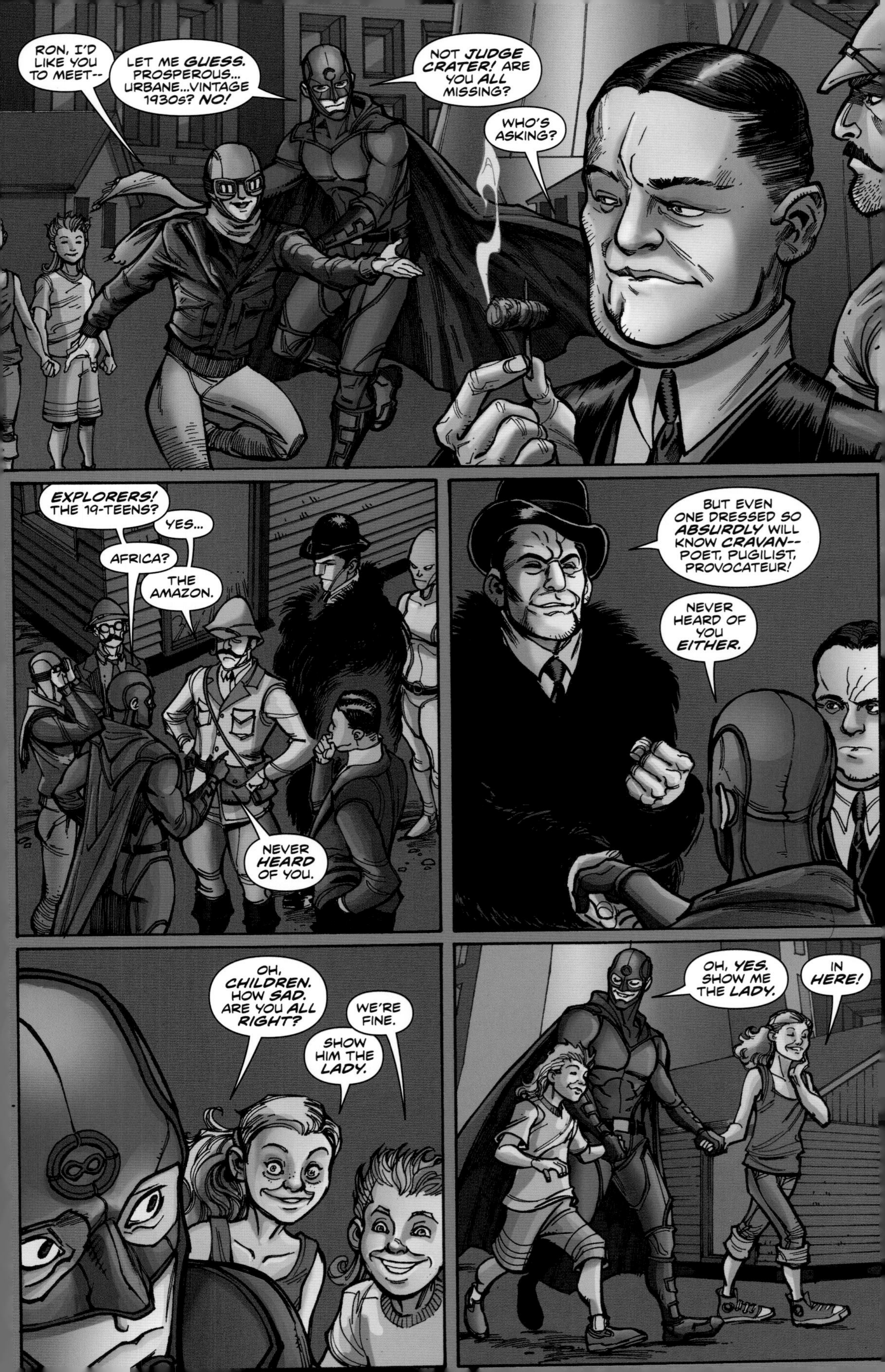
RON, I'D LIKE YOU TO MEET--
LET ME GUESS. PROSPEROUS... URBANE...VINTAGE 1930s? NO!
NOT JUDGE CRATER! ARE YOU ALL MISSING?
WHO'S ASKING?
EXPLORERS! THE 19-TEENS?
YES...
AFRICA?
THE AMAZON.
NEVER HEARD OF YOU.
BUT EVEN ONE DRESSED SO ABSURDLY WILL KNOW CRAVAN-- POET, PUGILIST, PROVOCATEUR!
NEVER HEARD OF YOU EITHER.
OH, CHILDREN. HOW SAD. ARE YOU ALL RIGHT?
WE'RE FINE.
SHOW HIM THE LADY.
OH, YES. SHOW ME THE LADY.
IN HERE!

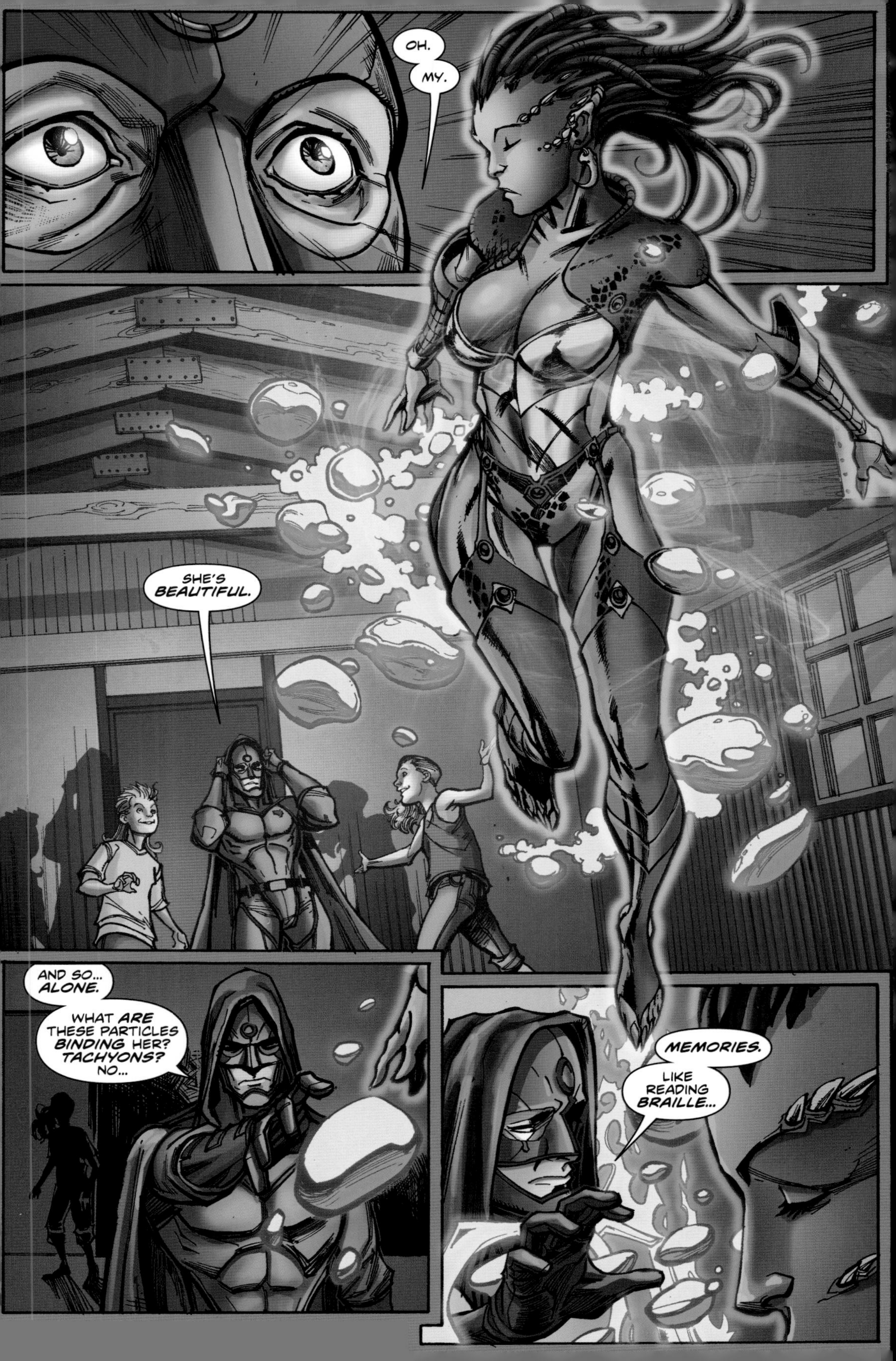
OH.
MY.
SHE'S BEAUTIFUL.
AND SO... ALONE.
WHAT ARE THESE PARTICLES BINDING HER? TACHYONS? NO...
MEMORIES.
LIKE READING BRAILLE...

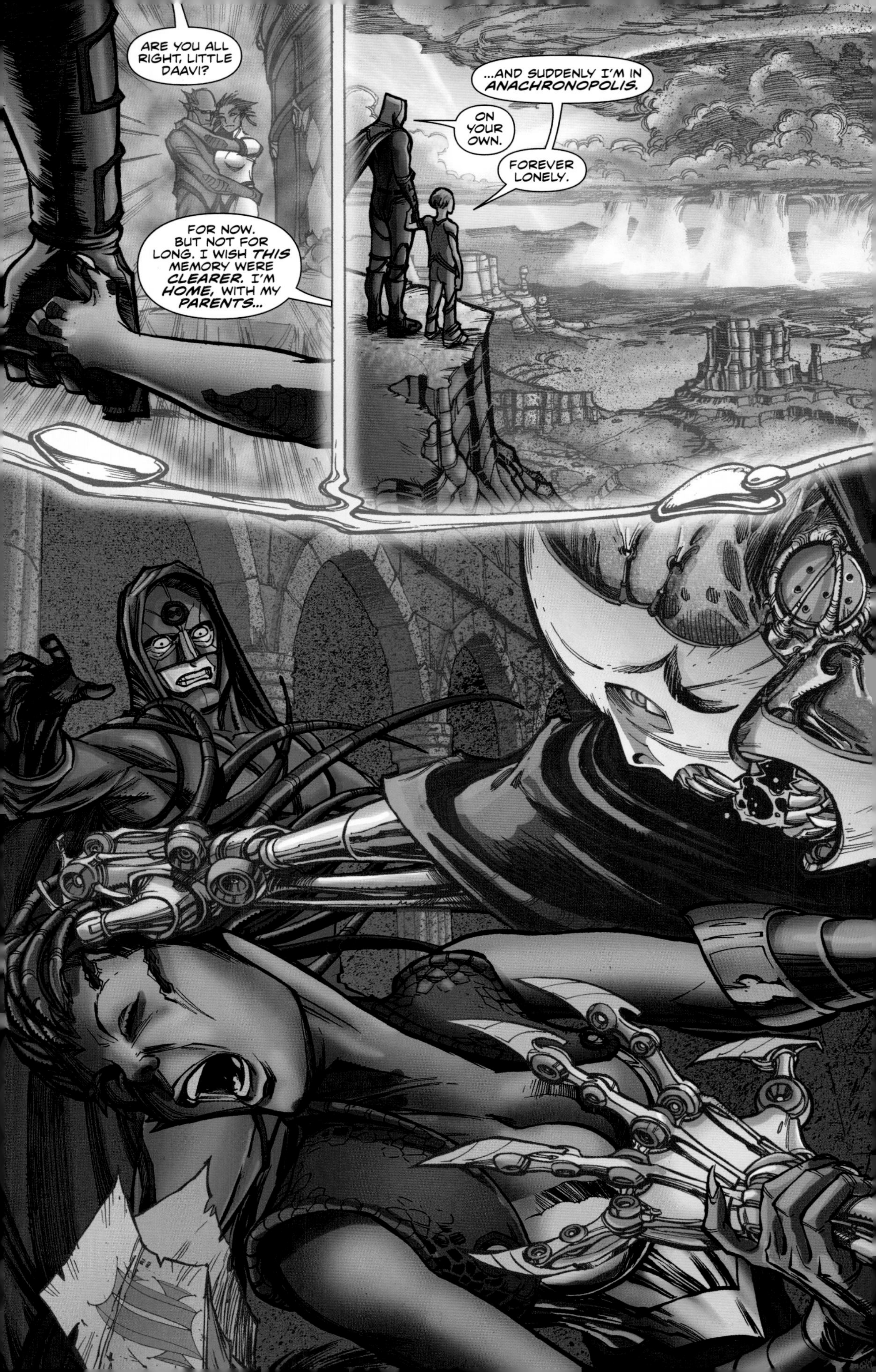
ARE YOU ALL RIGHT, LITTLE DAAVI?
FOR NOW. BUT NOT FOR LONG. I WISH *THIS* MEMORY WERE *CLEARER*. I'M *HOME*, WITH MY *PARENTS*...
...AND SUDDENLY I'M IN *ANACHRONOPOLIS*.
ON YOUR OWN.
FOREVER LONELY.

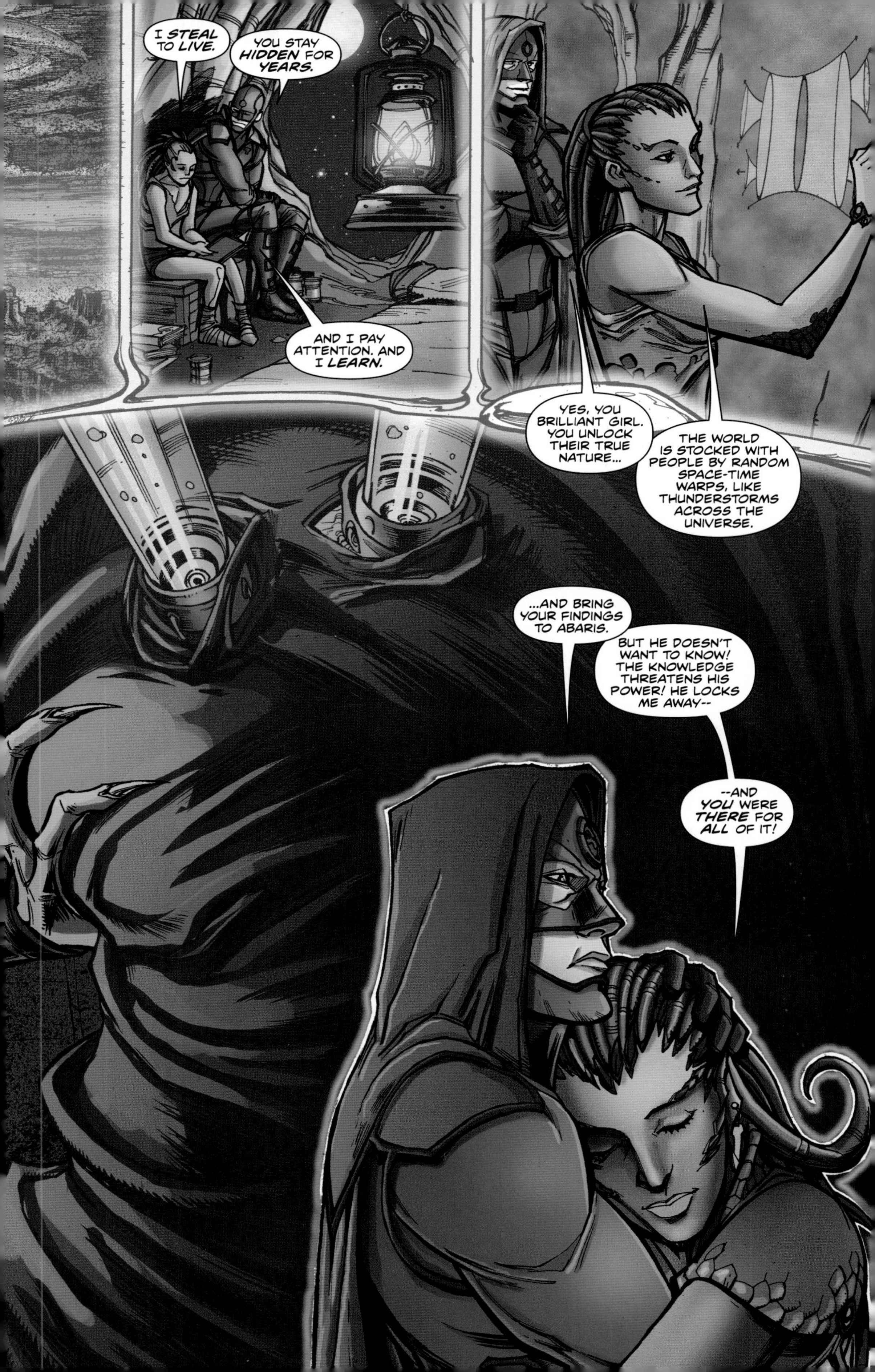
I STEAL TO LIVE.
YOU STAY HIDDEN FOR YEARS.
AND I PAY ATTENTION. AND I LEARN.
YES, YOU BRILLIANT GIRL. YOU UNLOCK THEIR TRUE NATURE...
THE WORLD IS STOCKED WITH PEOPLE BY RANDOM SPACE-TIME WARPS, LIKE THUNDERSTORMS ACROSS THE UNIVERSE.
...AND BRING YOUR FINDINGS TO ABARIS.
BUT HE DOESN'T WANT TO KNOW! THE KNOWLEDGE THREATENS HIS POWER! HE LOCKS ME AWAY--
--AND YOU WERE THERE FOR ALL OF IT!

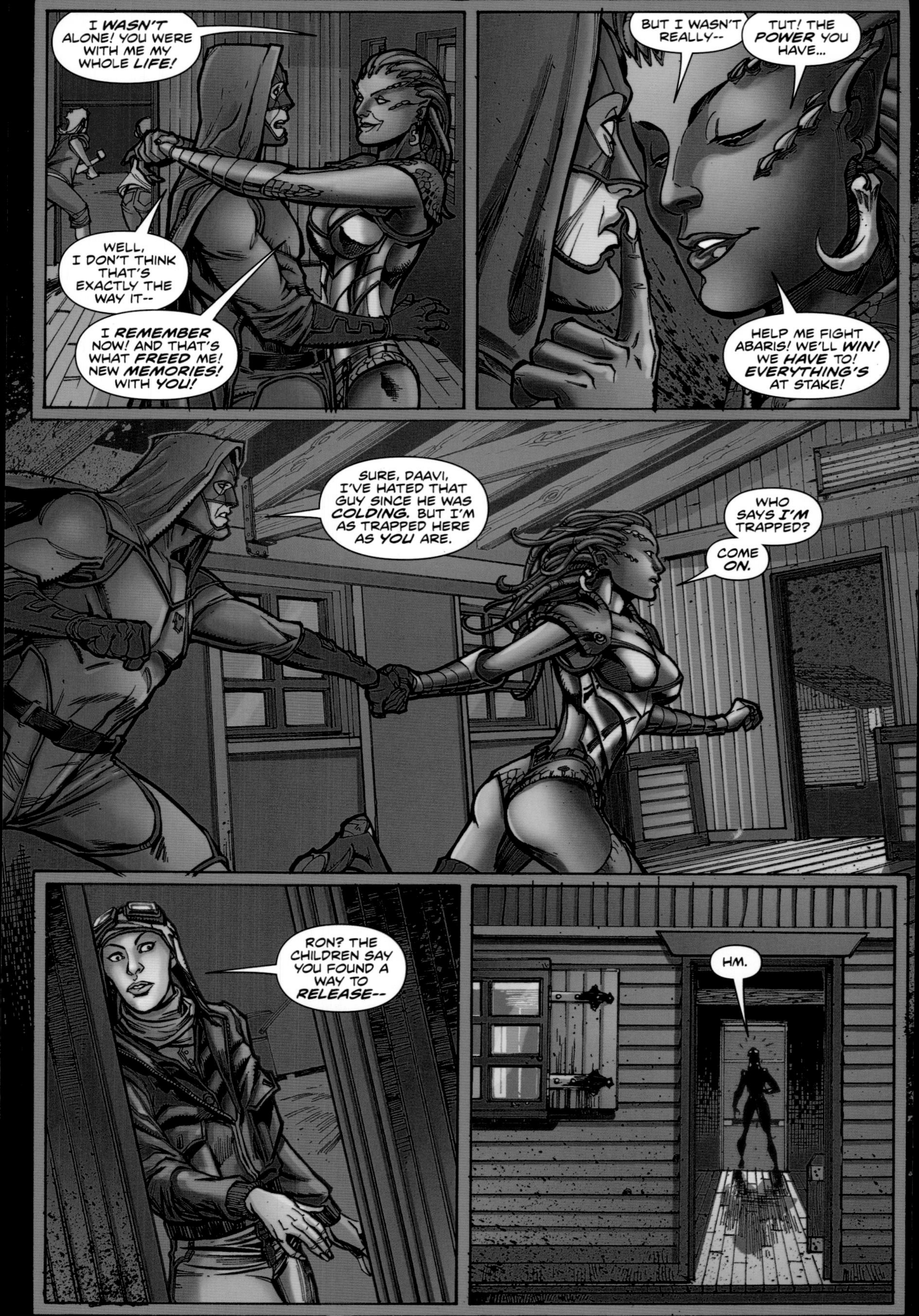
I WASN'T ALONE! YOU WERE WITH ME MY WHOLE LIFE!
WELL, I DON'T THINK THAT'S EXACTLY THE WAY IT--
I REMEMBER NOW! AND THAT'S WHAT FREED ME! NEW MEMORIES! WITH YOU!
BUT I WASN'T REALLY--
TUT! THE POWER YOU HAVE...
HELP ME FIGHT ABARIS! WE'LL WIN! WE HAVE TO! EVERYTHING'S AT STAKE!
SURE, DAAVI, I'VE HATED THAT GUY SINCE HE WAS COLDING. BUT I'M AS TRAPPED HERE AS YOU ARE.
WHO SAYS I'M TRAPPED?
COME ON.
RON? THE CHILDREN SAY YOU FOUND A WAY TO RELEASE--
HM.

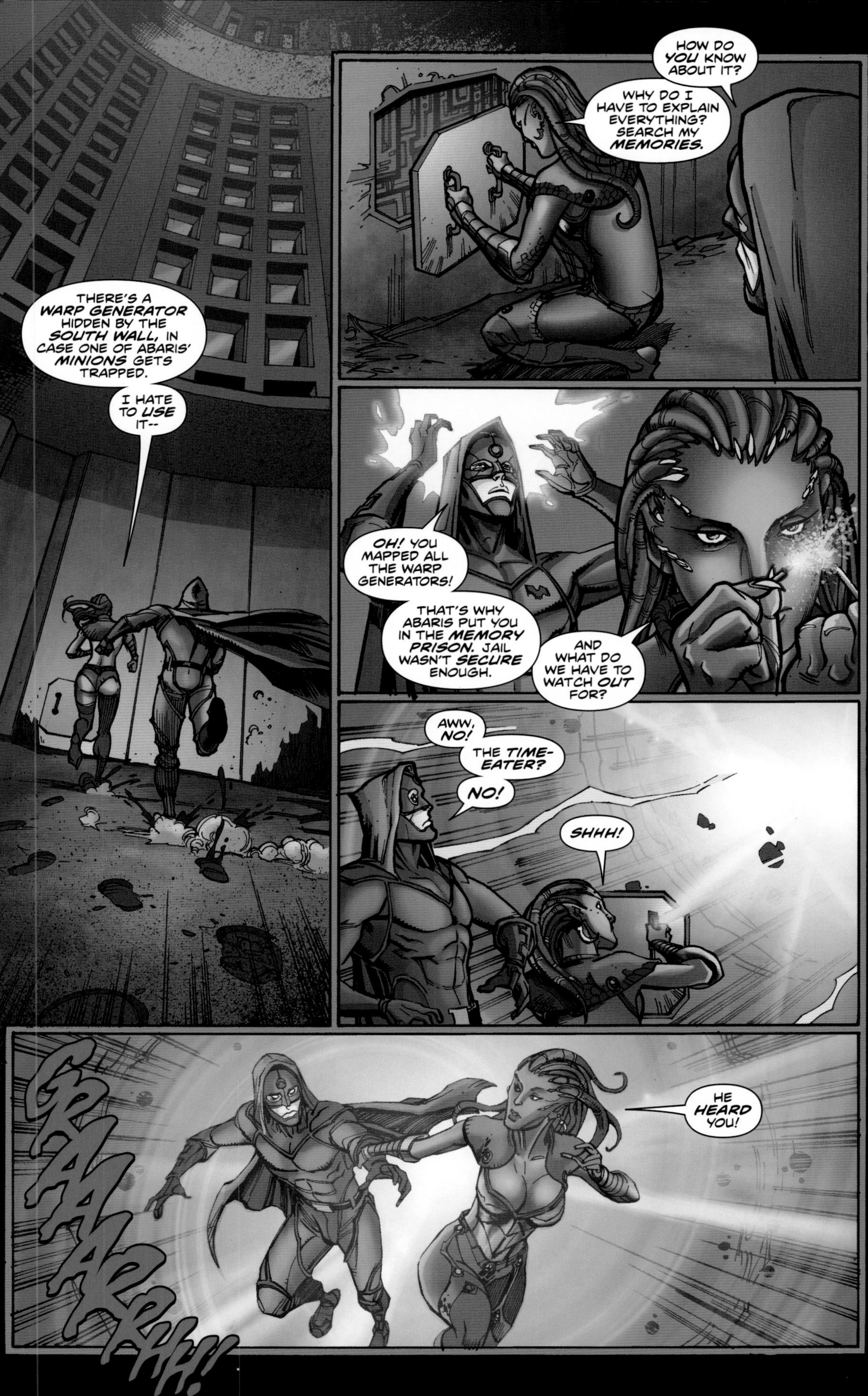

THERE'S A WARP GENERATOR HIDDEN BY THE SOUTH WALL, IN CASE ONE OF ABARIS' MINIONS GETS TRAPPED.
I HATE TO USE IT--
HOW DO YOU KNOW ABOUT IT?
WHY DO I HAVE TO EXPLAIN EVERYTHING? SEARCH MY MEMORIES.
OH! YOU MAPPED ALL THE WARP GENERATORS!
THAT'S WHY ABARIS PUT YOU IN THE MEMORY PRISON. JAIL WASN'T SECURE ENOUGH.
AND WHAT DO WE HAVE TO WATCH OUT FOR?
AWW, NO!
THE TIME-EATER?
NO!
SHHH!
GRAAARRHH!
HE HEARD YOU!

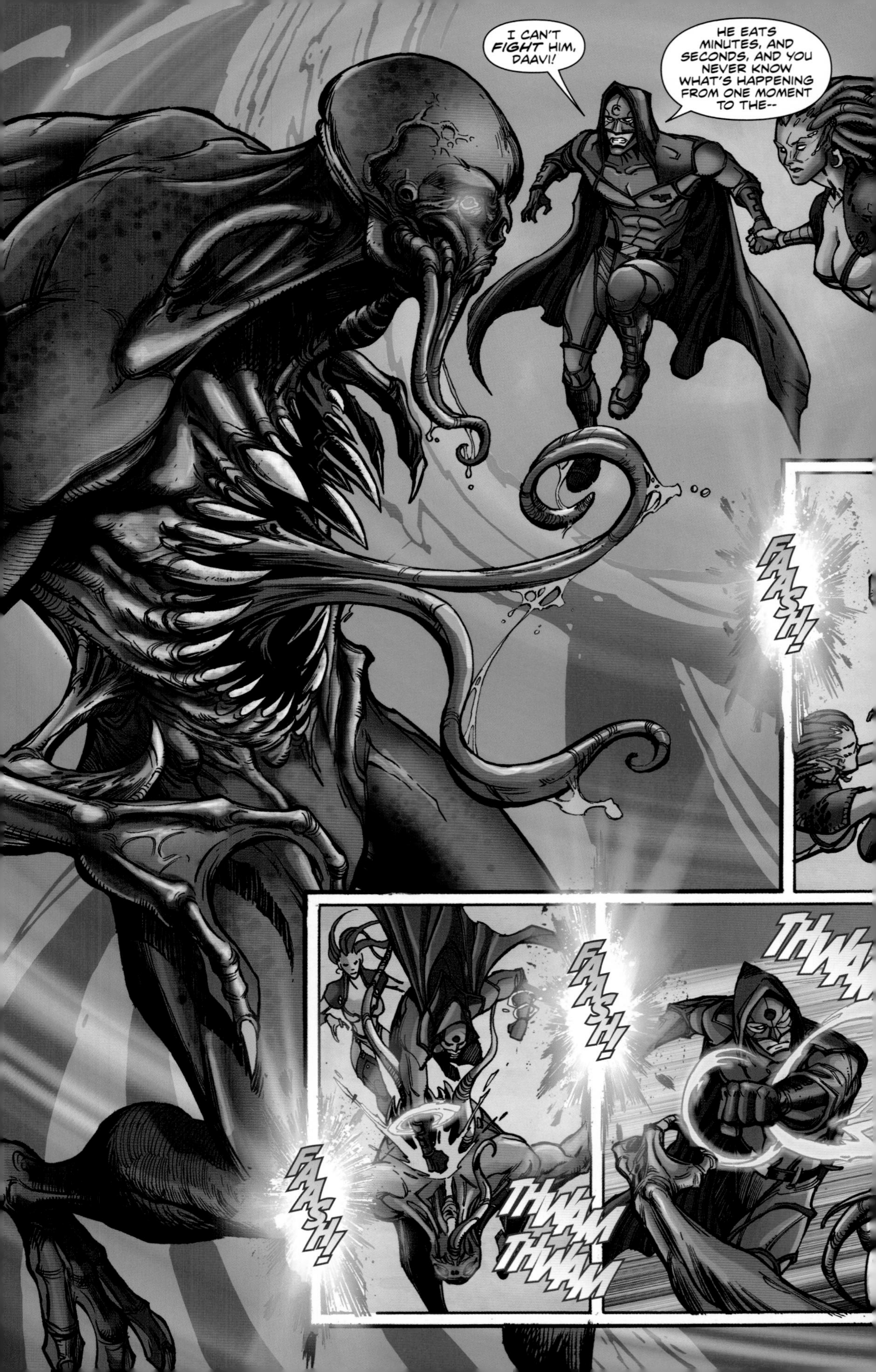
I CAN'T *FIGHT* HIM, DAAVI!
HE EATS MINUTES, AND SECONDS, AND YOU NEVER KNOW WHAT'S HAPPENING FROM ONE MOMENT TO THE--
FAASH!
FAASH!
FAASH!
THWAM THWAM
THWAM

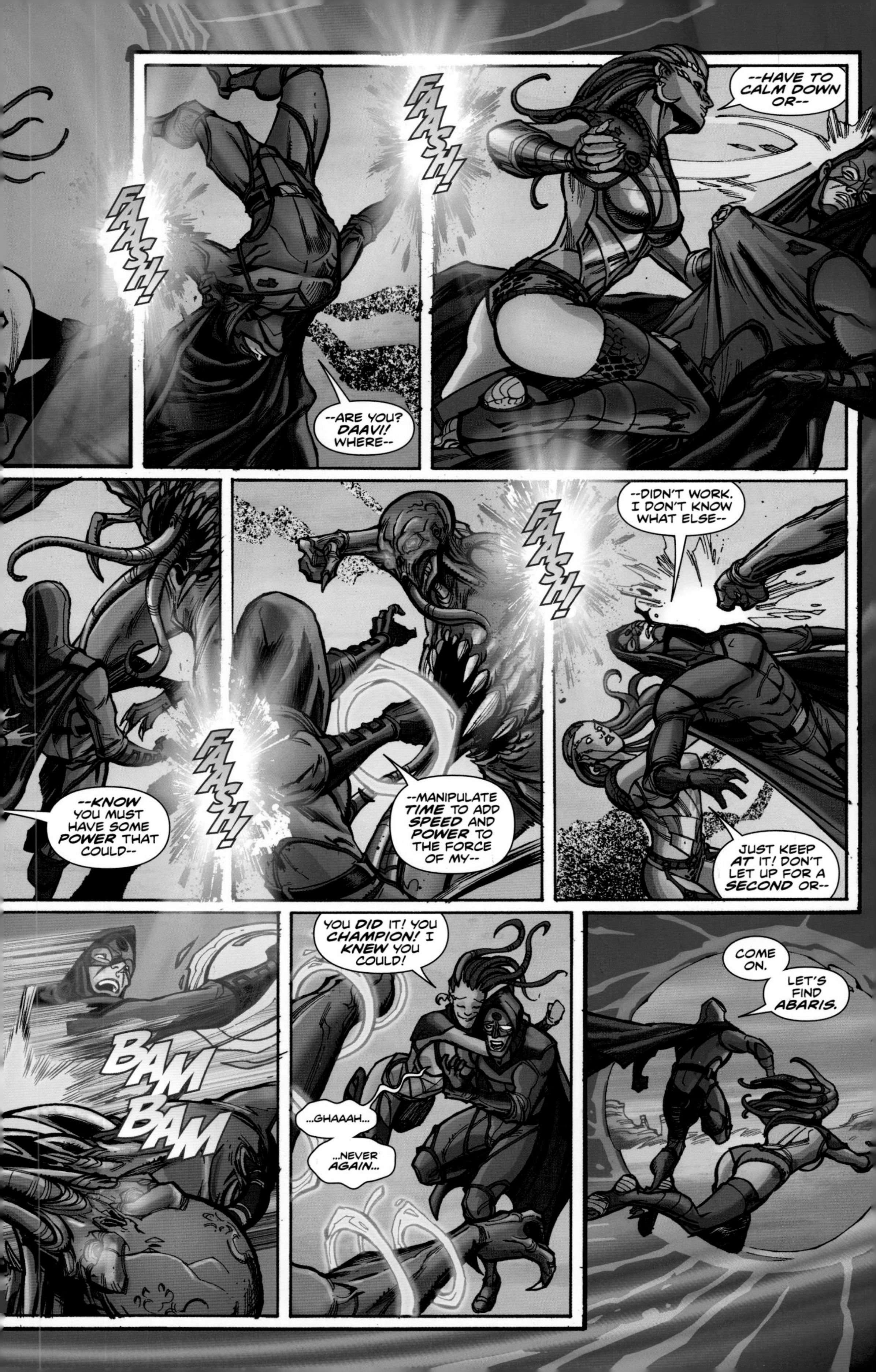FAASH!
FAASH!
--ARE YOU? DAAVI! WHERE--
--HAVE TO CALM DOWN OR--
--KNOW YOU MUST HAVE SOME POWER THAT COULD--
FAASH!
--MANIPULATE TIME TO ADD SPEED AND POWER TO THE FORCE OF MY--
FAASH!
--DIDN'T WORK. I DON'T KNOW WHAT ELSE--
JUST KEEP AT IT! DON'T LET UP FOR A SECOND OR--
BAM BAM
YOU DID IT! YOU CHAMPION! I KNEW YOU COULD!
...GHAAAH...
...NEVER AGAIN...
COME ON.
LET'S FIND ABARIS.

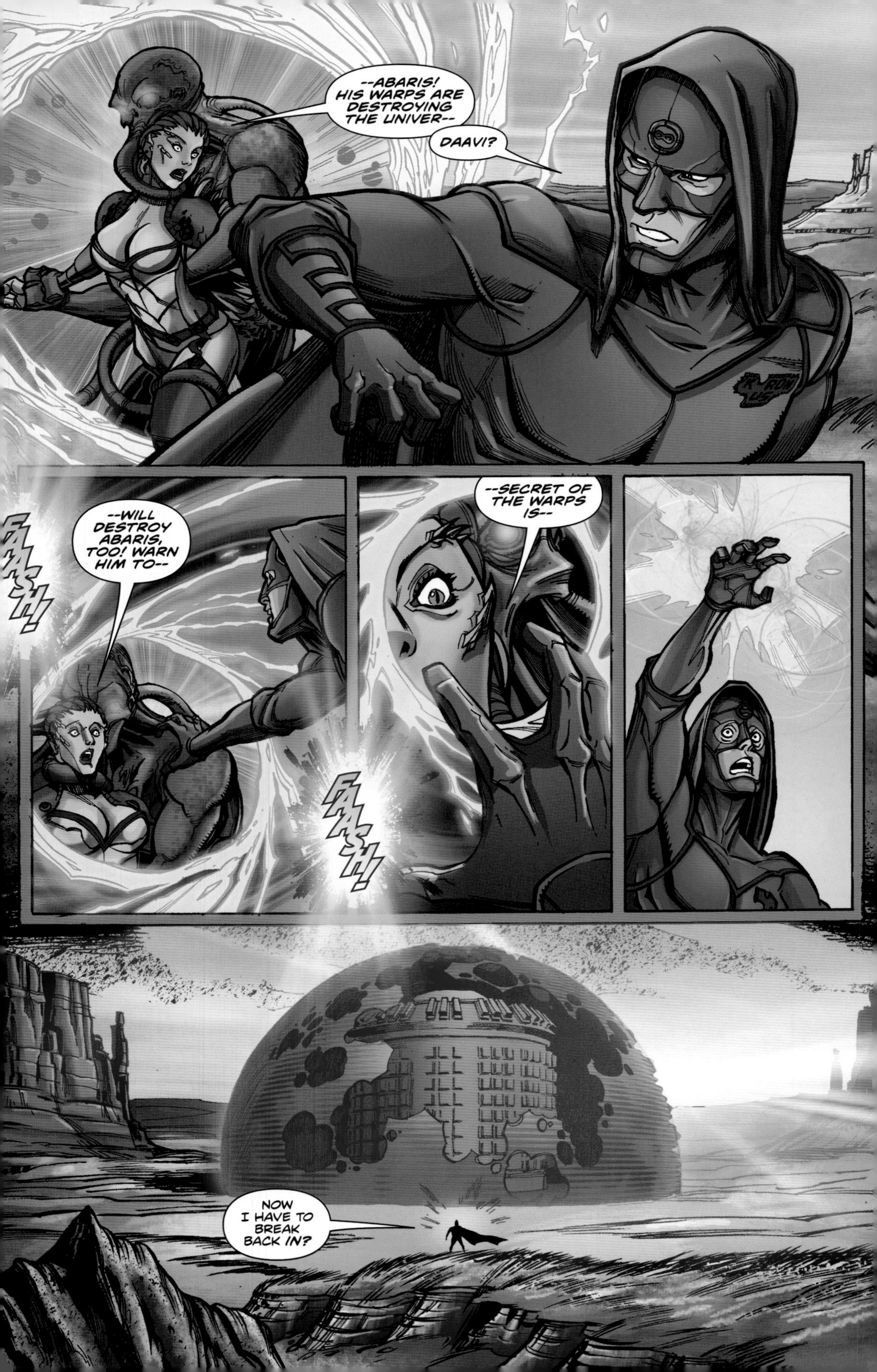
--ABARIS! HIS WARPS ARE DESTROYING THE UNIVER--
DAAVI?
FAASH!
--WILL DESTROY ABARIS, TOO! WARN HIM TO--
--SECRET OF THE WARPS IS--
FAASH!
NOW I HAVE TO BREAK BACK IN?

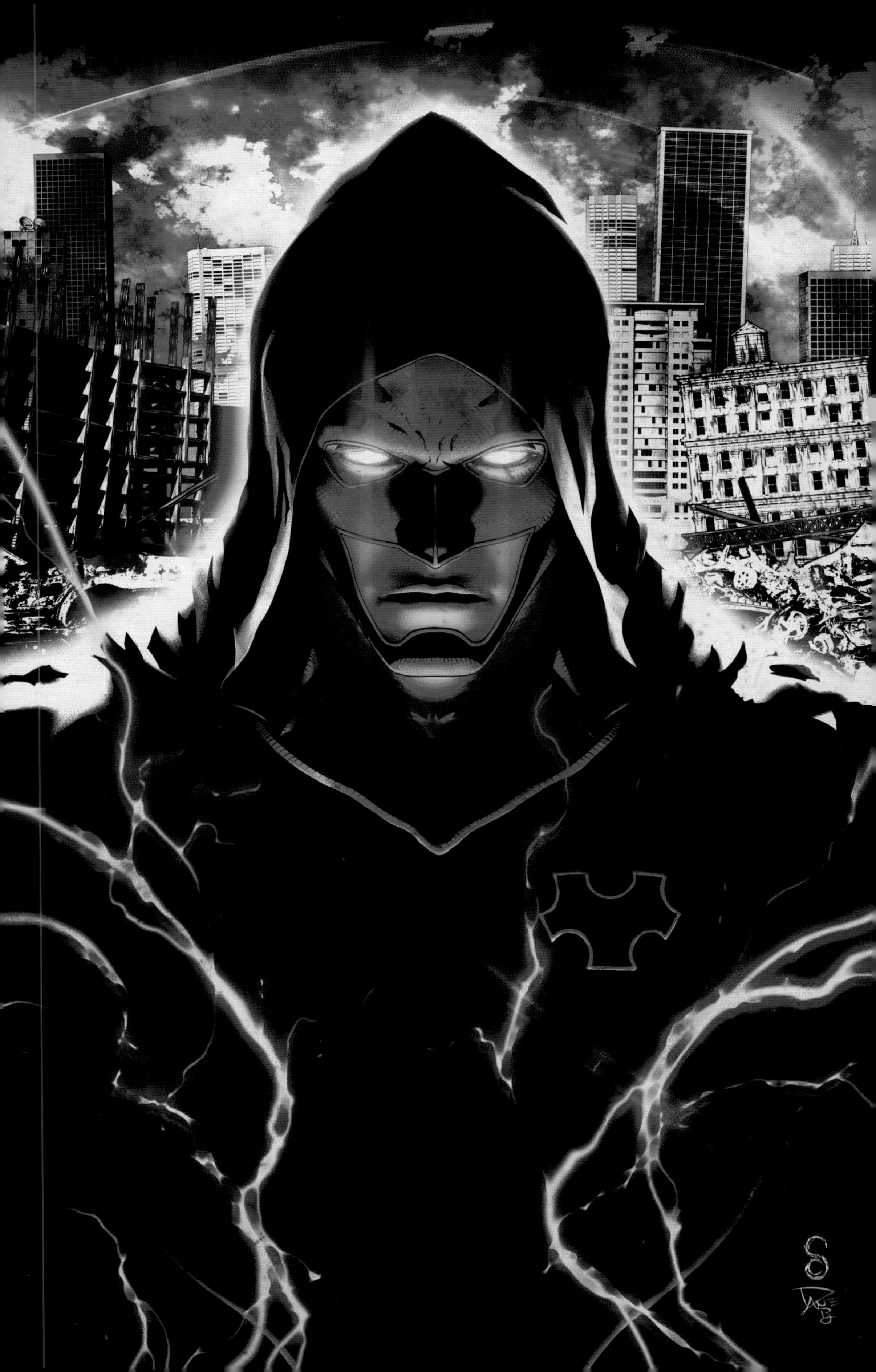

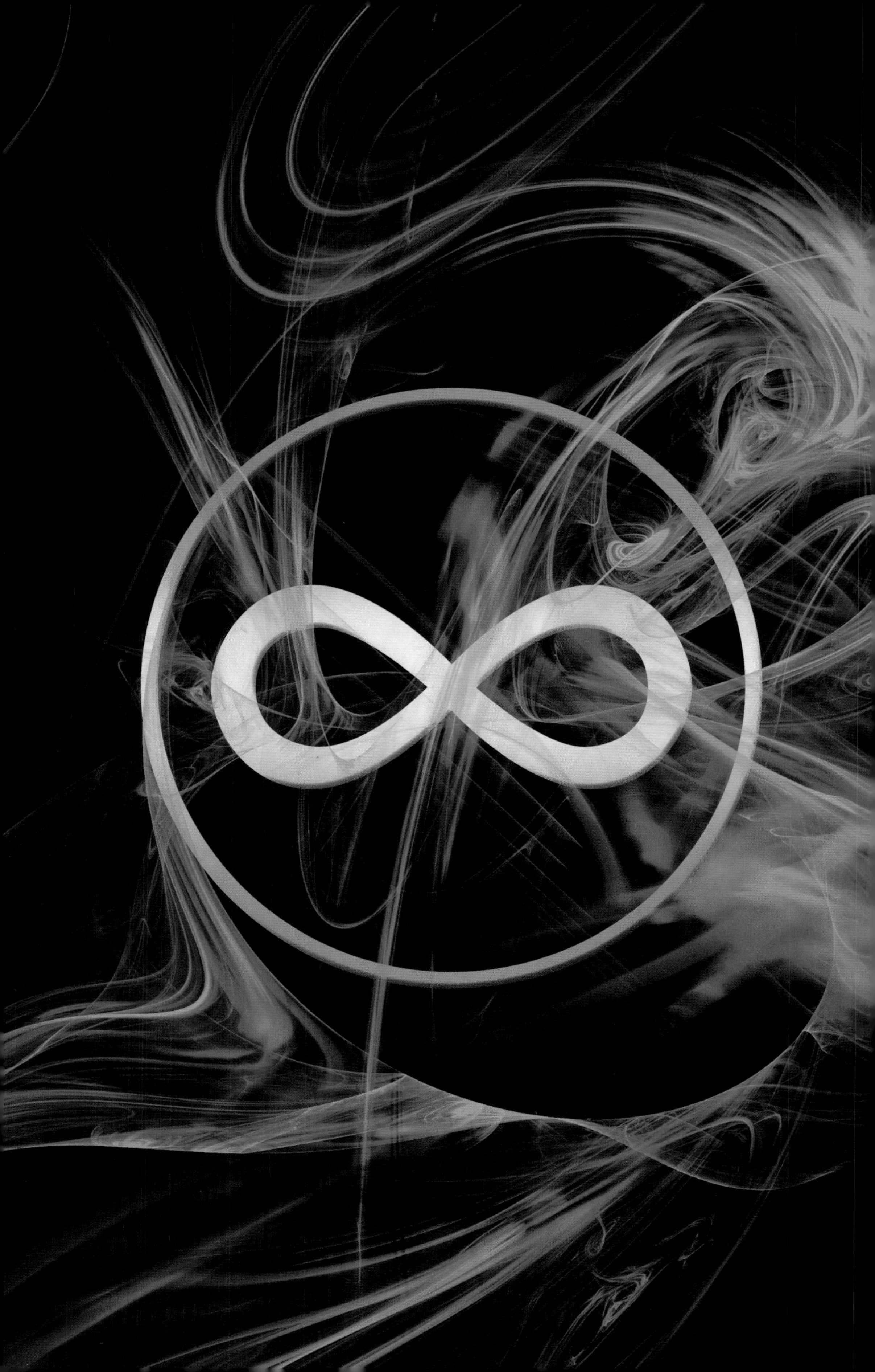

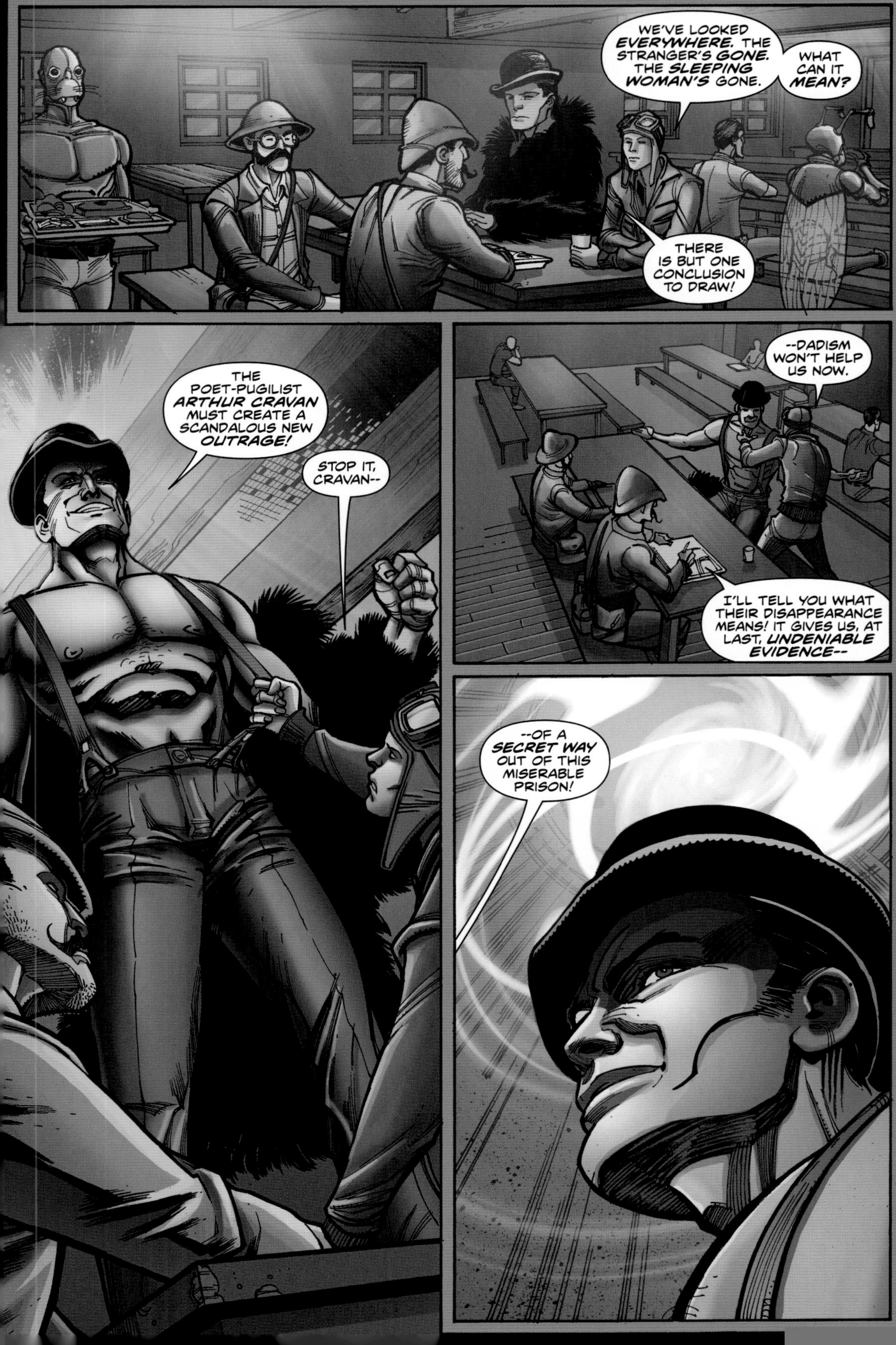
WE'VE LOOKED EVERYWHERE. THE STRANGER'S GONE. THE SLEEPING WOMAN'S GONE.
WHAT CAN IT MEAN?
THERE IS BUT ONE CONCLUSION TO DRAW!
THE POET-PUGILIST ARTHUR CRAVAN MUST CREATE A SCANDALOUS NEW OUTRAGE!
STOP IT, CRAVAN--
--DADISM WON'T HELP US NOW.
I'LL TELL YOU WHAT THEIR DISAPPEARANCE MEANS! IT GIVES US, AT LAST, UNDENIABLE EVIDENCE--
--OF A SECRET WAY OUT OF THIS MISERABLE PRISON!

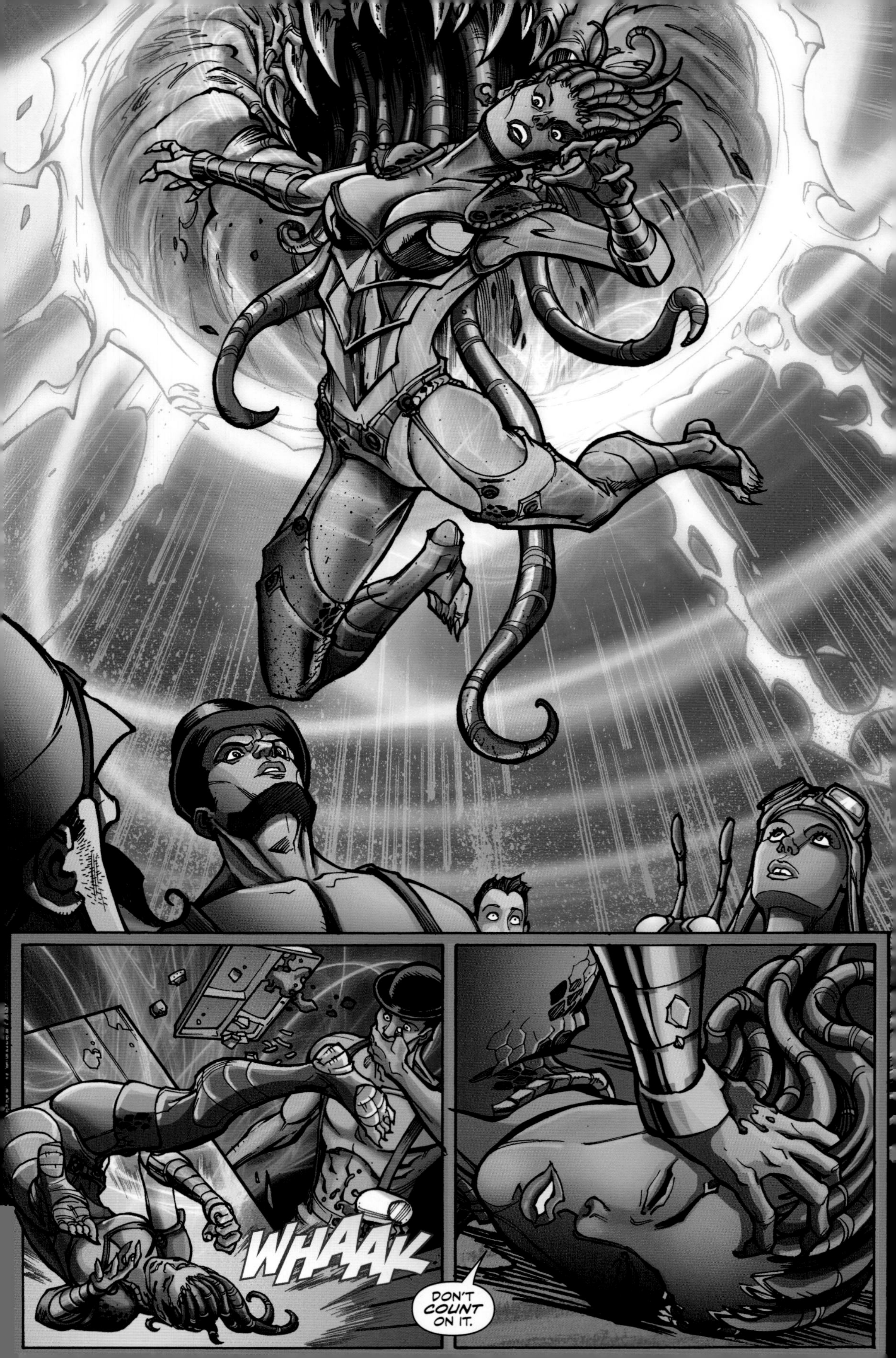
WHAAK
DON'T COUNT ON IT.

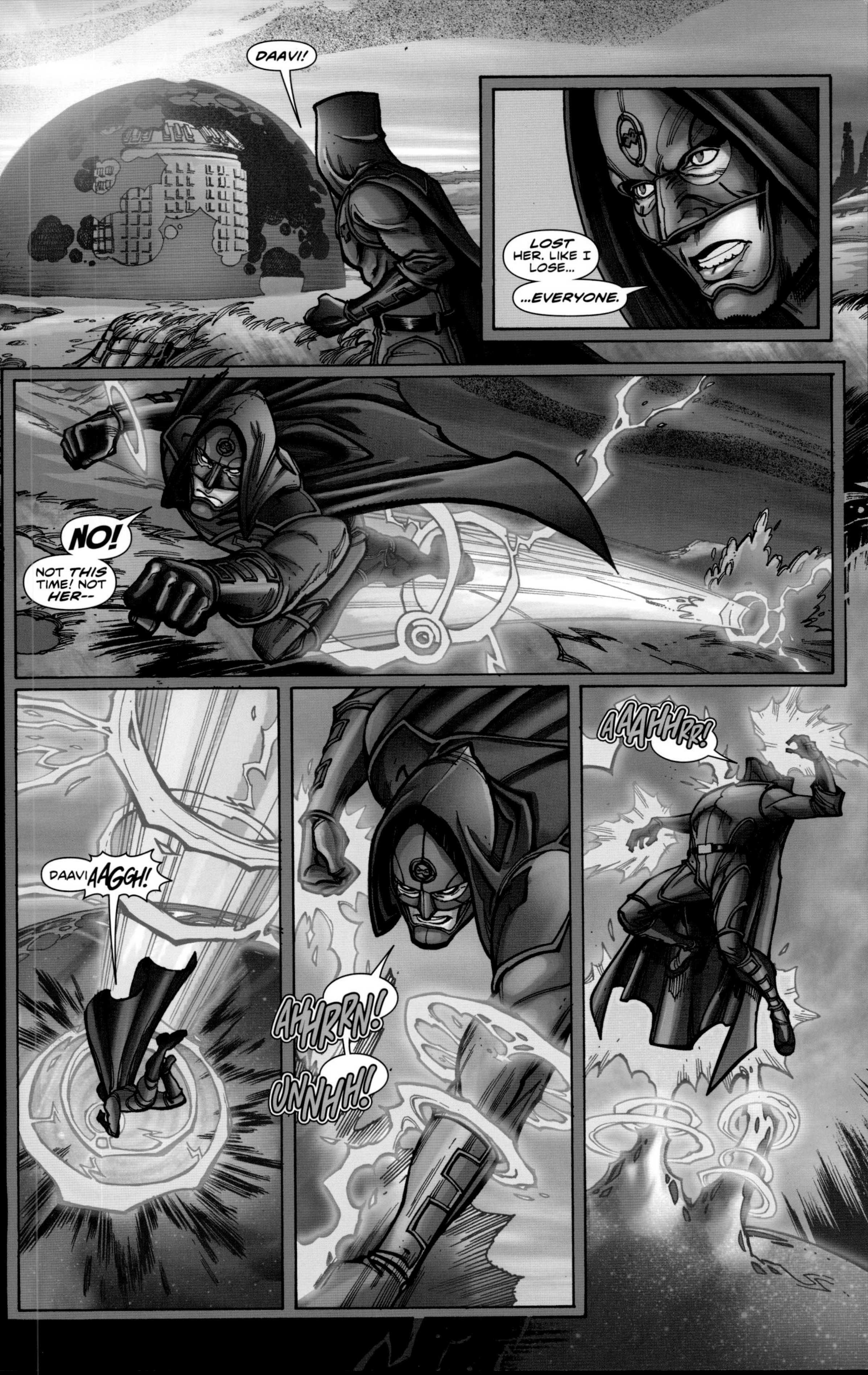
DAAVI!
LOST HER. LIKE I LOSE...
...EVERYONE.
NO!
NOT THIS TIME! NOT HER--
DAAVI AAGGH!
AHHRRN!
UNNHH!
AAAHHRR!

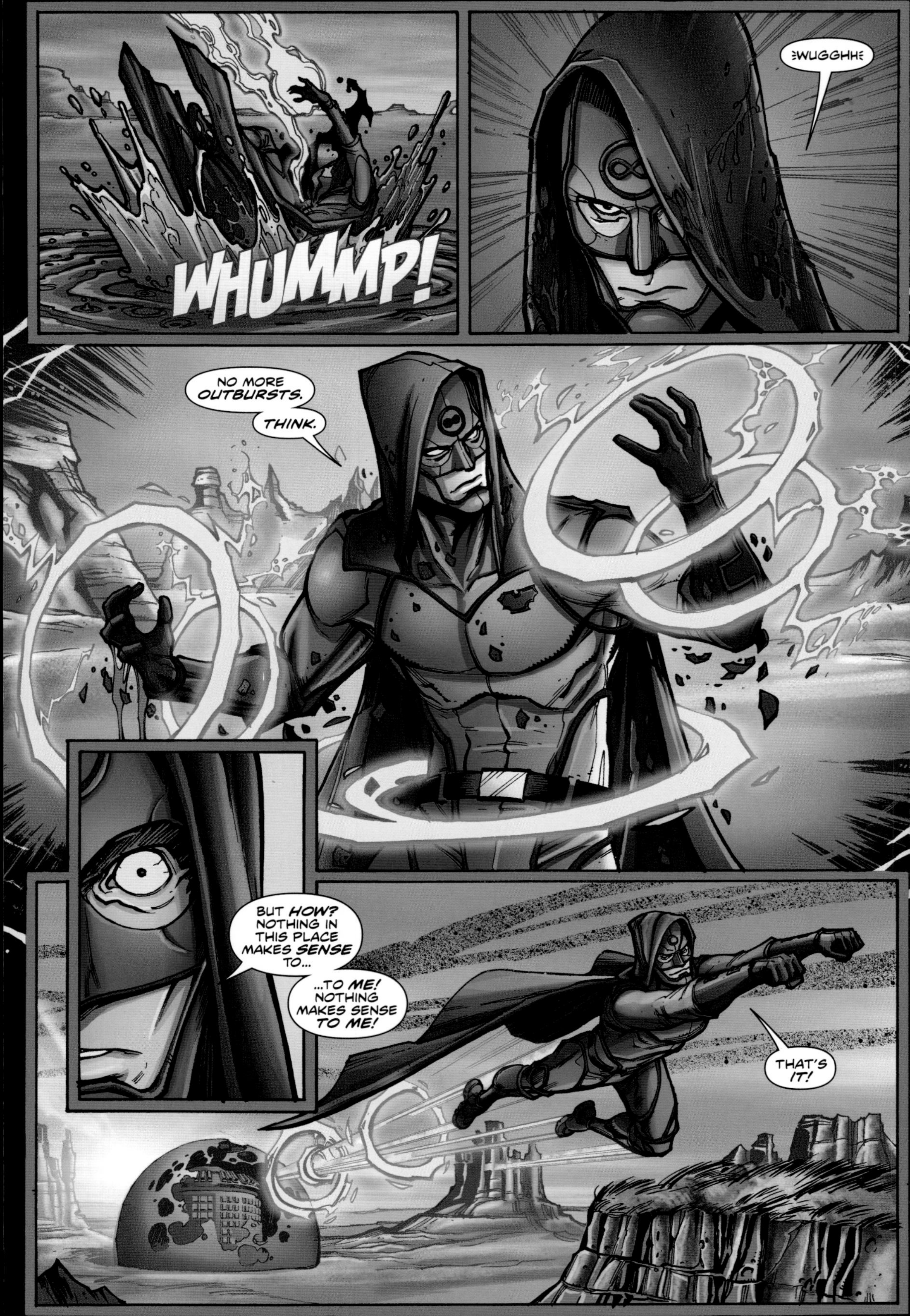
WHUMMP!
WUGGHH
NO MORE OUTBURSTS.
THINK.
BUT HOW? NOTHING IN THIS PLACE MAKES SENSE TO...
...TO ME! NOTHING MAKES SENSE TO ME!
THAT'S IT!

IF YOU'RE TRYING TO TELL ME *TRAVELER* ESCAPED WITH *DAAVI--*

NO, HE DIDN'T! EXACTLY. SIR.

THE *TIME EATER* MANAGED TO RECAPTURE *HER--*

BUT NOT *HIM?* I DON'T REMEMBER TRAVELER BEING THIS *IMPRESSIVE* SO EARLY IN HIS CAREER.

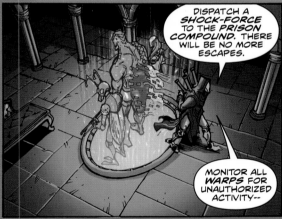

DISPATCH A *SHOCK-FORCE* TO THE *PRISON COMPOUND.* THERE WILL BE NO MORE ESCAPES.

MONITOR ALL *WARPS* FOR UNAUTHORIZED ACTIVITY--

--AND ALERT ALL *FREEGANGS!* TRAVELER IS TO BE BROUGHT *HERE,* TO *ME,* ALIVE--

--BUT NOT NECESSARILY *UNHURT.*

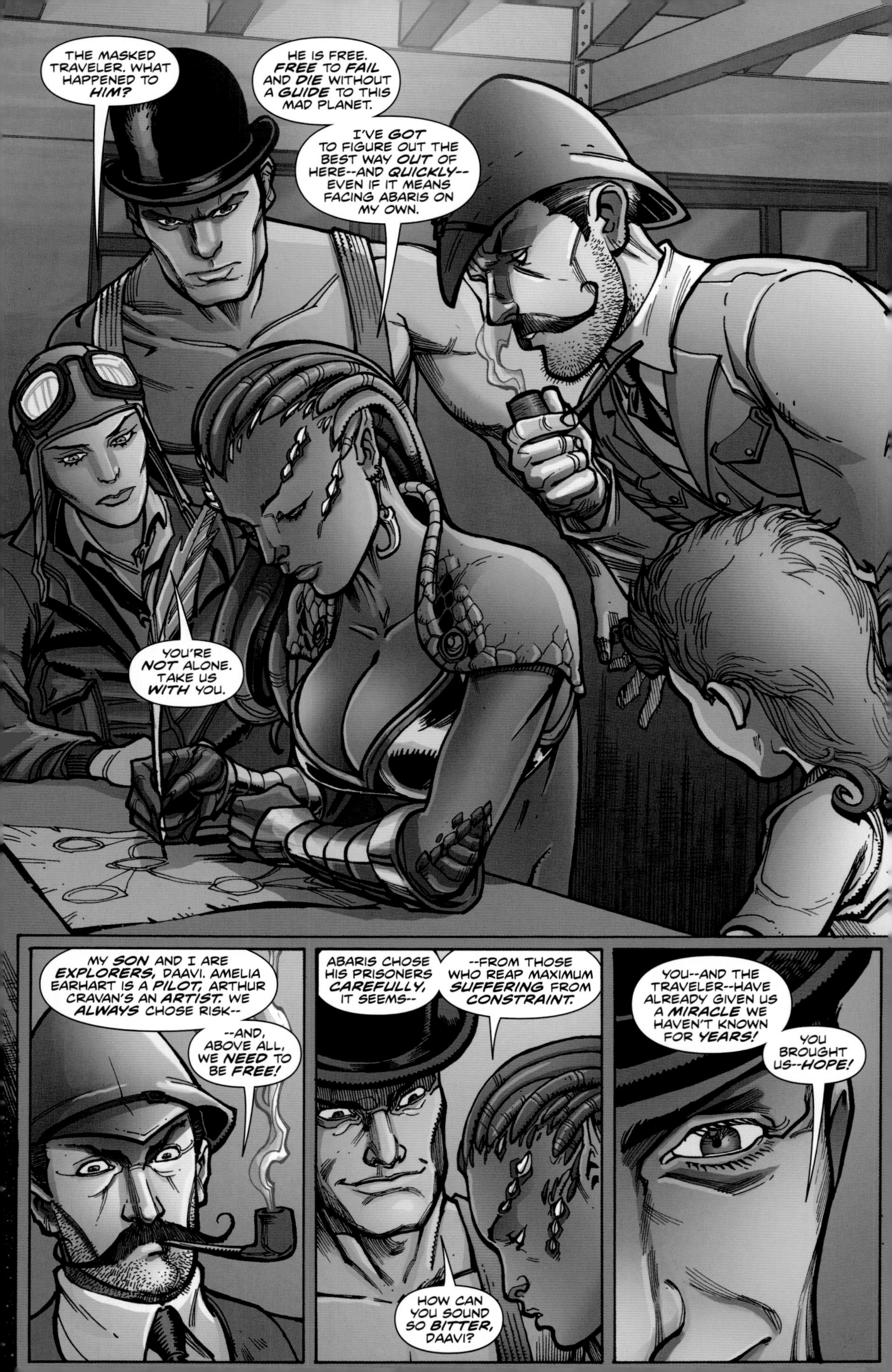
THE MASKED TRAVELER. WHAT HAPPENED TO HIM?
HE IS FREE. FREE TO FAIL AND DIE WITHOUT A GUIDE TO THIS MAD PLANET.
I'VE GOT TO FIGURE OUT THE BEST WAY OUT OF HERE--AND QUICKLY--EVEN IF IT MEANS FACING ABARIS ON MY OWN.
YOU'RE NOT ALONE. TAKE US WITH YOU.
MY SON AND I ARE EXPLORERS, DAAVI. AMELIA EARHART IS A PILOT, ARTHUR CRAVAN'S AN ARTIST. WE ALWAYS CHOSE RISK--
--AND, ABOVE ALL, WE NEED TO BE FREE!
ABARIS CHOSE HIS PRISONERS CAREFULLY, IT SEEMS--
--FROM THOSE WHO REAP MAXIMUM SUFFERING FROM CONSTRAINT.
HOW CAN YOU SOUND SO BITTER, DAAVI?
YOU--AND THE TRAVELER--HAVE ALREADY GIVEN US A MIRACLE WE HAVEN'T KNOWN FOR YEARS!
YOU BROUGHT US--HOPE!

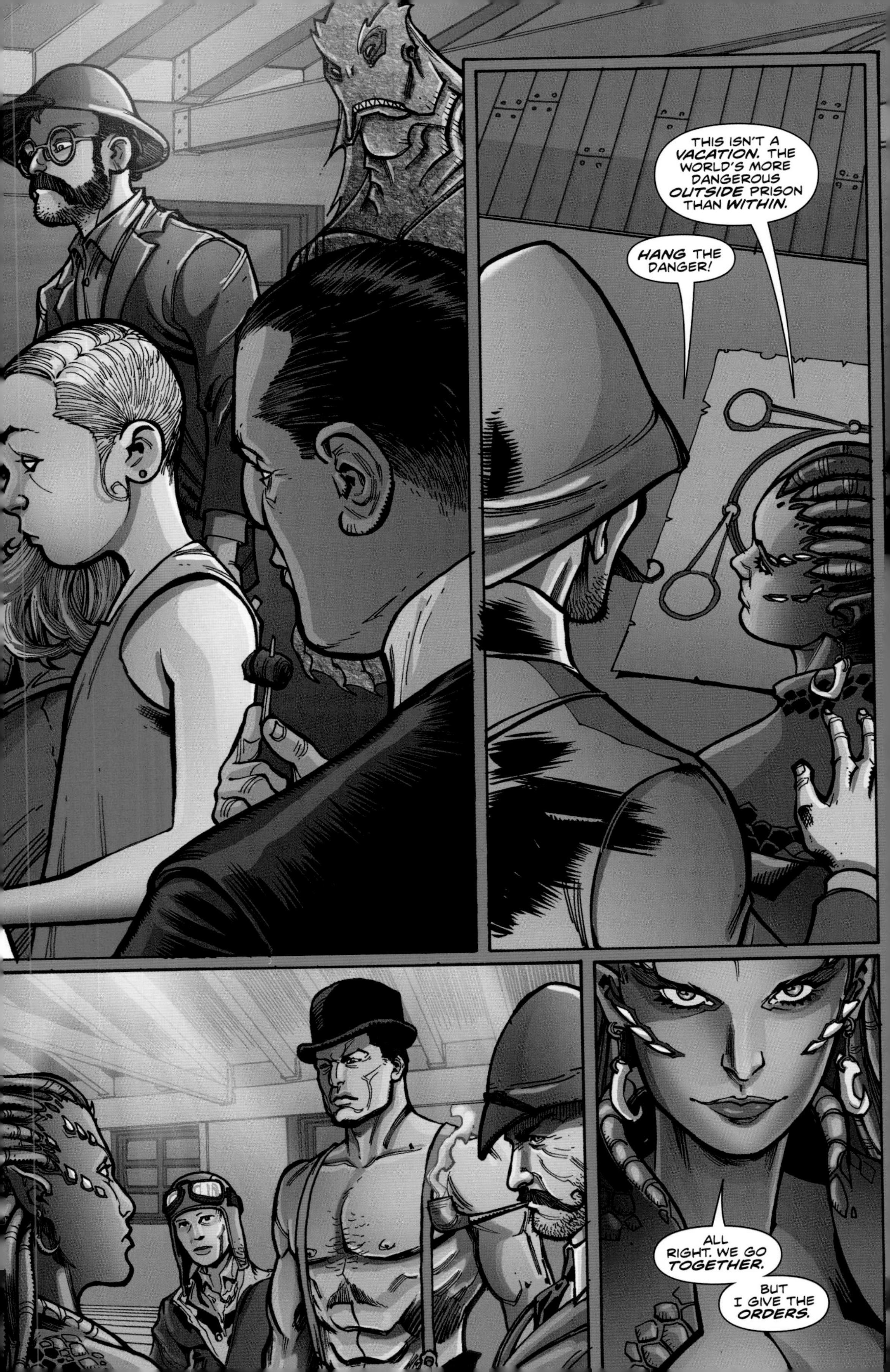
THIS ISN'T A VACATION. THE WORLD'S MORE DANGEROUS OUTSIDE PRISON THAN WITHIN.
HANG THE DANGER!
ALL RIGHT. WE GO TOGETHER.
BUT I GIVE THE ORDERS.

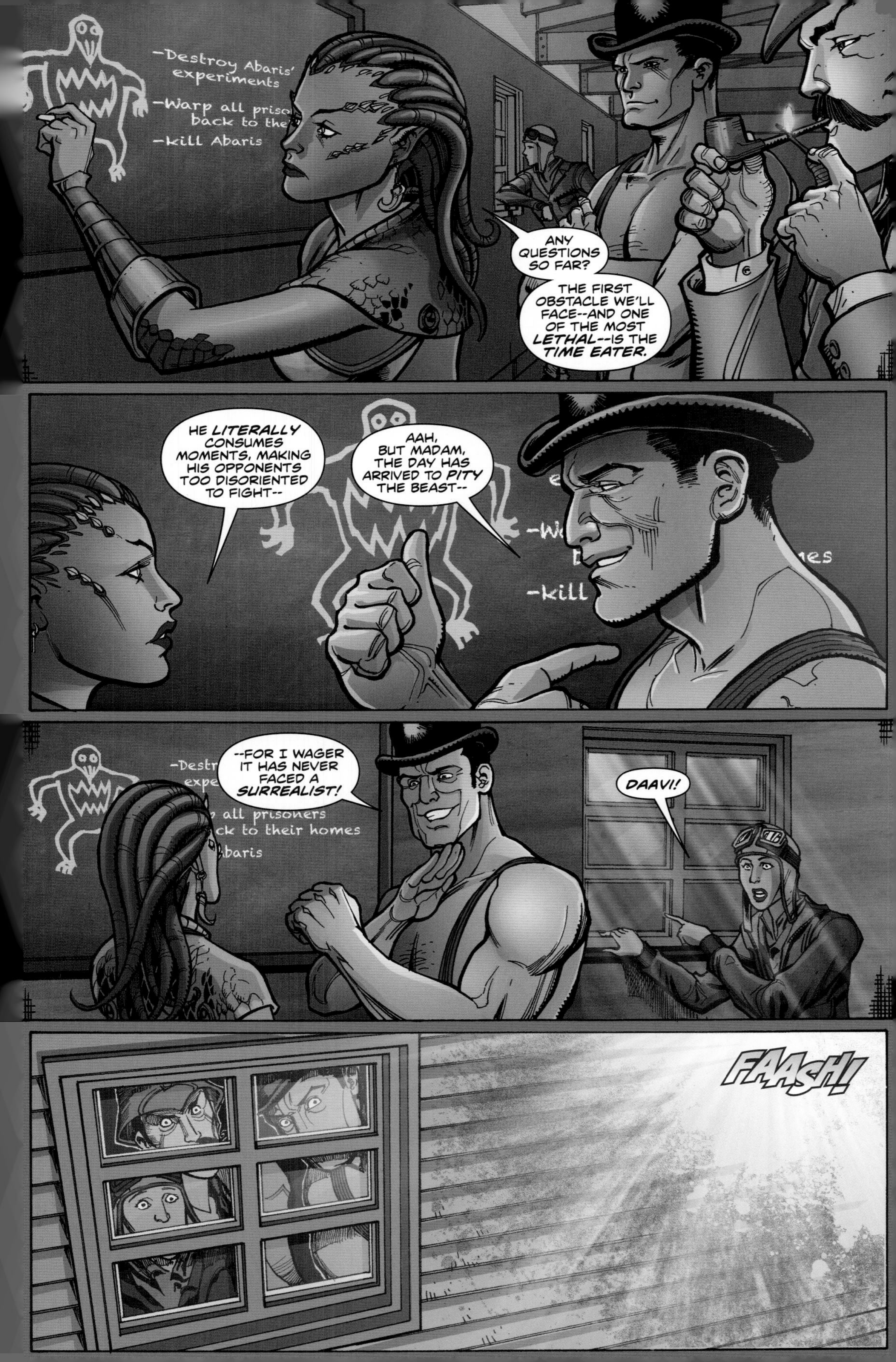
-Destroy Abaris' experiments
-Warp all prisoners back to their homes
-kill Abaris
ANY QUESTIONS SO FAR?
THE FIRST OBSTACLE WE'LL FACE--AND ONE OF THE MOST *LETHAL*--IS THE *TIME EATER.*
HE *LITERALLY* CONSUMES MOMENTS, MAKING HIS OPPONENTS TOO DISORIENTED TO FIGHT--
AAH, BUT MADAM, THE DAY HAS ARRIVED TO *PITY* THE BEAST--
--FOR I WAGER IT HAS NEVER FACED A *SURREALIST!*
DAAVI!
FAASH!

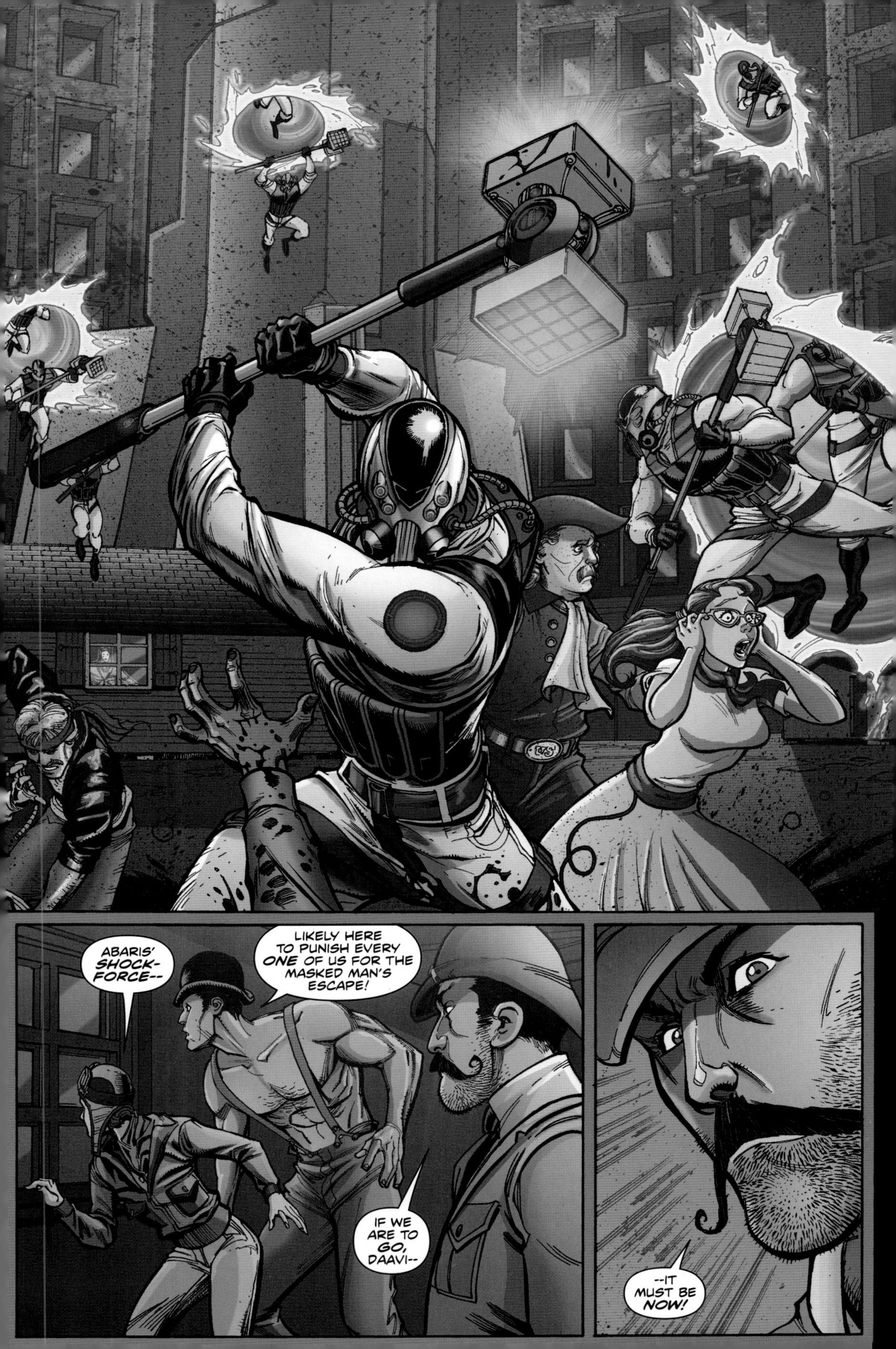
ABARIS' SHOCK-FORCE--
LIKELY HERE TO PUNISH EVERY ONE OF US FOR THE MASKED MAN'S ESCAPE!
IF WE ARE TO GO, DAAVI--
--IT MUST BE NOW!

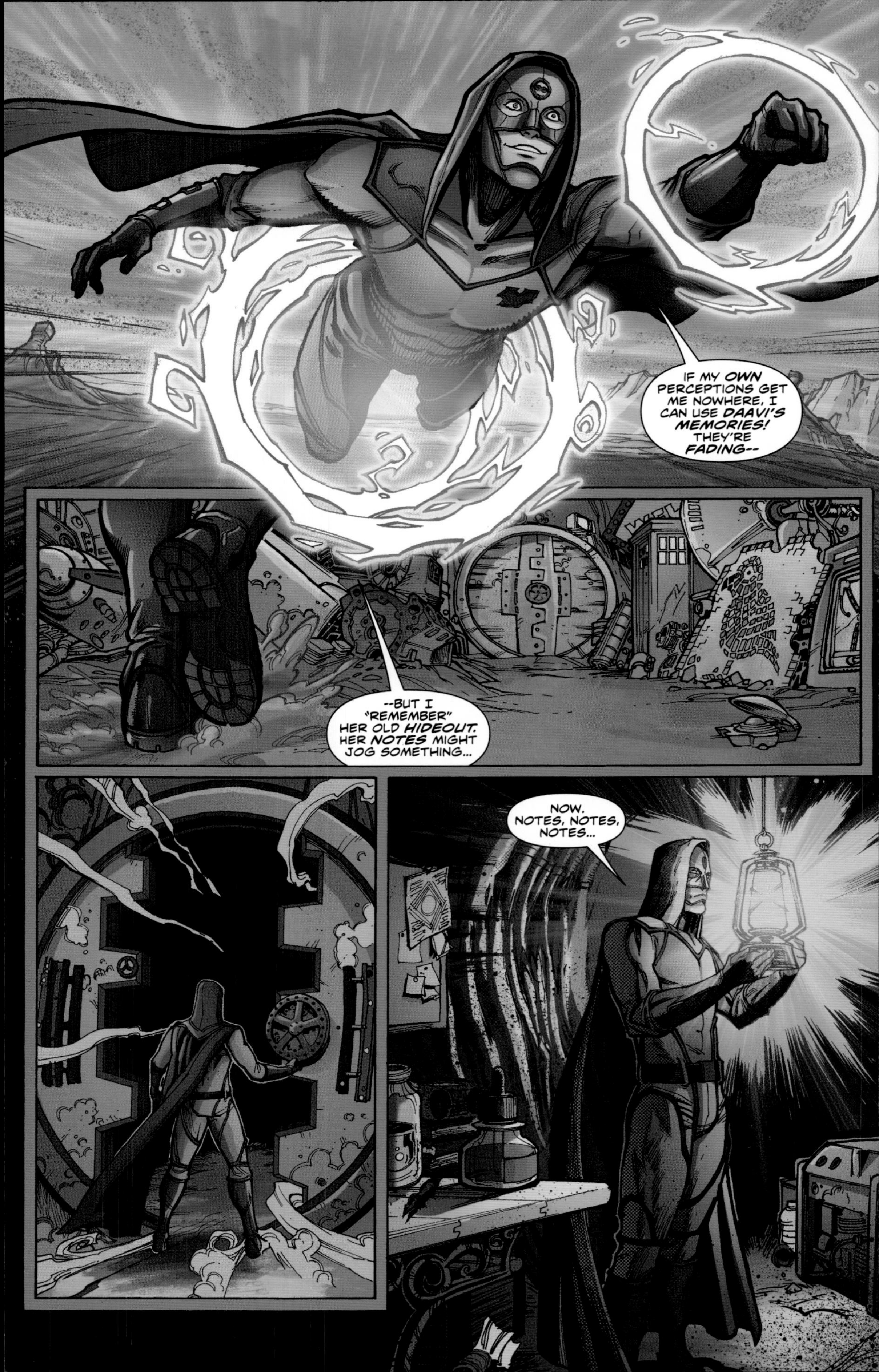
IF MY OWN PERCEPTIONS GET ME NOWHERE, I CAN USE DAAVI'S MEMORIES! THEY'RE FADING--
--BUT I "REMEMBER" HER OLD HIDEOUT. HER NOTES MIGHT JOG SOMETHING...
NOW. NOTES, NOTES, NOTES...

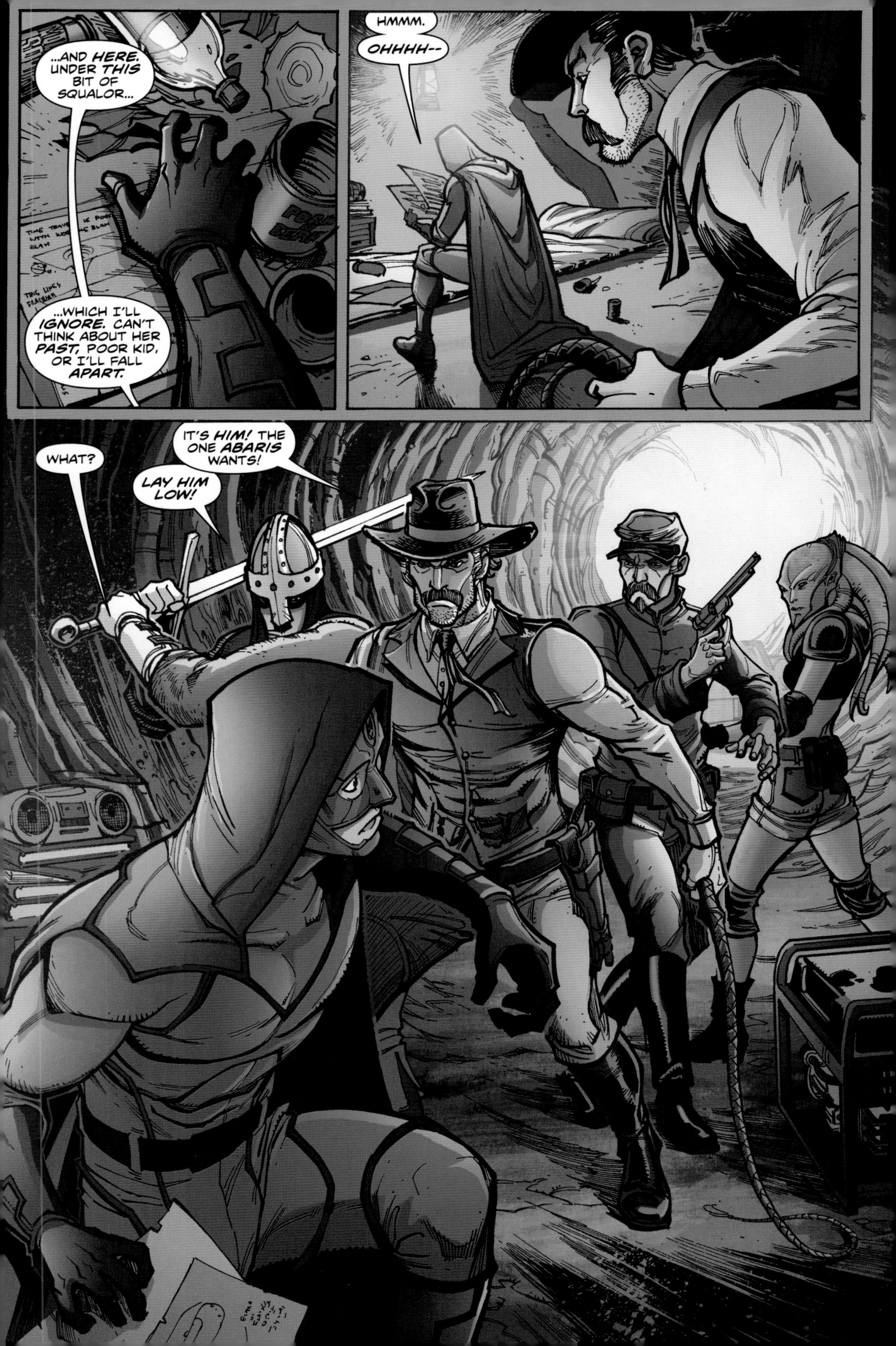

...AND HERE. UNDER THIS BIT OF SQUALOR...
...WHICH I'LL IGNORE. CAN'T THINK ABOUT HER PAST, POOR KID, OR I'LL FALL APART.
HMMM.
OHHHH--
WHAT?
IT'S HIM! THE ONE ABARIS WANTS!
LAY HIM LOW!

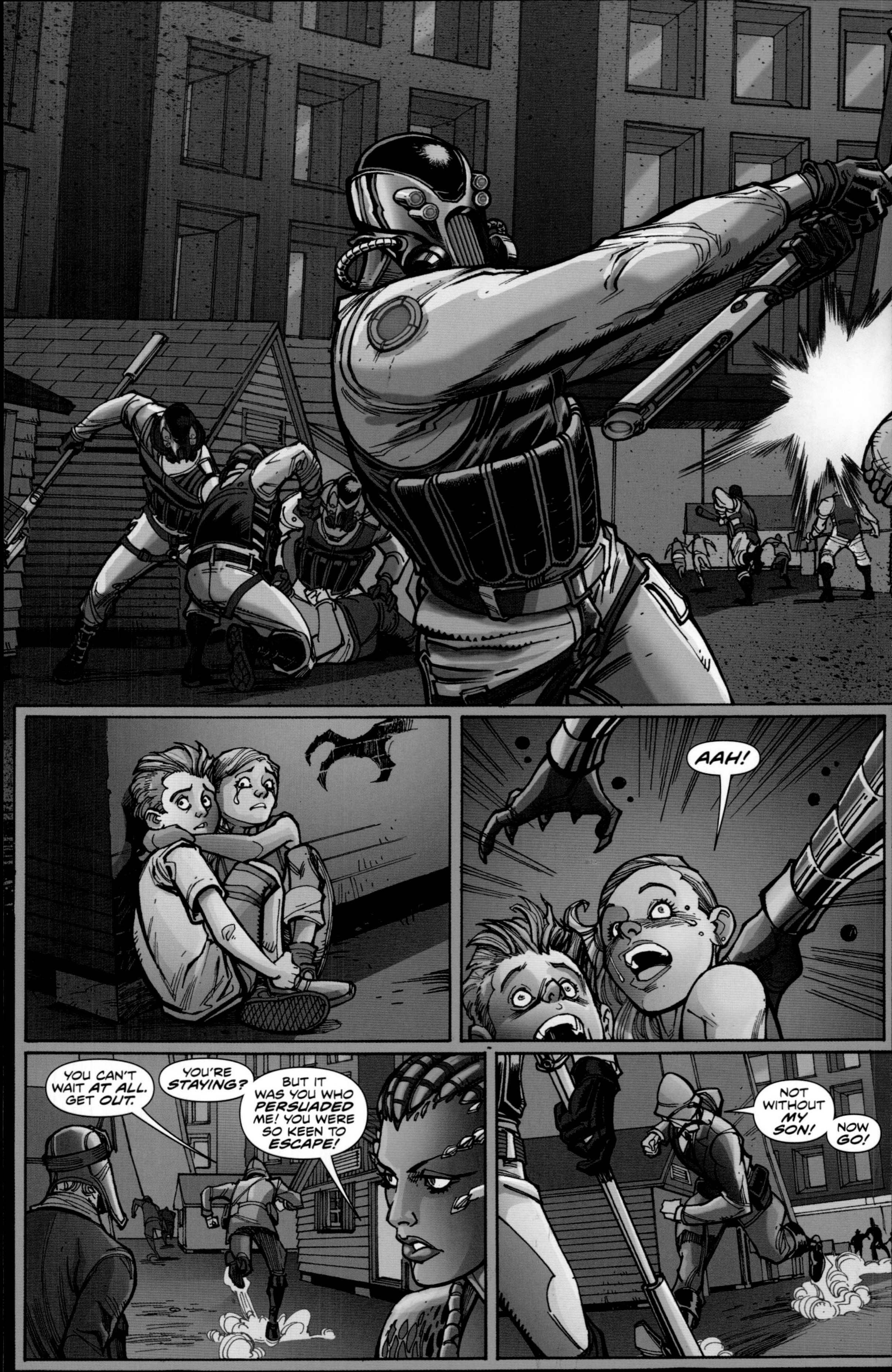
AAH!
YOU CAN'T WAIT AT ALL. GET OUT.
YOU'RE STAYING?
BUT IT WAS YOU WHO PERSUADED ME! YOU WERE SO KEEN TO ESCAPE!
NOT WITHOUT MY SON!
NOW GO!

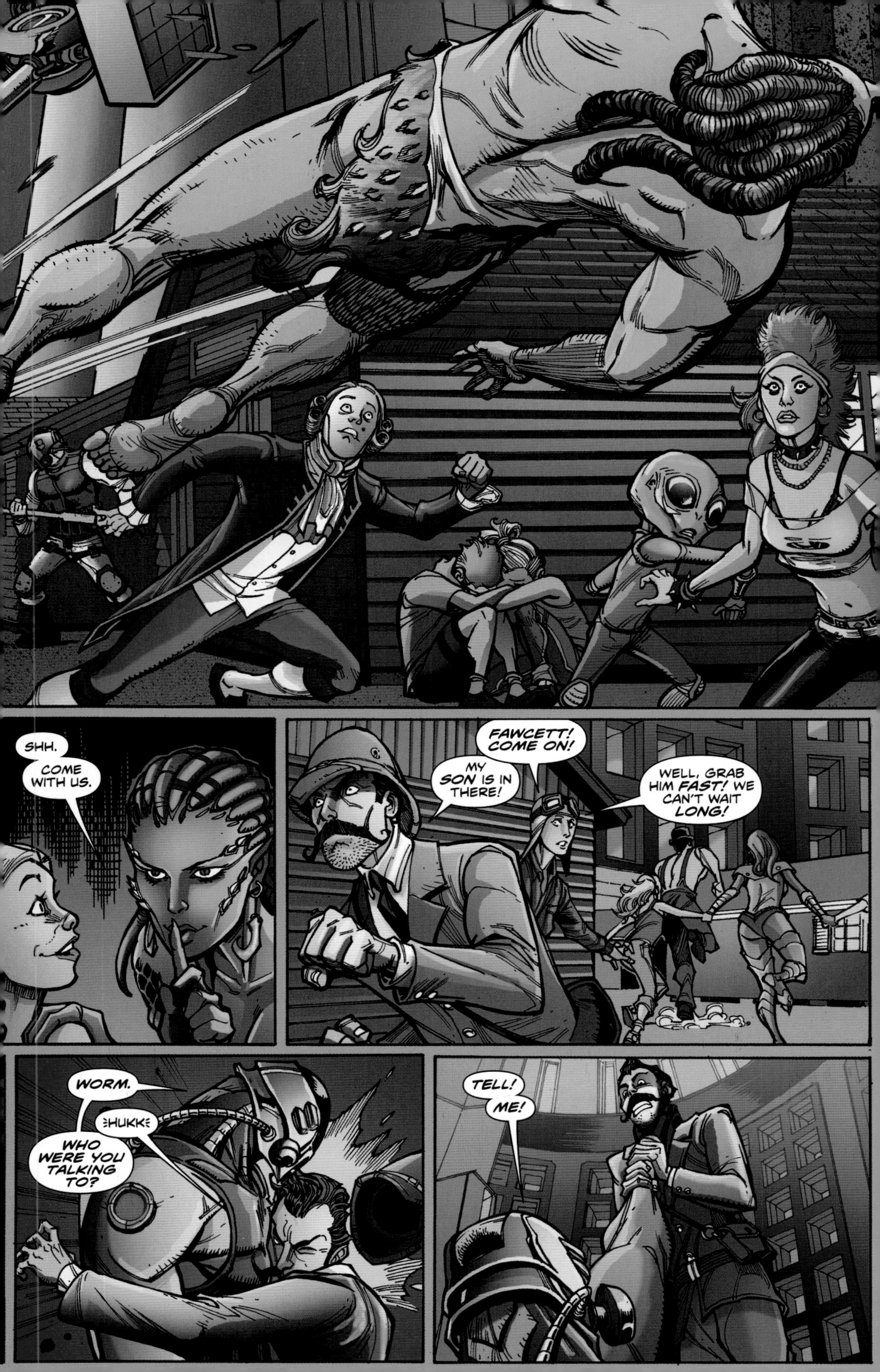
SHH.
COME WITH US.
MY SON IS IN THERE!
FAWCETT! COME ON!
WELL, GRAB HIM FAST! WE CAN'T WAIT LONG!
WORM.
HUKK
WHO WERE YOU TALKING TO?
TELL!
ME!

KRAK!

AAH!

CURSE ME...

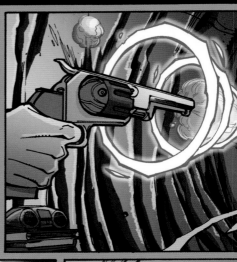

--WELL, IT'S *YOUR* BAD LUCK.

HER NOTES *TAUGHT* ME SOMETHING IMPORTANT. ABOUT THE WARPS.

--I GET TO *UNDO* SOMETHING IMPORTANT.

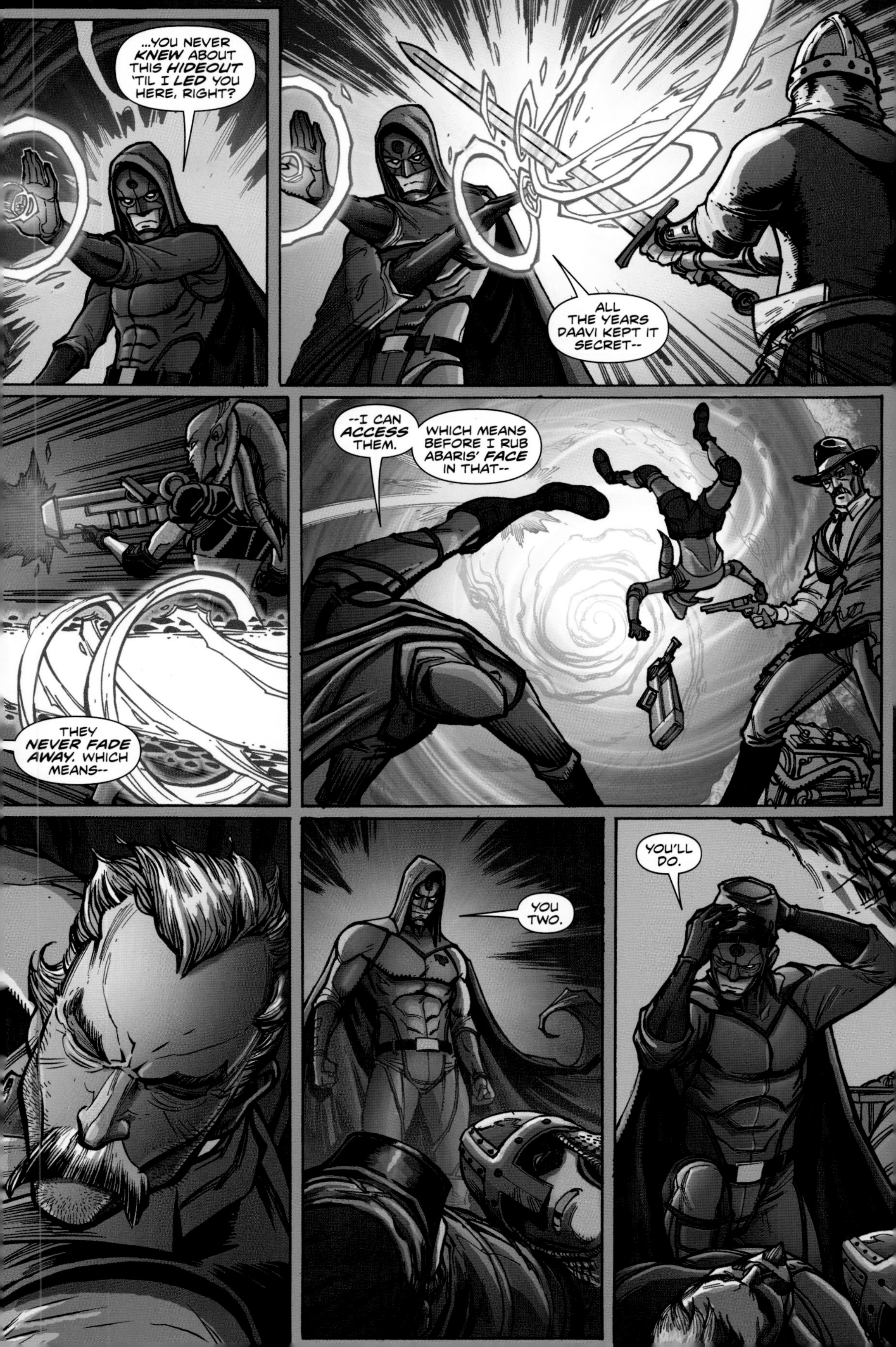
...YOU NEVER KNEW ABOUT THIS HIDEOUT 'TIL I LED YOU HERE, RIGHT?
ALL THE YEARS DAAVI KEPT IT SECRET--
THEY NEVER FADE AWAY. WHICH MEANS--
--I CAN ACCESS THEM.
WHICH MEANS BEFORE I RUB ABARIS' FACE IN THAT--
YOU TWO.
YOU'LL DO.

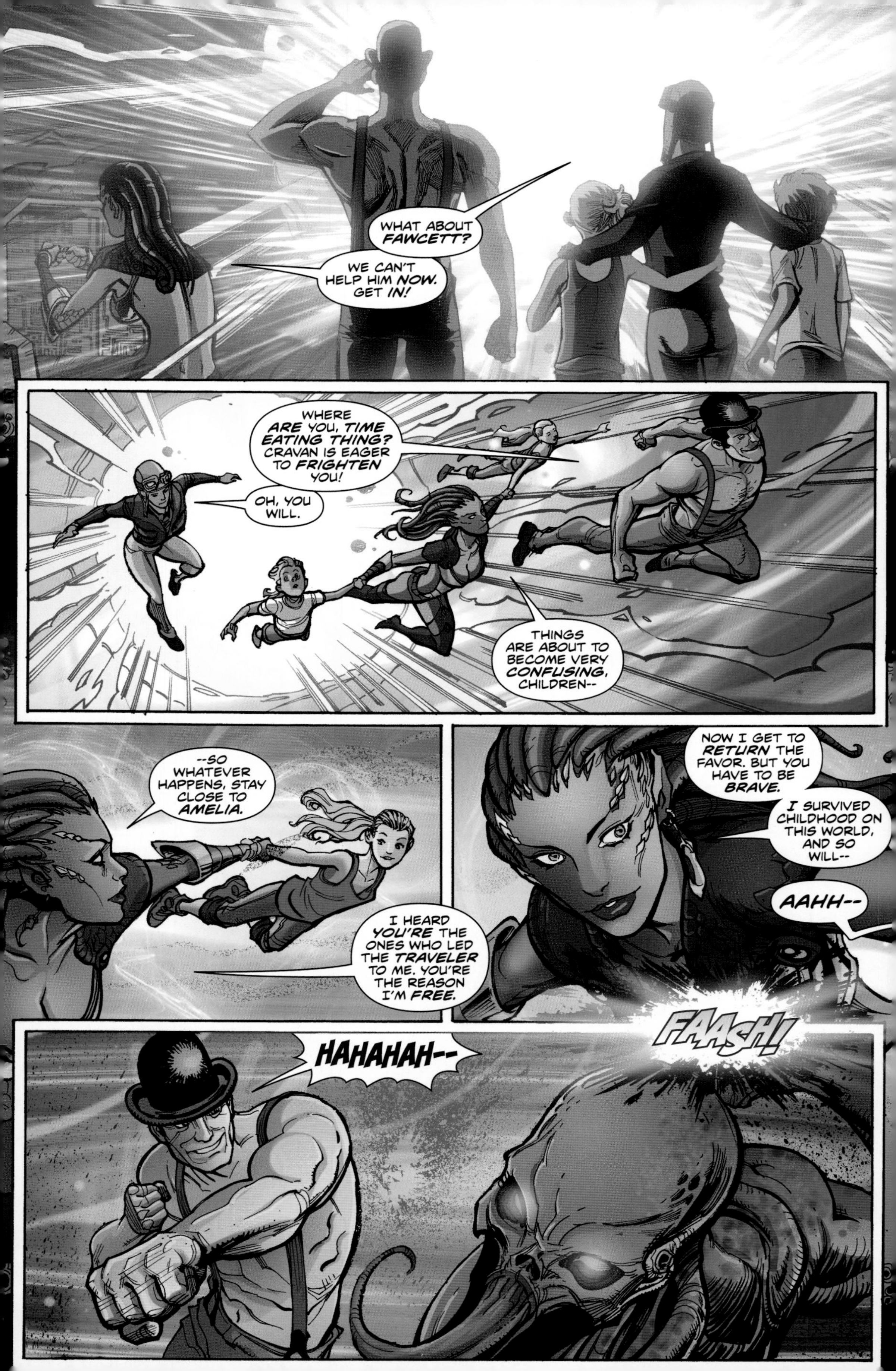
WHAT ABOUT FAWCETT?
WE CAN'T HELP HIM NOW. GET IN!
WHERE ARE YOU, TIME EATING THING? CRAVAN IS EAGER TO FRIGHTEN YOU!
OH, YOU WILL.
THINGS ARE ABOUT TO BECOME VERY CONFUSING, CHILDREN--
--SO WHATEVER HAPPENS, STAY CLOSE TO AMELIA.
I HEARD YOU'RE THE ONES WHO LED THE TRAVELER TO ME. YOU'RE THE REASON I'M FREE.
NOW I GET TO RETURN THE FAVOR. BUT YOU HAVE TO BE BRAVE.
I SURVIVED CHILDHOOD ON THIS WORLD, AND SO WILL--
AAHH--
FAASH!
HAHAHAH--

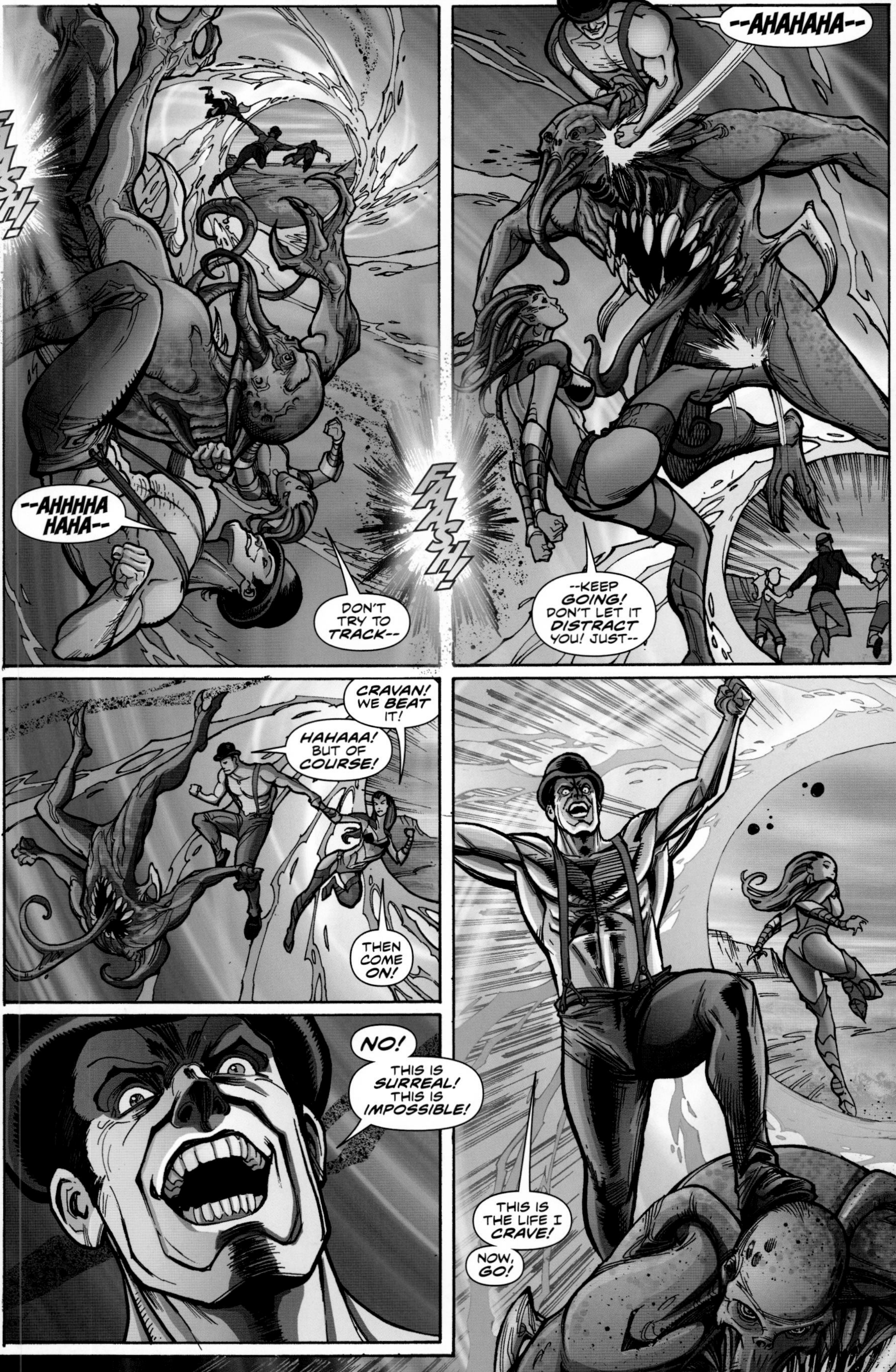

FLASH!
--AHHHHA HAHA--
DON'T TRY TO TRACK--
FLASH!
--AHAHAHA--
--KEEP GOING! DON'T LET IT DISTRACT YOU! JUST--
CRAVAN! WE BEAT IT!
HAHAAA! BUT OF COURSE!
THEN COME ON!
NO!
THIS IS SURREAL! THIS IS IMPOSSIBLE!
THIS IS THE LIFE I CRAVE!
NOW, GO!

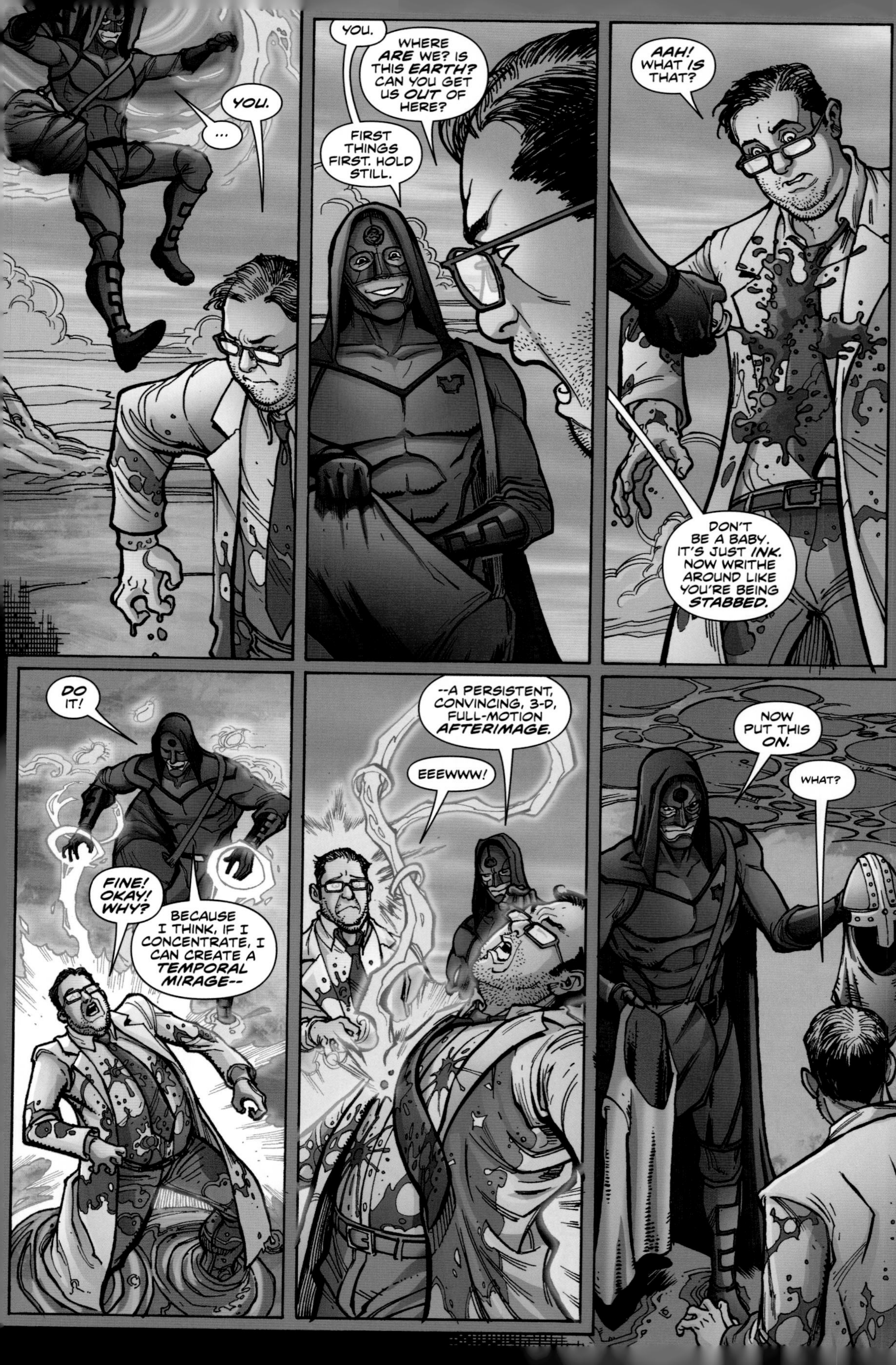
...
YOU.
YOU.
WHERE ARE WE? IS THIS EARTH? CAN YOU GET US OUT OF HERE?
FIRST THINGS FIRST. HOLD STILL.
AAH! WHAT IS THAT?
DON'T BE A BABY. IT'S JUST INK. NOW WRITHE AROUND LIKE YOU'RE BEING STABBED.
DO IT!
FINE! OKAY! WHY?
BECAUSE I THINK, IF I CONCENTRATE, I CAN CREATE A TEMPORAL MIRAGE--
--A PERSISTENT, CONVINCING, 3-D, FULL-MOTION AFTERIMAGE.
EEEWWW!
NOW PUT THIS ON.
WHAT?

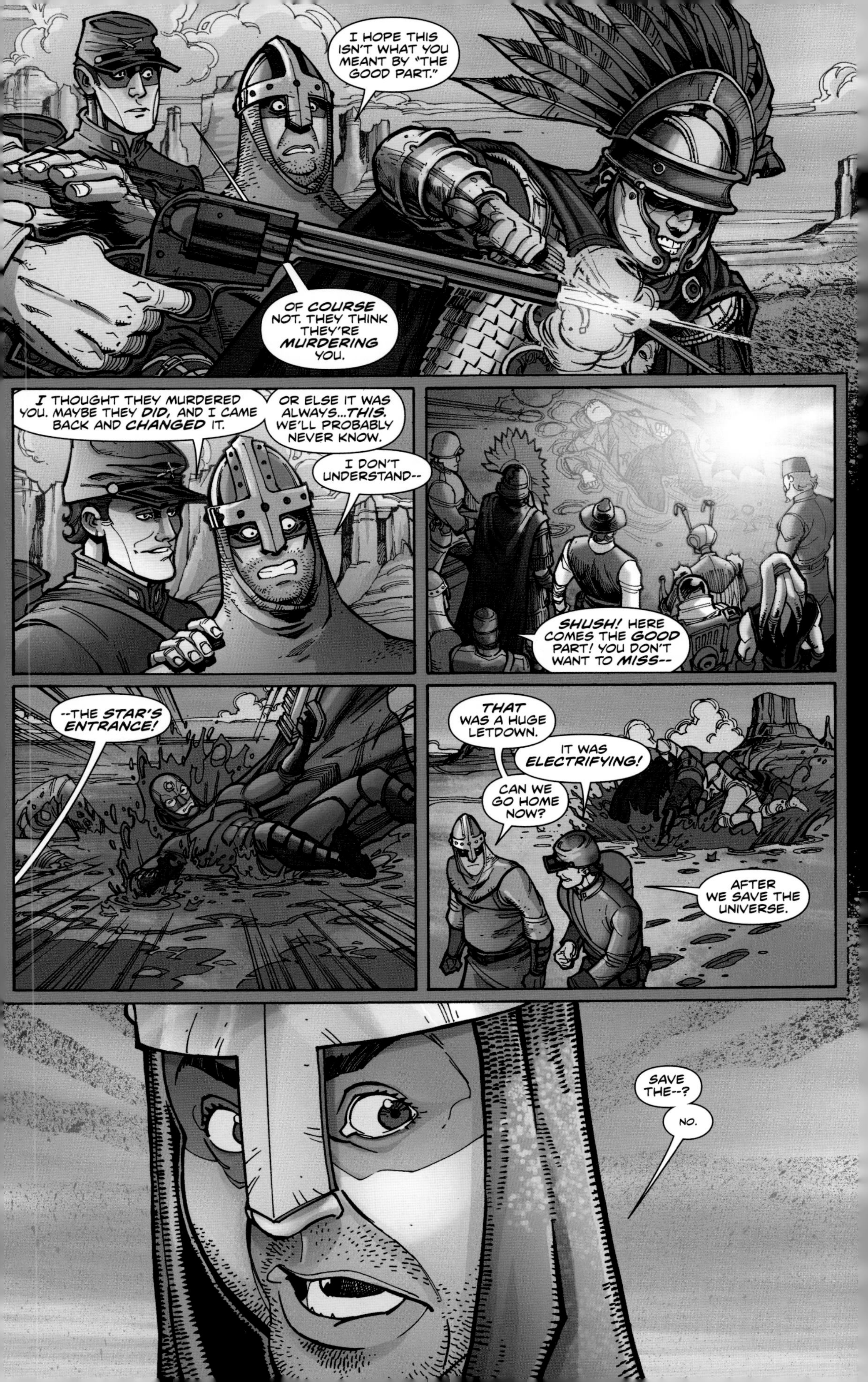
I HOPE THIS ISN'T WHAT YOU MEANT BY "THE GOOD PART."
OF COURSE NOT. THEY THINK THEY'RE MURDERING YOU.
I THOUGHT THEY MURDERED YOU. MAYBE THEY DID, AND I CAME BACK AND CHANGED IT.
OR ELSE IT WAS ALWAYS...THIS. WE'LL PROBABLY NEVER KNOW.
I DON'T UNDERSTAND--
SHUSH! HERE COMES THE GOOD PART! YOU DON'T WANT TO MISS--
--THE STAR'S ENTRANCE!
THAT WAS A HUGE LETDOWN.
IT WAS ELECTRIFYING!
CAN WE GO HOME NOW?
AFTER WE SAVE THE UNIVERSE.
SAVE THE--?
NO.

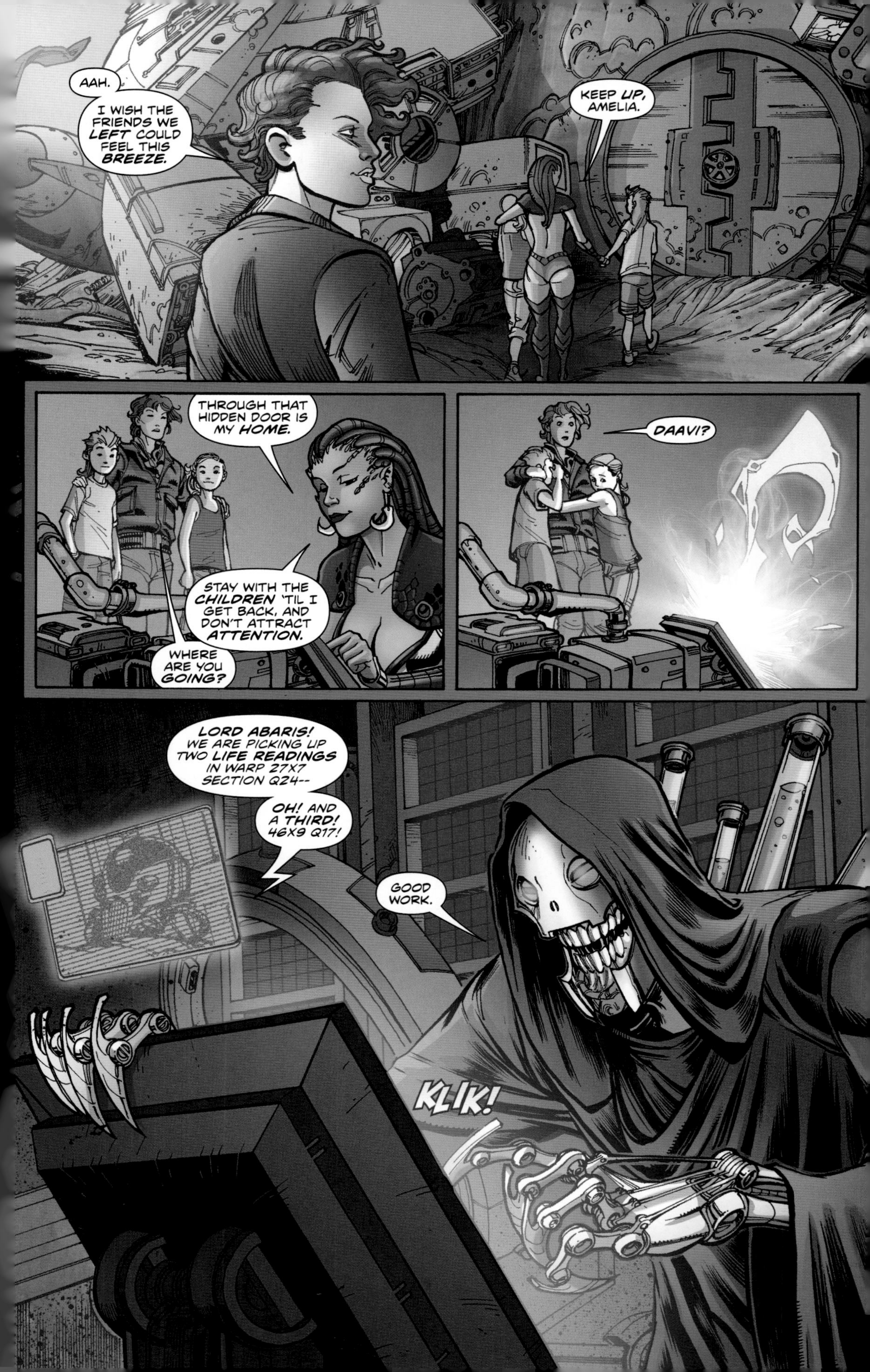
AAH.
I WISH THE FRIENDS WE LEFT COULD FEEL THIS BREEZE.
KEEP UP, AMELIA.
THROUGH THAT HIDDEN DOOR IS MY HOME.
STAY WITH THE CHILDREN 'TIL I GET BACK, AND DON'T ATTRACT ATTENTION.
WHERE ARE YOU GOING?
DAAVI?
LORD ABARIS! WE ARE PICKING UP TWO LIFE READINGS IN WARP 27X7 SECTION Q24--
OH! AND A THIRD! 46X9 Q17!
GOOD WORK.
KLIK!

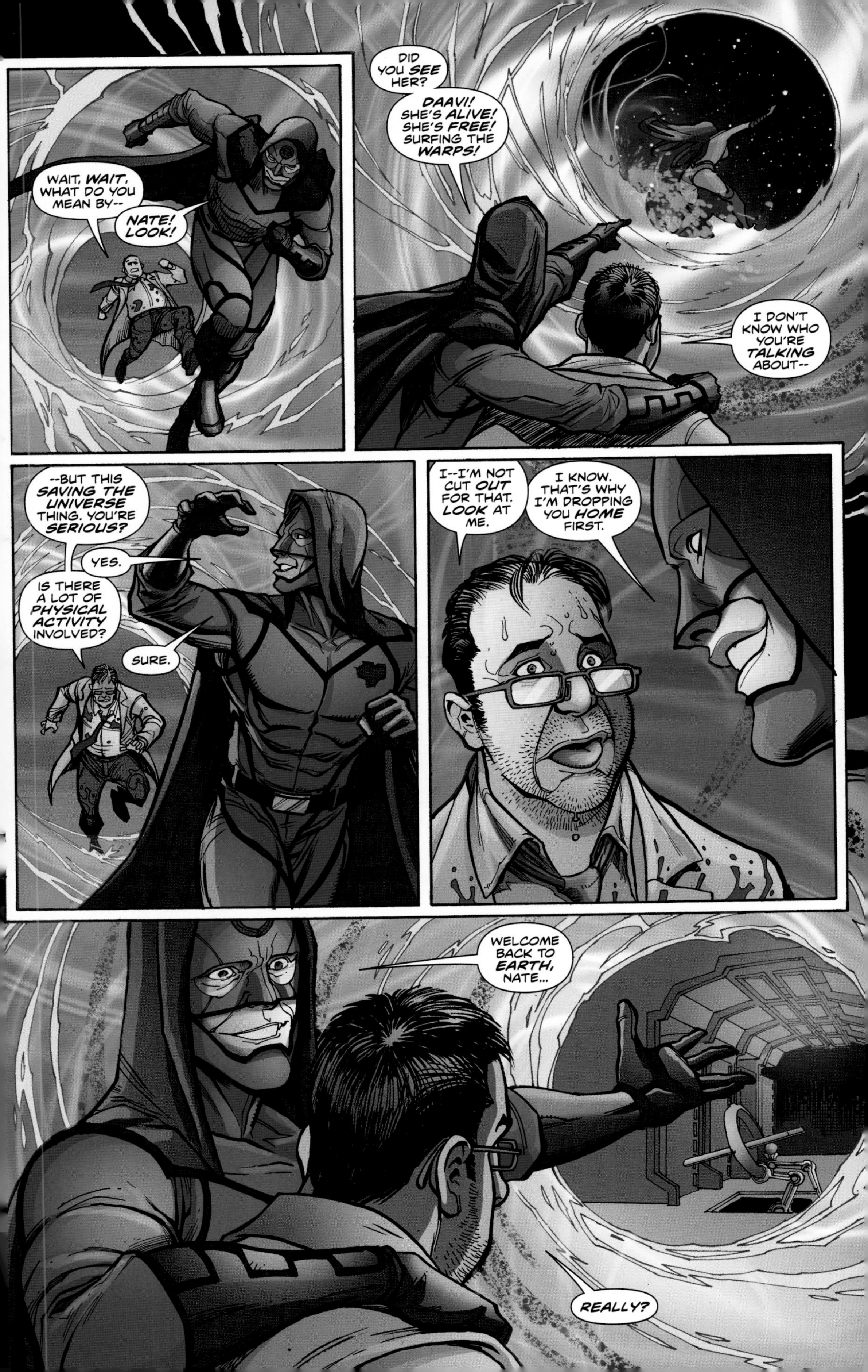
WAIT, WAIT, WHAT DO YOU MEAN BY--
NATE! LOOK!
DID YOU SEE HER?
DAAVI! SHE'S ALIVE! SHE'S FREE! SURFING THE WARPS!
I DON'T KNOW WHO YOU'RE TALKING ABOUT--
--BUT THIS SAVING THE UNIVERSE THING. YOU'RE SERIOUS?
YES.
IS THERE A LOT OF PHYSICAL ACTIVITY INVOLVED?
SURE.
I--I'M NOT CUT OUT FOR THAT. LOOK AT ME.
I KNOW. THAT'S WHY I'M DROPPING YOU HOME FIRST.
WELCOME BACK TO EARTH, NATE...
REALLY?

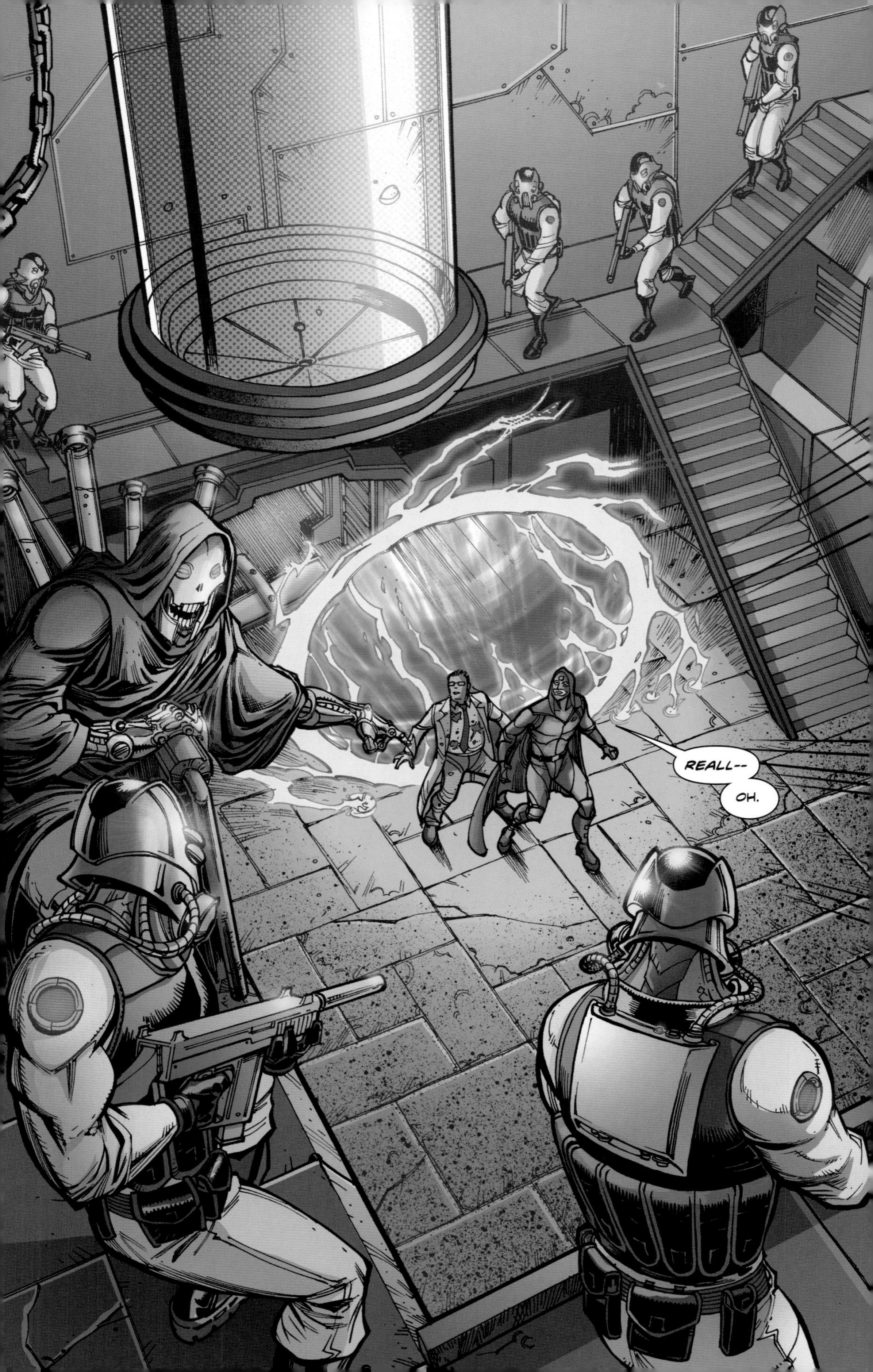
REALL--
OH.

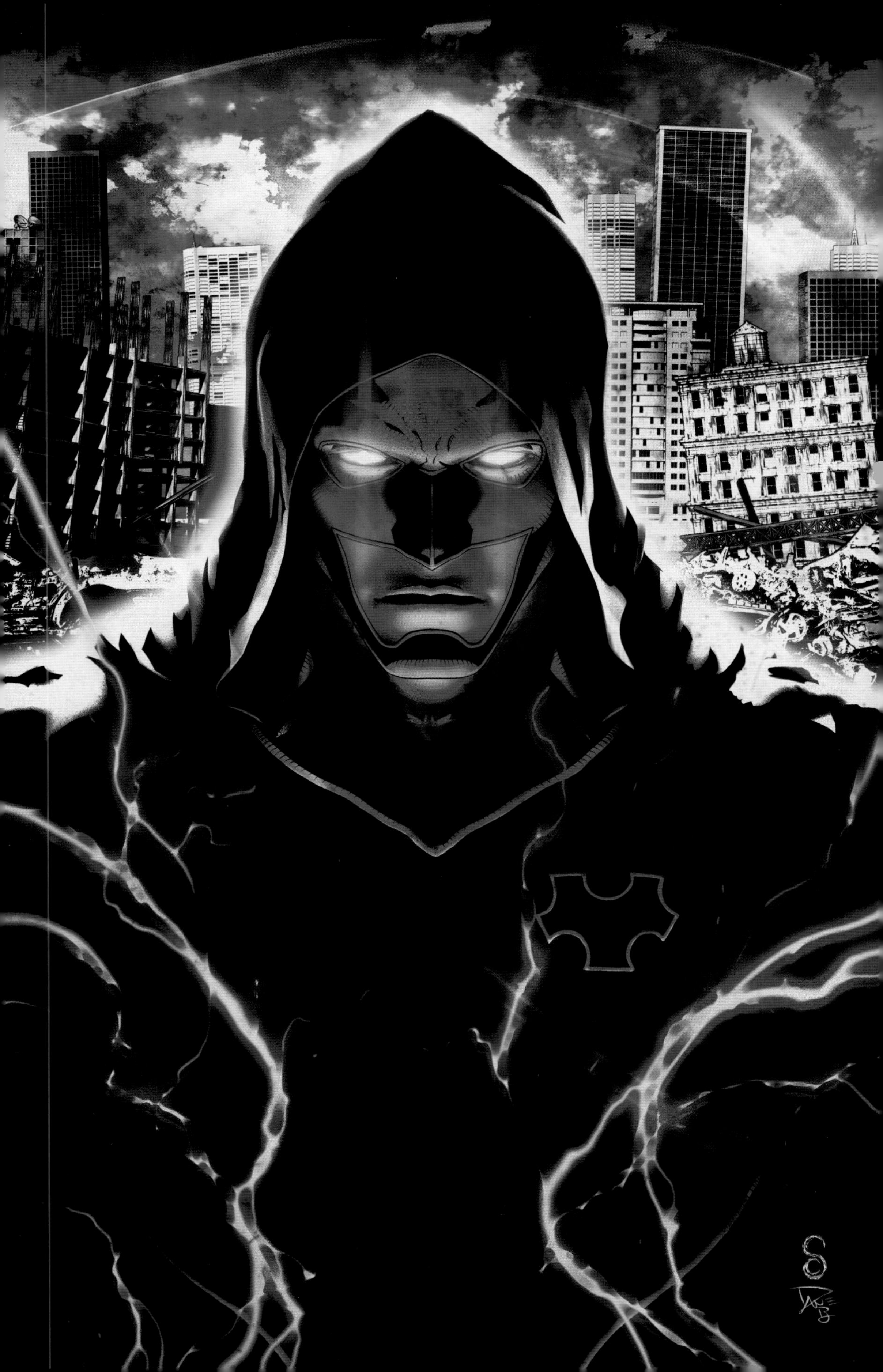

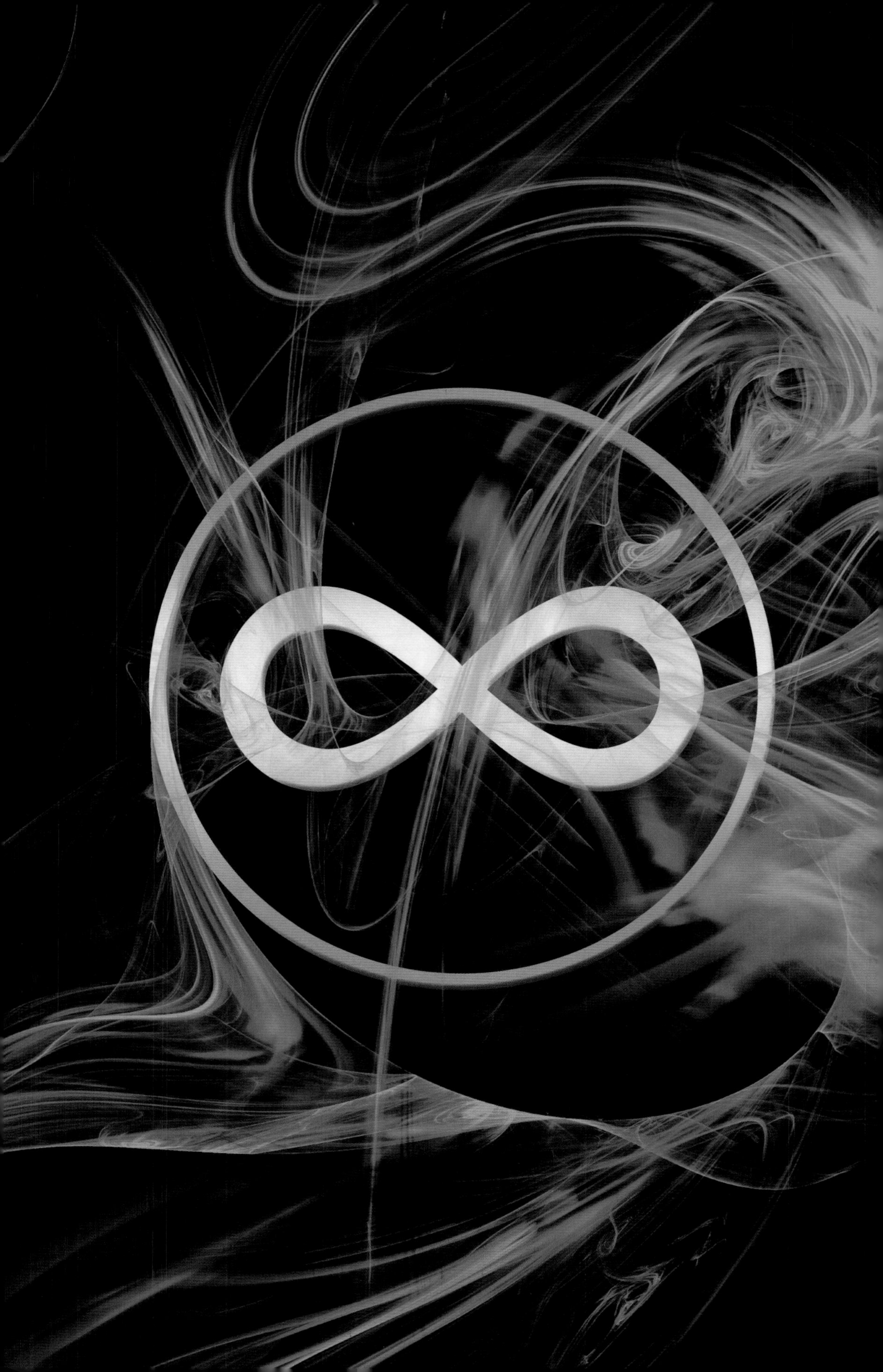

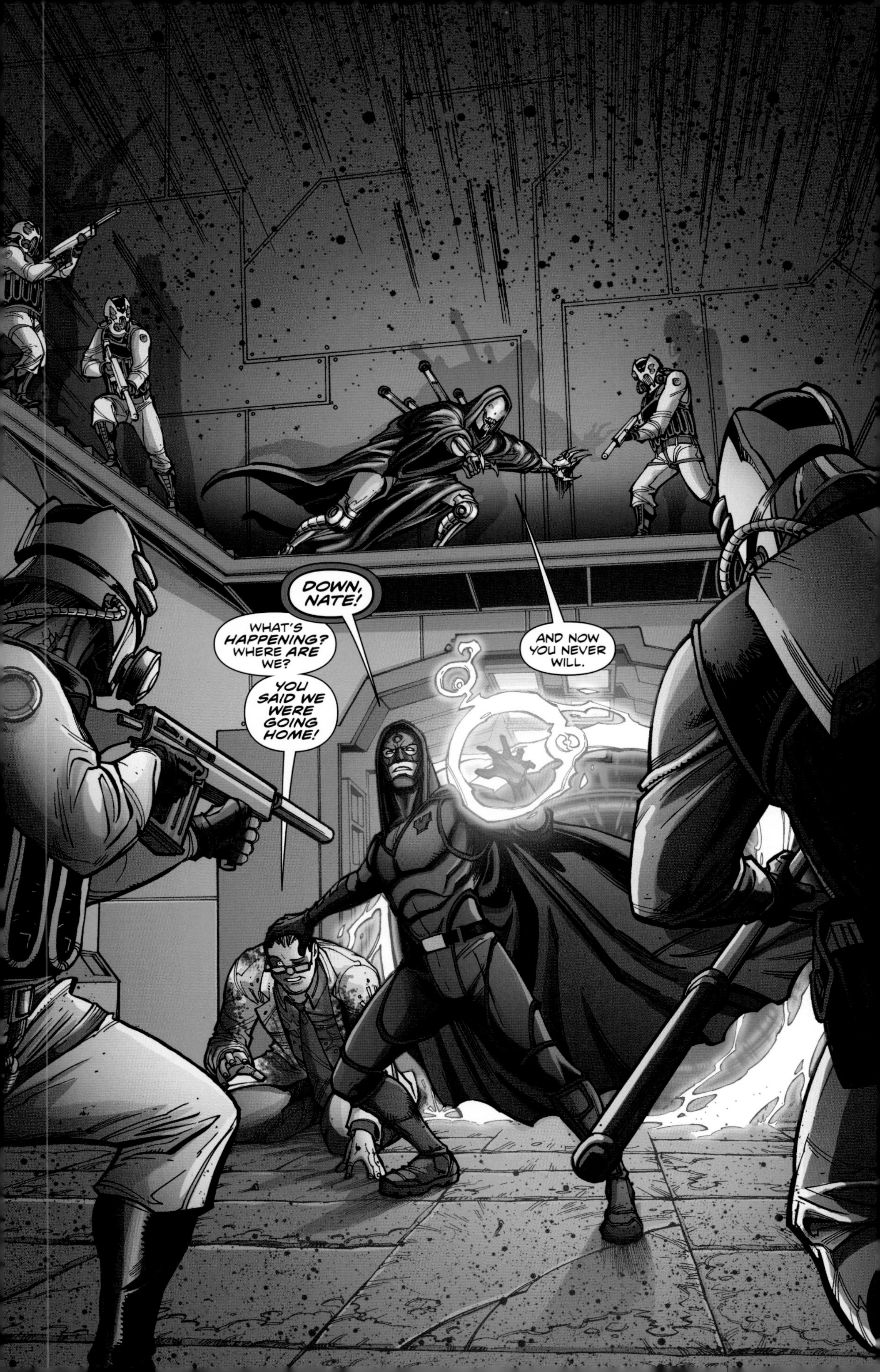
WHAT'S HAPPENING? WHERE ARE WE?
YOU SAID WE WERE GOING HOME!
DOWN, NATE!
AND NOW YOU NEVER WILL.

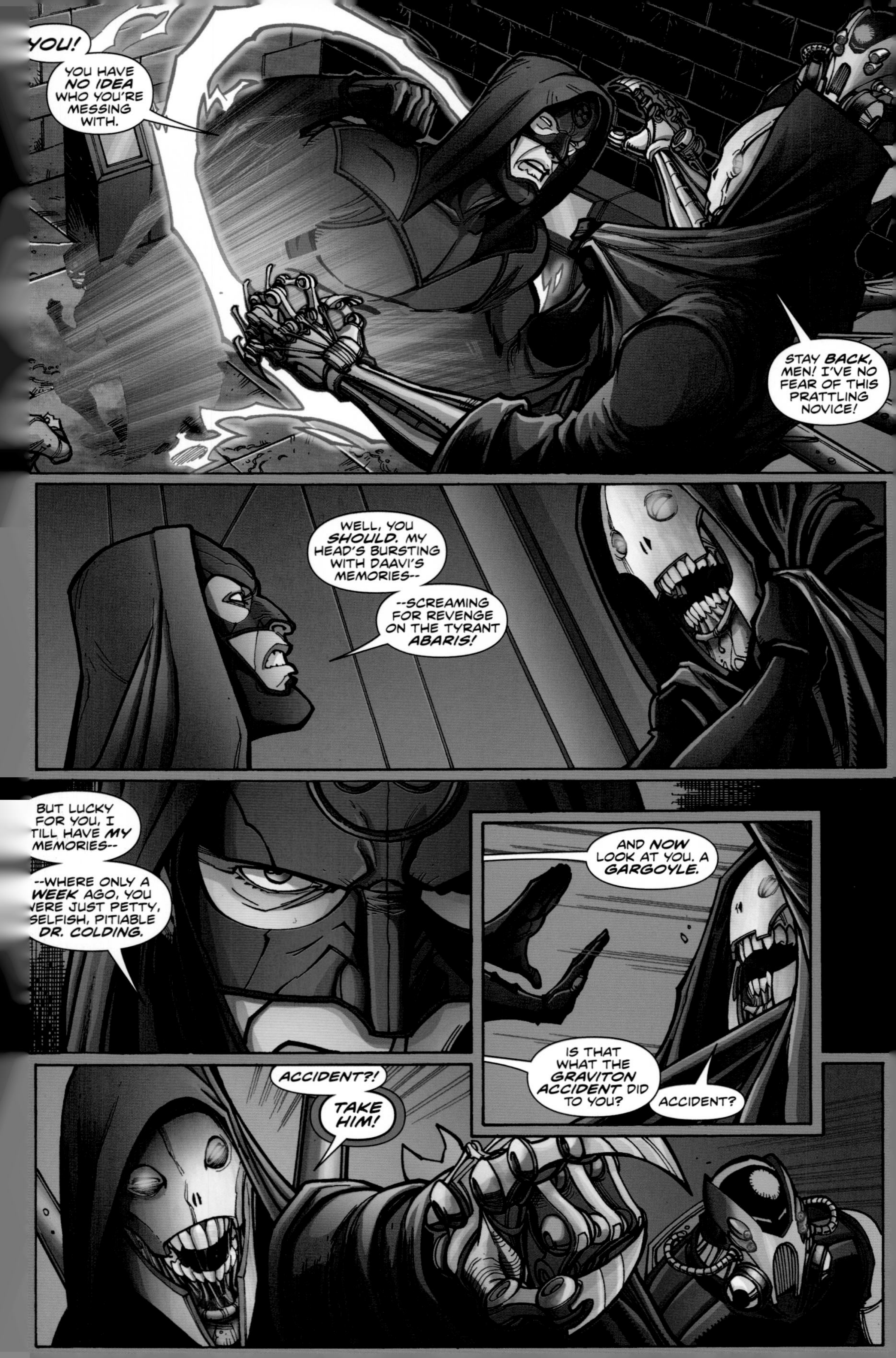
YOU!
YOU HAVE NO IDEA WHO YOU'RE MESSING WITH.
STAY BACK, MEN! I'VE NO FEAR OF THIS PRATTLING NOVICE!
WELL, YOU SHOULD. MY HEAD'S BURSTING WITH DAAVI'S MEMORIES--
--SCREAMING FOR REVENGE ON THE TYRANT ABARIS!
BUT LUCKY FOR YOU, I TILL HAVE MY MEMORIES--
--WHERE ONLY A WEEK AGO, YOU WERE JUST PETTY, SELFISH, PITIABLE DR. COLDING.
AND NOW LOOK AT YOU. A GARGOYLE.
IS THAT WHAT THE GRAVITON ACCIDENT DID TO YOU?
ACCIDENT?
ACCIDENT?!
TAKE HIM!

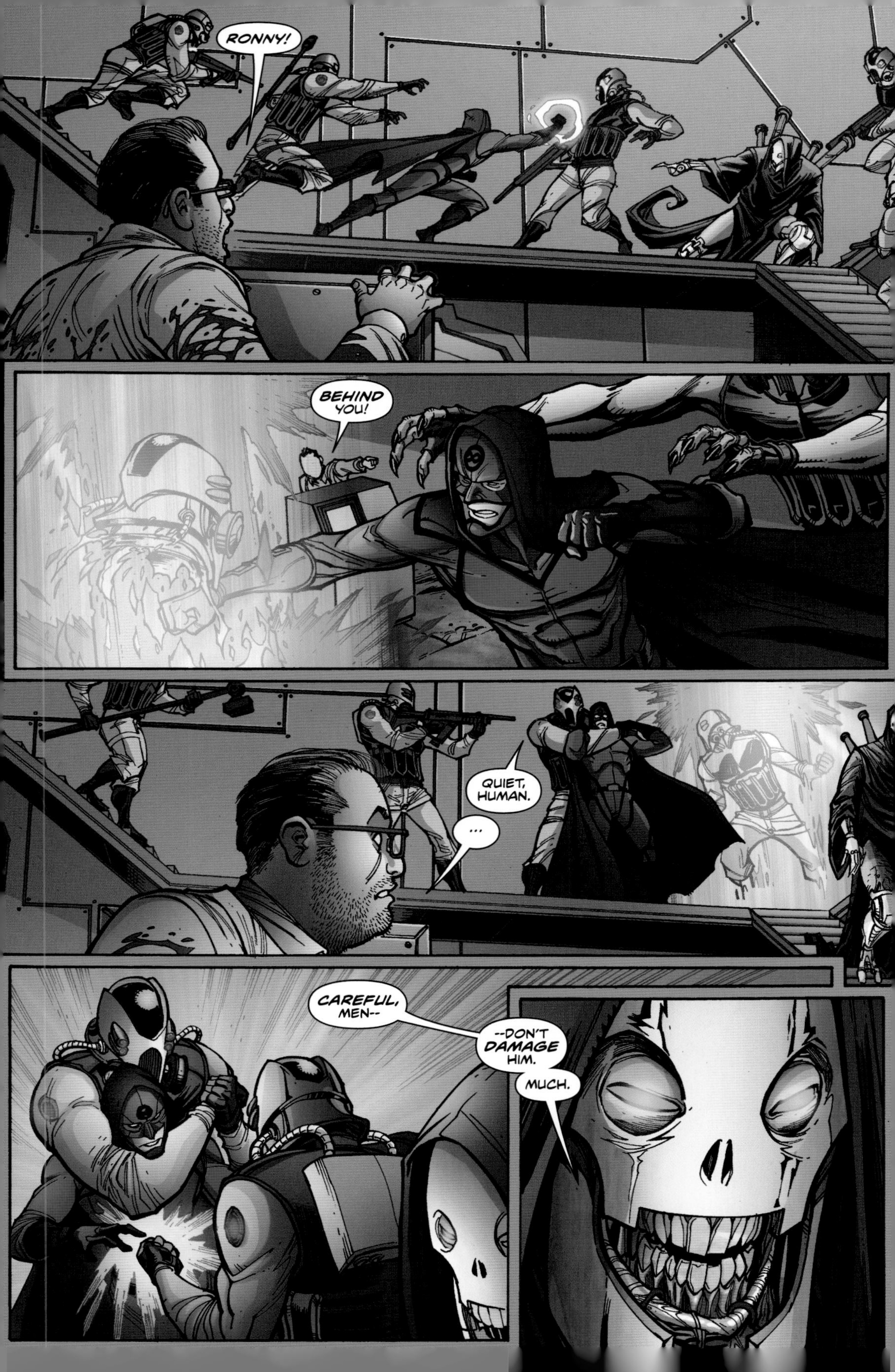
RONNY!
BEHIND YOU!
QUIET, HUMAN.
...
CAREFUL, MEN--
--DON'T DAMAGE HIM.
MUCH.

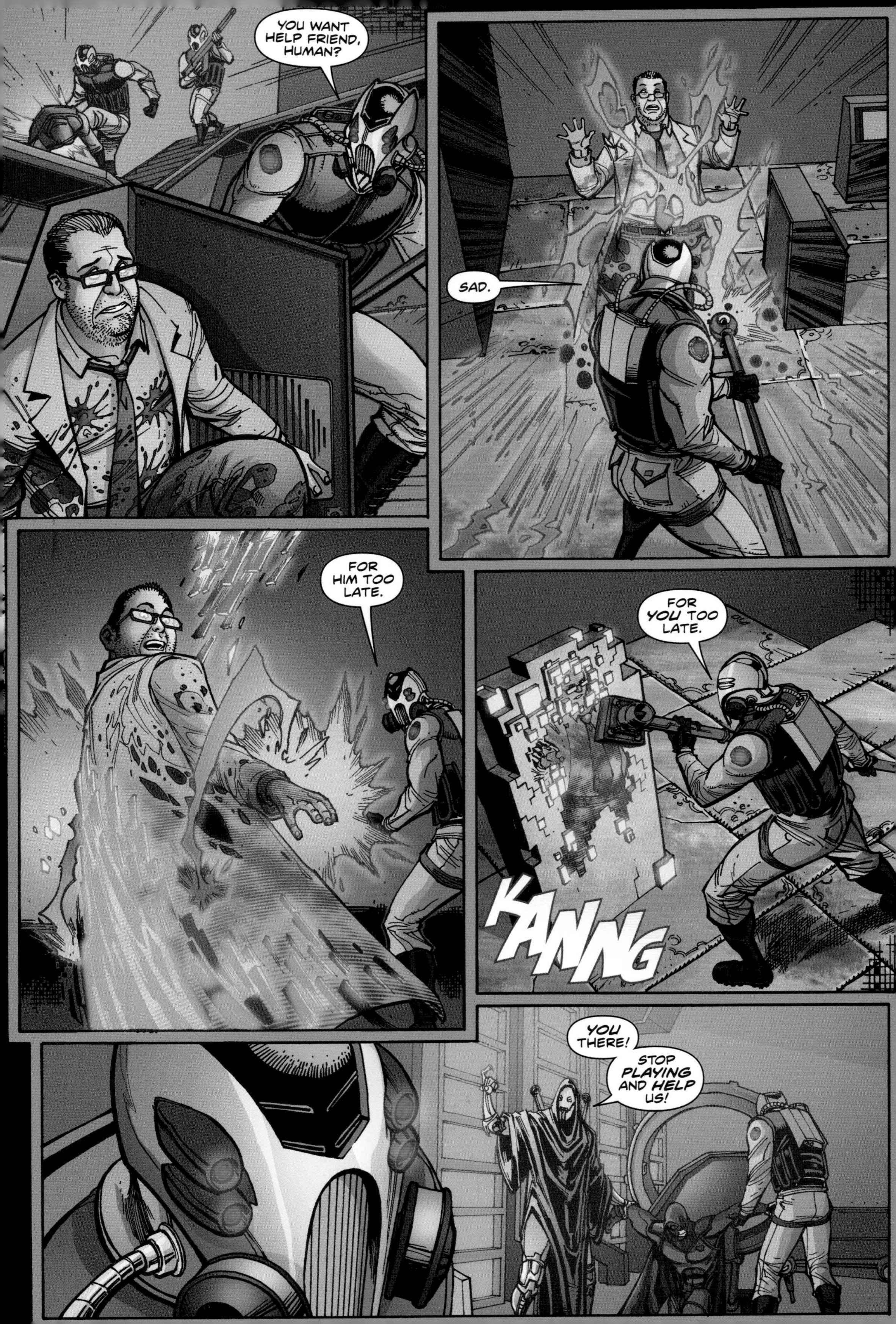

YOU WANT HELP FRIEND, HUMAN?
SAD.
FOR HIM TOO LATE.
FOR YOU TOO LATE.
KANNG
YOU THERE!
STOP PLAYING AND HELP US!

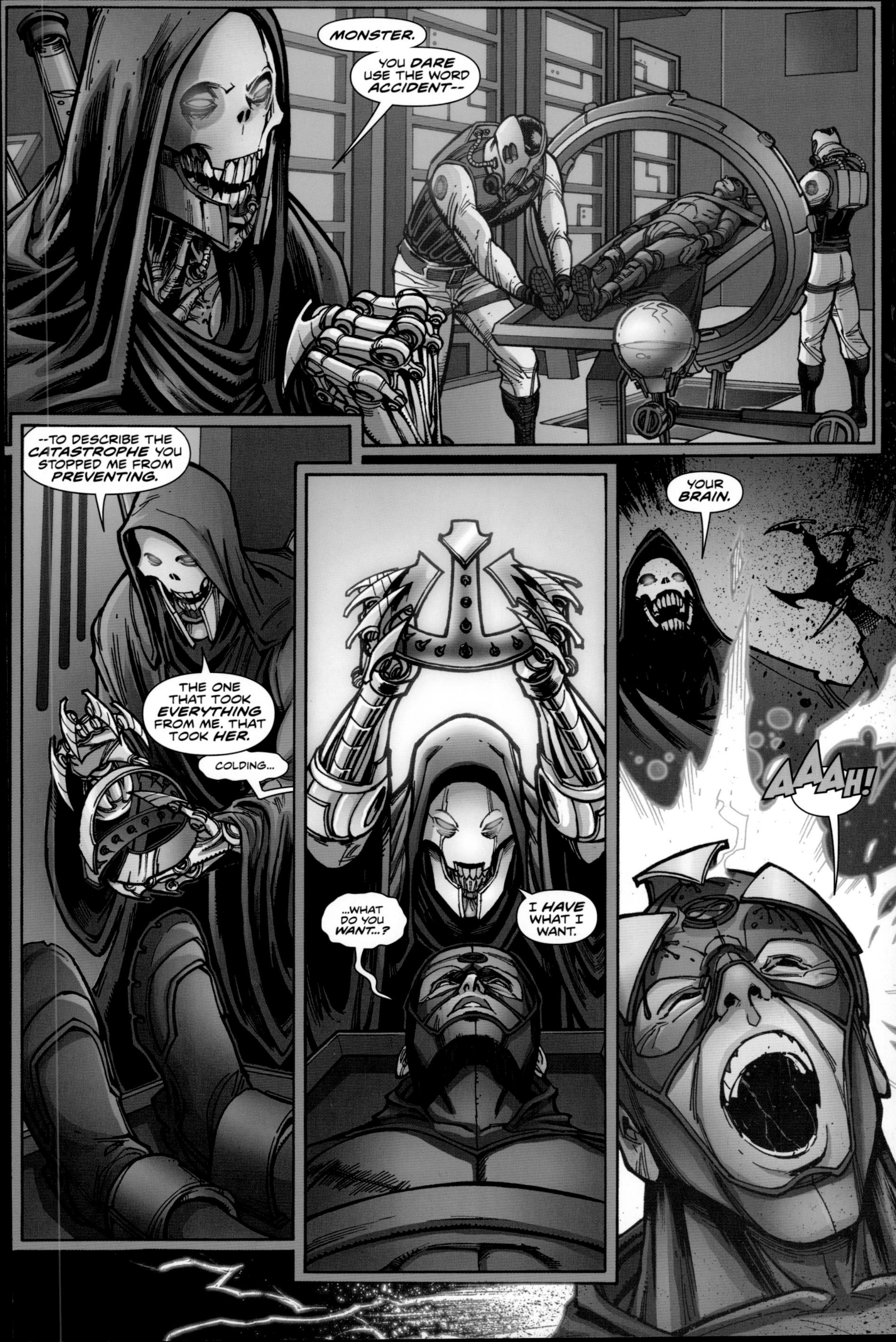
MONSTER.
YOU DARE USE THE WORD ACCIDENT--
--TO DESCRIBE THE CATASTROPHE YOU STOPPED ME FROM PREVENTING.
THE ONE THAT TOOK EVERYTHING FROM ME. THAT TOOK HER.
COLDING...
...WHAT DO YOU WANT...?
I HAVE WHAT I WANT.
YOUR BRAIN.
AAAH!

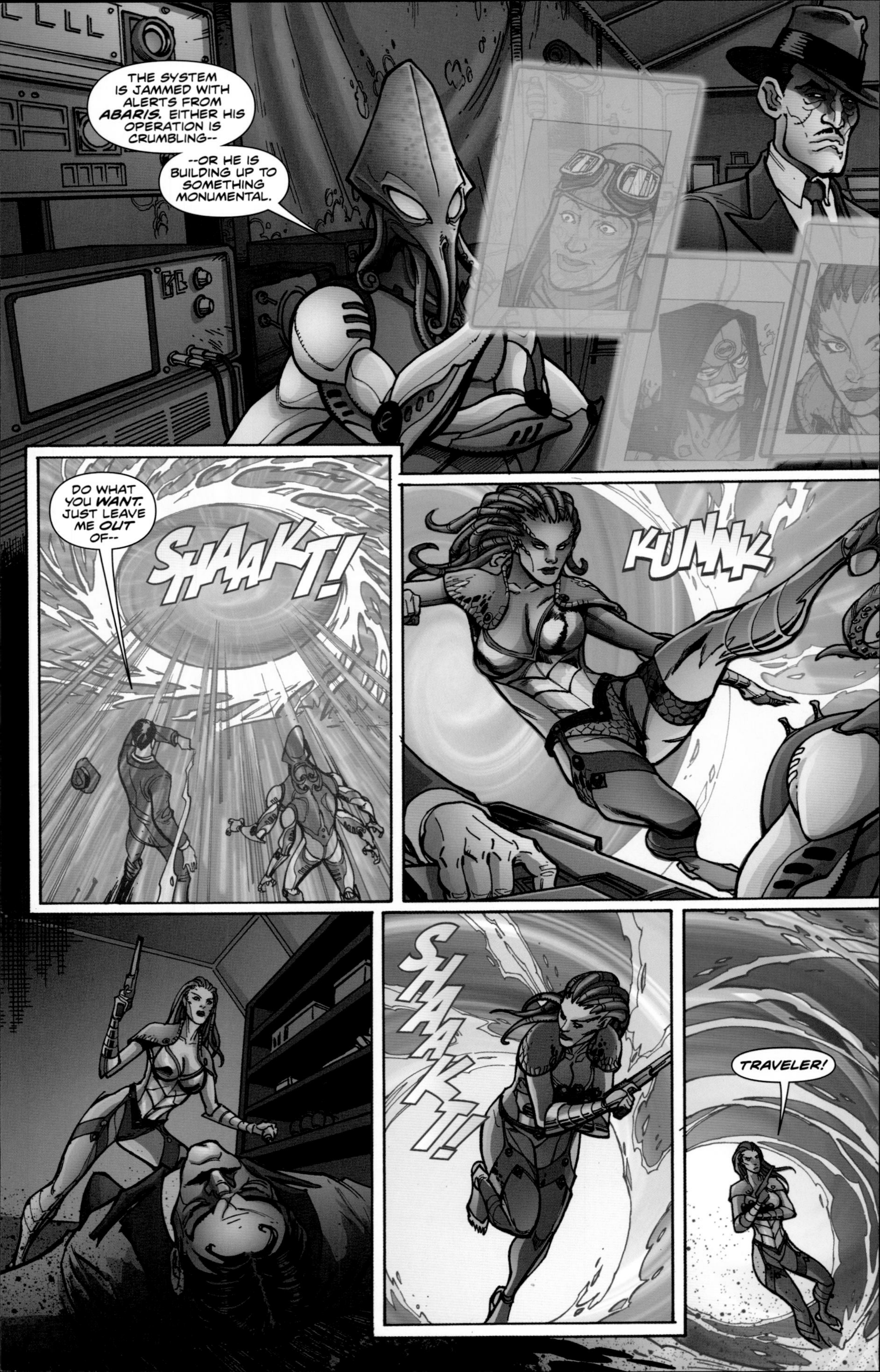
THE SYSTEM IS JAMMED WITH ALERTS FROM ABARIS. EITHER HIS OPERATION IS CRUMBLING--
--OR HE IS BUILDING UP TO SOMETHING MONUMENTAL.
DO WHAT YOU WANT. JUST LEAVE ME OUT OF--
SHAAKT!
KUNNK
SHAAKT!
TRAVELER!

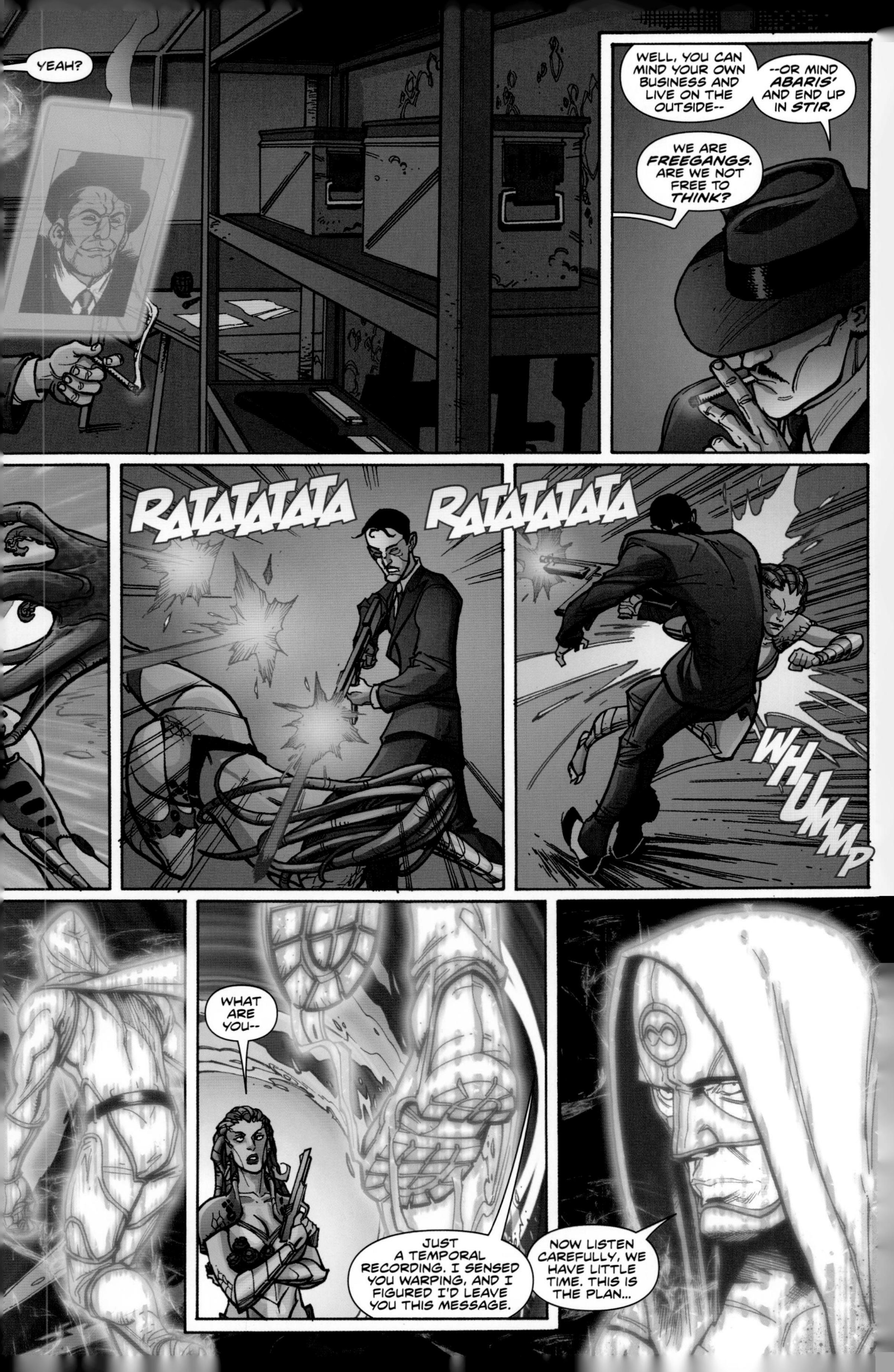
YEAH?
WELL, YOU CAN MIND YOUR OWN BUSINESS AND LIVE ON THE OUTSIDE--
--OR MIND ABARIS' AND END UP IN STIR.
WE ARE FREEGANGS. ARE WE NOT FREE TO THINK?
RATATATATA
RATATATATA
WHUMMP
WHAT ARE YOU--
JUST A TEMPORAL RECORDING. I SENSED YOU WARPING, AND I FIGURED I'D LEAVE YOU THIS MESSAGE.
NOW LISTEN CAREFULLY, WE HAVE LITTLE TIME. THIS IS THE PLAN...

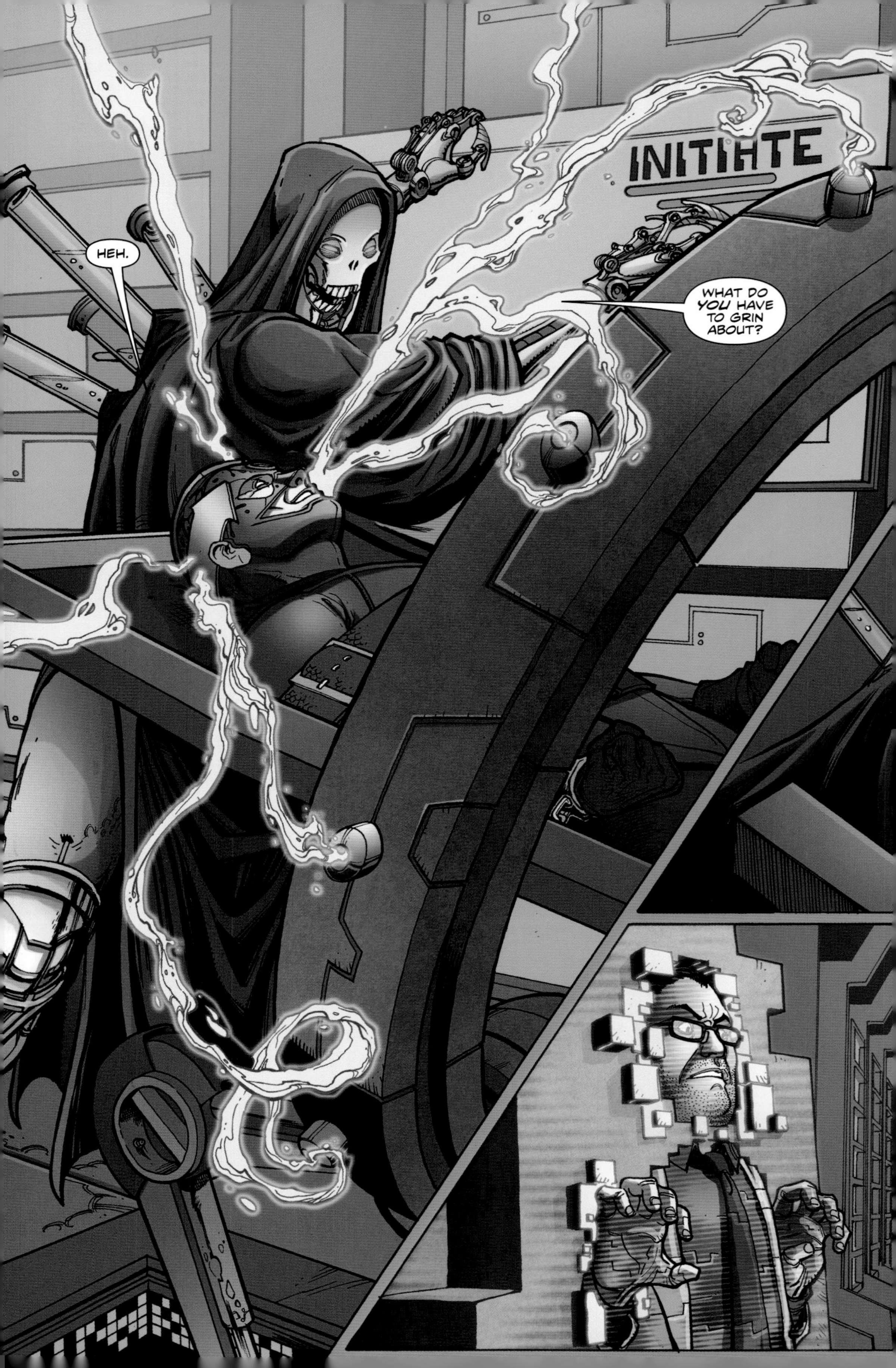
INITIATE
HEH.
WHAT DO YOU HAVE TO GRIN ABOUT?

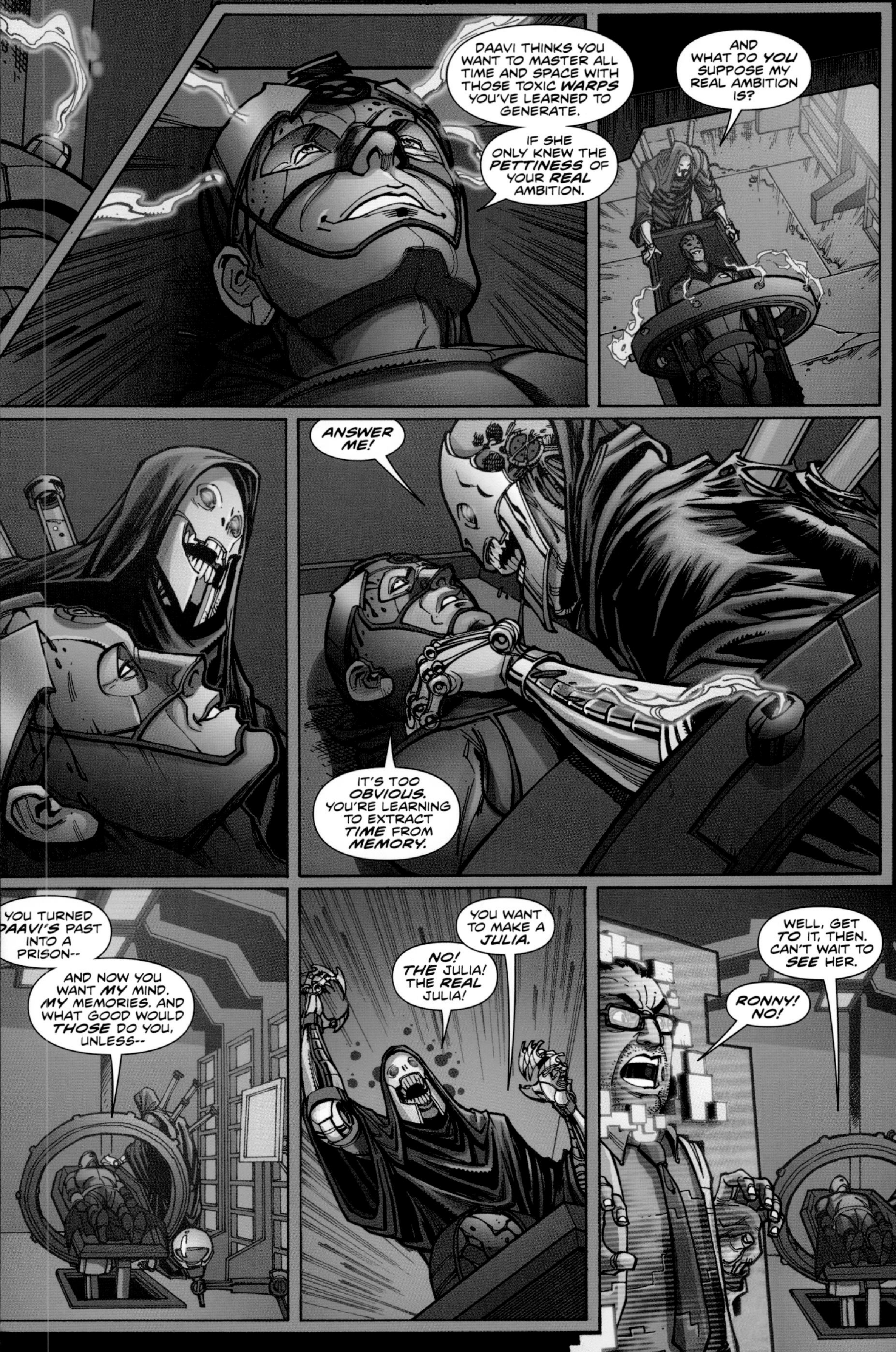

DAAVI THINKS YOU WANT TO MASTER ALL TIME AND SPACE WITH THOSE TOXIC WARPS YOU'VE LEARNED TO GENERATE.
IF SHE ONLY KNEW THE PETTINESS OF YOUR REAL AMBITION.
AND WHAT DO YOU SUPPOSE MY REAL AMBITION IS?
ANSWER ME!
IT'S TOO OBVIOUS. YOU'RE LEARNING TO EXTRACT TIME FROM MEMORY.
YOU TURNED DAAVI'S PAST INTO A PRISON--
AND NOW YOU WANT MY MIND. MY MEMORIES. AND WHAT GOOD WOULD THOSE DO YOU, UNLESS--
YOU WANT TO MAKE A JULIA.
NO! THE JULIA! THE REAL JULIA!
WELL, GET TO IT, THEN. CAN'T WAIT TO SEE HER.
RONNY! NO!

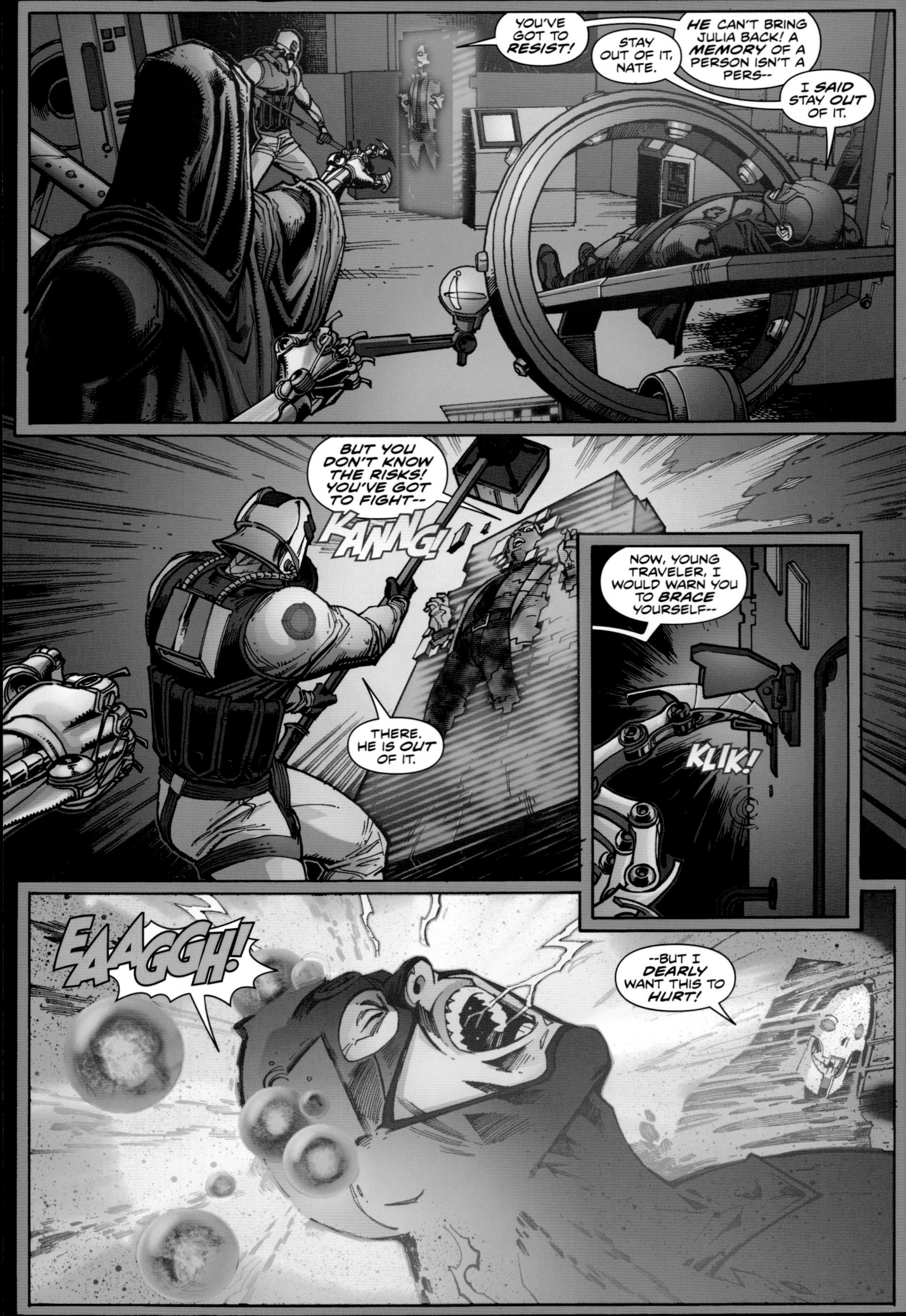

YOU'VE GOT TO RESIST!
STAY OUT OF IT, NATE.
HE CAN'T BRING JULIA BACK! A MEMORY OF A PERSON ISN'T A PERS--
I SAID STAY OUT OF IT.
BUT YOU DON'T KNOW THE RISKS! YOU'VE GOT TO FIGHT--
KANNG!
THERE. HE IS OUT OF IT.
NOW, YOUNG TRAVELER, I WOULD WARN YOU TO BRACE YOURSELF--
KLIK!
EAAGGH!
--BUT I DEARLY WANT THIS TO HURT!

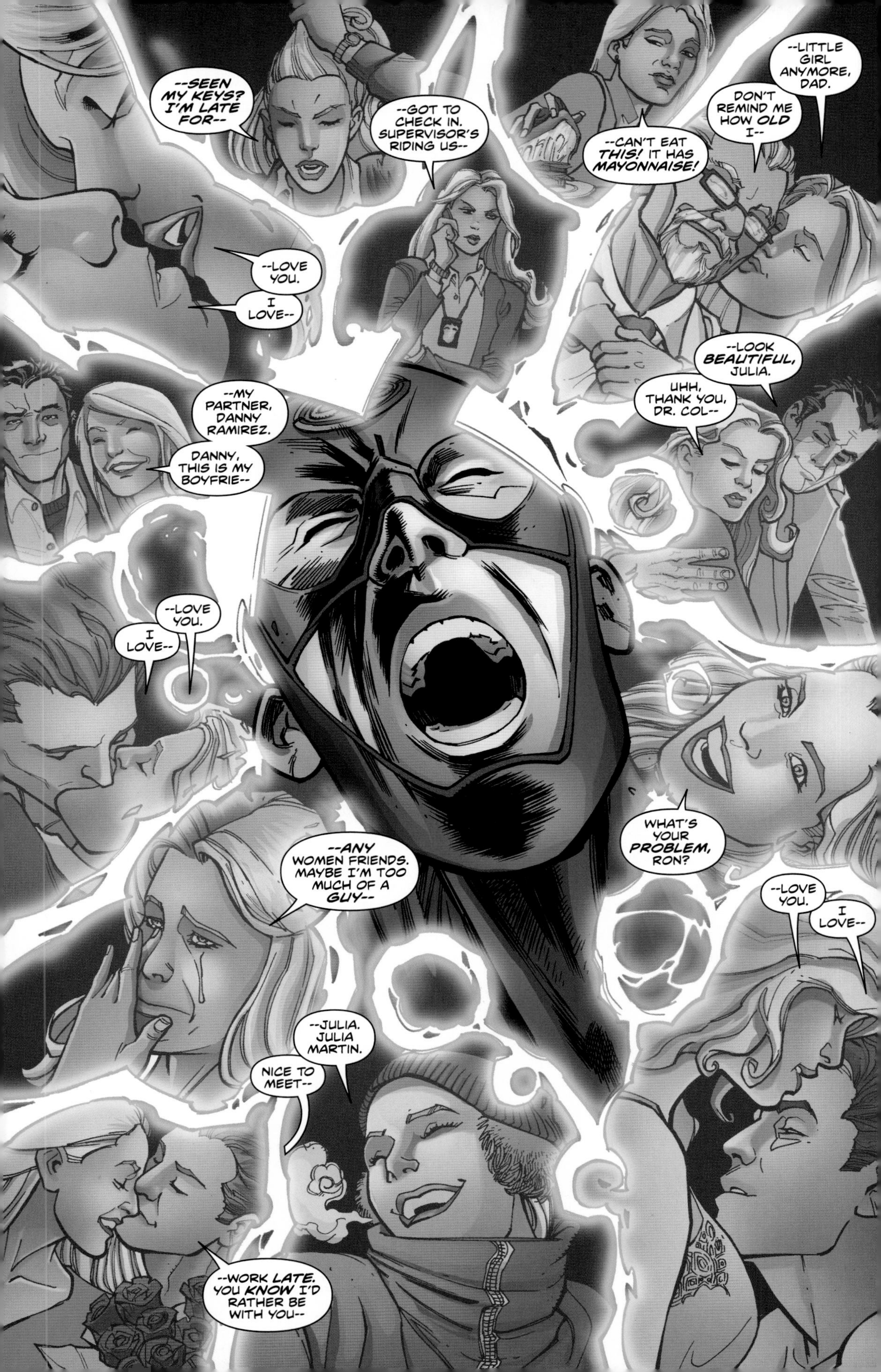
--SEEN MY KEYS? I'M LATE FOR--
--GOT TO CHECK IN. SUPERVISOR'S RIDING US--
--CAN'T EAT THIS! IT HAS MAYONNAISE!
--LITTLE GIRL ANYMORE, DAD.
DON'T REMIND ME HOW OLD I--
--LOVE YOU.
I LOVE--
--MY PARTNER, DANNY RAMIREZ.
DANNY, THIS IS MY BOYFRIE--
--LOOK BEAUTIFUL, JULIA.
UHH, THANK YOU, DR. COL--
--LOVE YOU.
I LOVE--
WHAT'S YOUR PROBLEM, RON?
--ANY WOMEN FRIENDS. MAYBE I'M TOO MUCH OF A GUY--
--LOVE YOU.
I LOVE--
--JULIA. JULIA MARTIN.
NICE TO MEET--
--WORK LATE. YOU KNOW I'D RATHER BE WITH YOU--

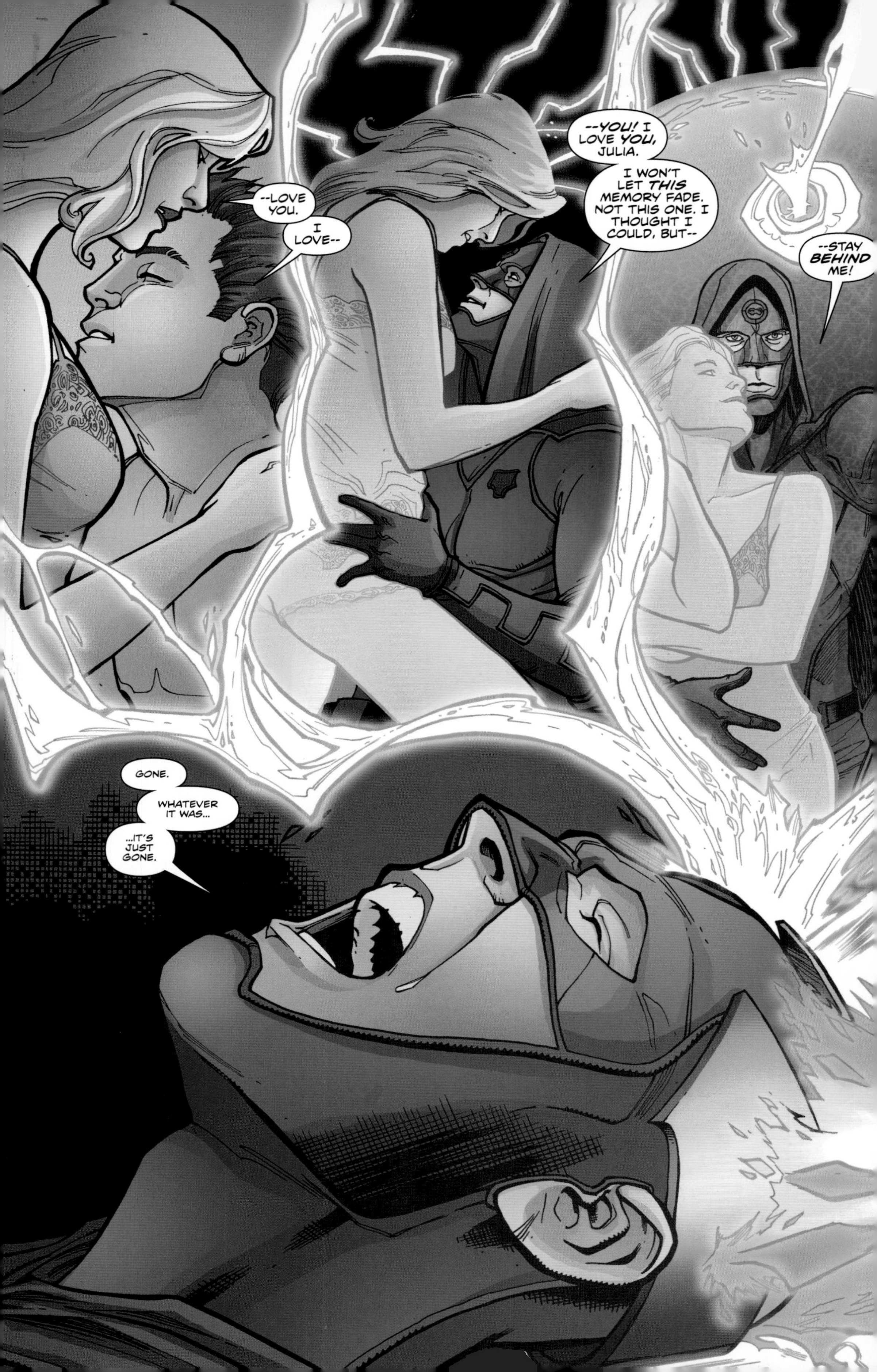
--LOVE YOU.
I LOVE--
--YOU! I LOVE YOU, JULIA.
I WON'T LET THIS MEMORY FADE. NOT THIS ONE. I THOUGHT I COULD, BUT--
--STAY BEHIND ME!
GONE.
WHATEVER IT WAS...
...IT'S JUST GONE.

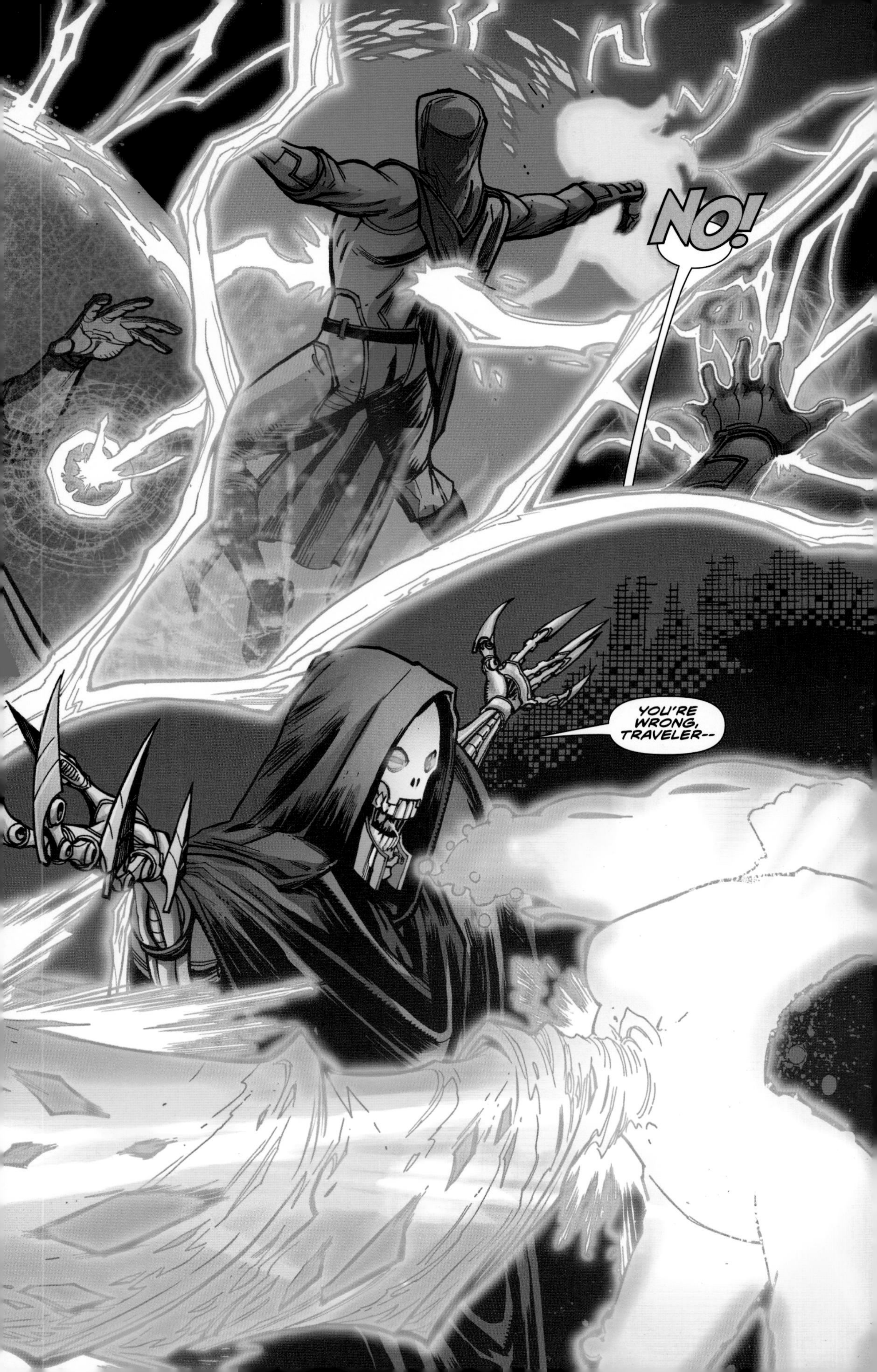
NO!
YOU'RE WRONG, TRAVELER--

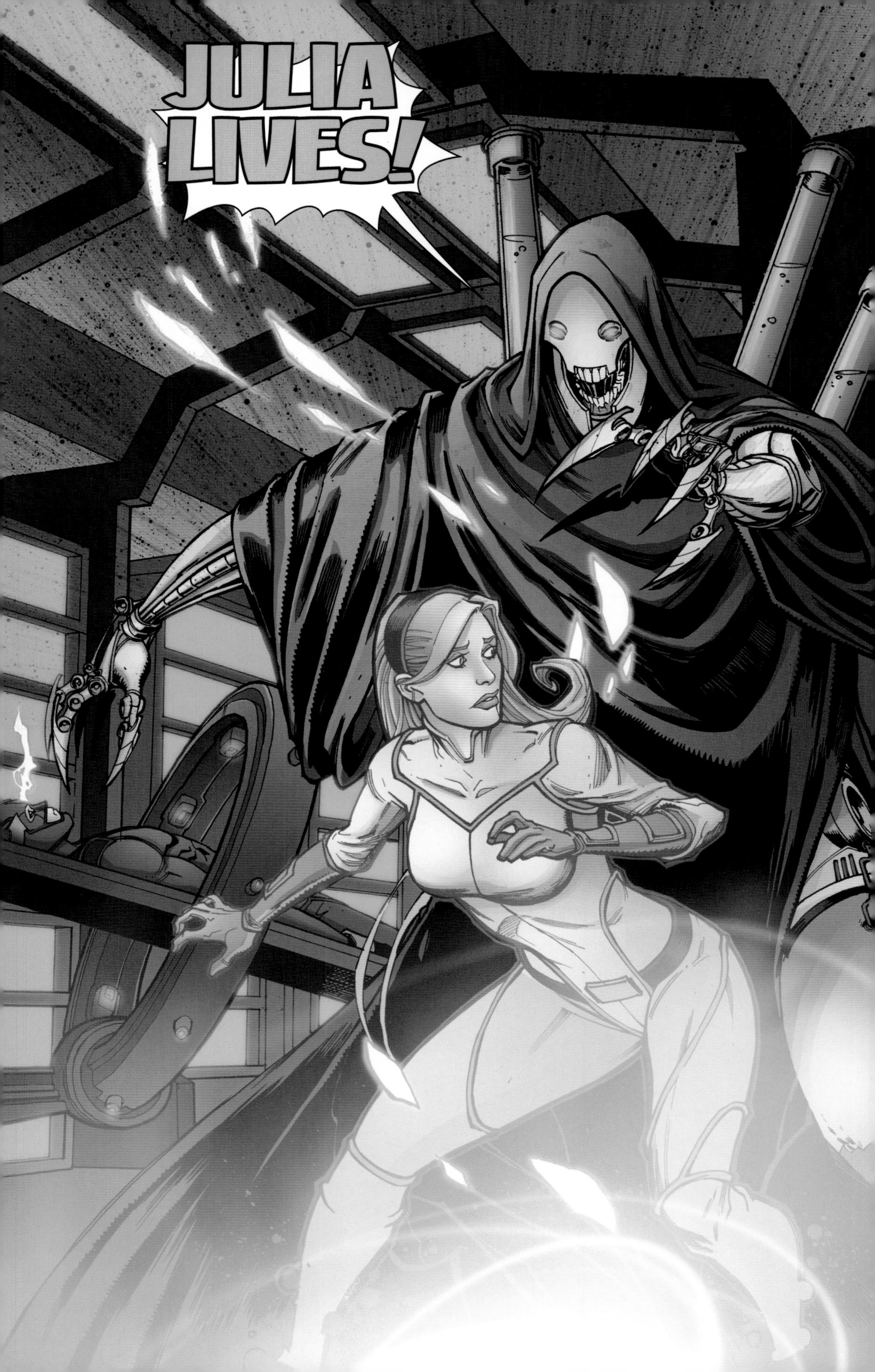
JULIA LIVES!

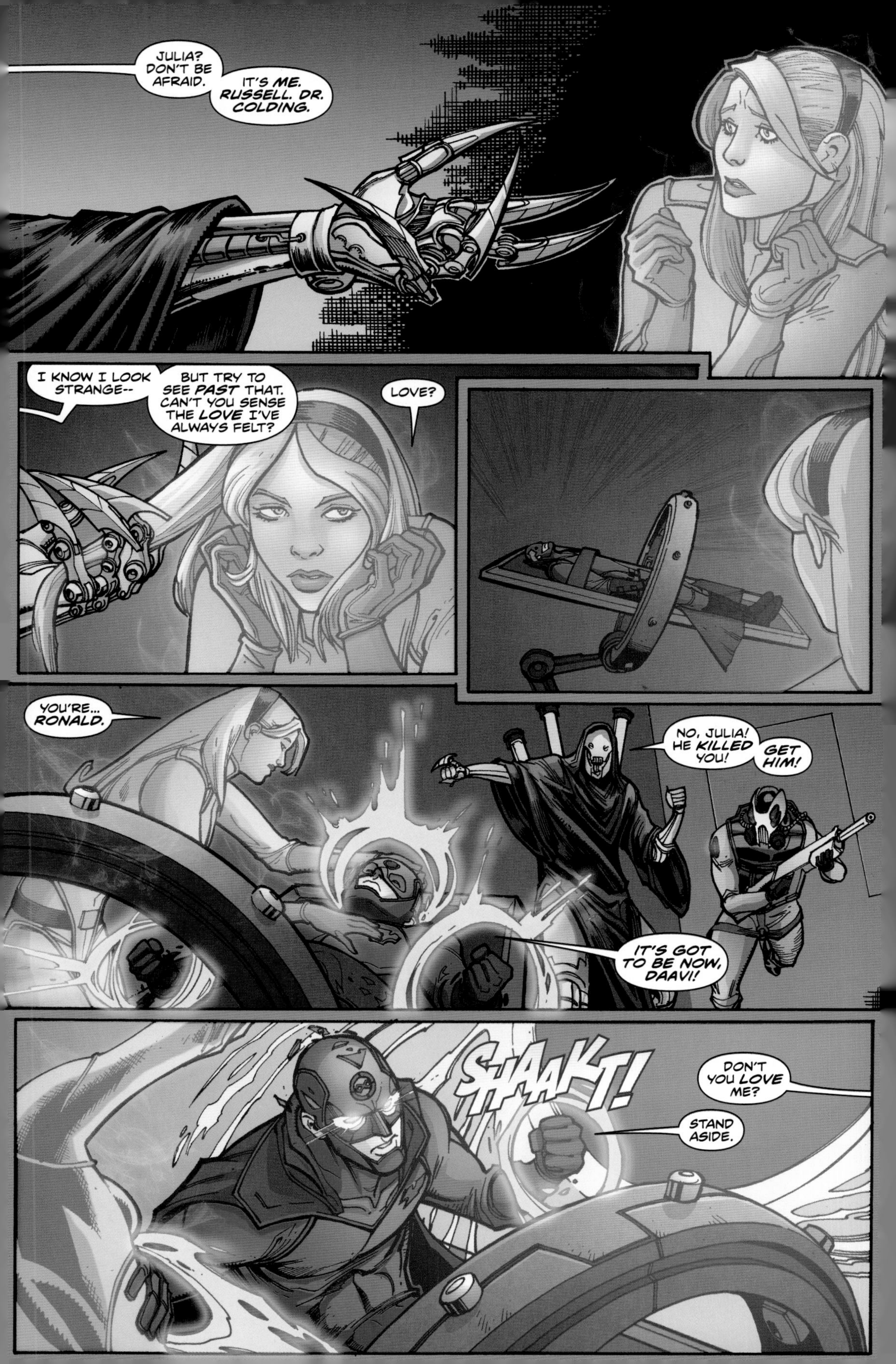
JULIA? DON'T BE AFRAID.
IT'S ME. RUSSELL. DR. COLDING.
I KNOW I LOOK STRANGE--
BUT TRY TO SEE PAST THAT. CAN'T YOU SENSE THE LOVE I'VE ALWAYS FELT?
LOVE?
YOU'RE... RONALD.
NO, JULIA! HE KILLED YOU!
GET HIM!
IT'S GOT TO BE NOW, DAAVI!
SHAAKT!
DON'T YOU LOVE ME?
STAND ASIDE.

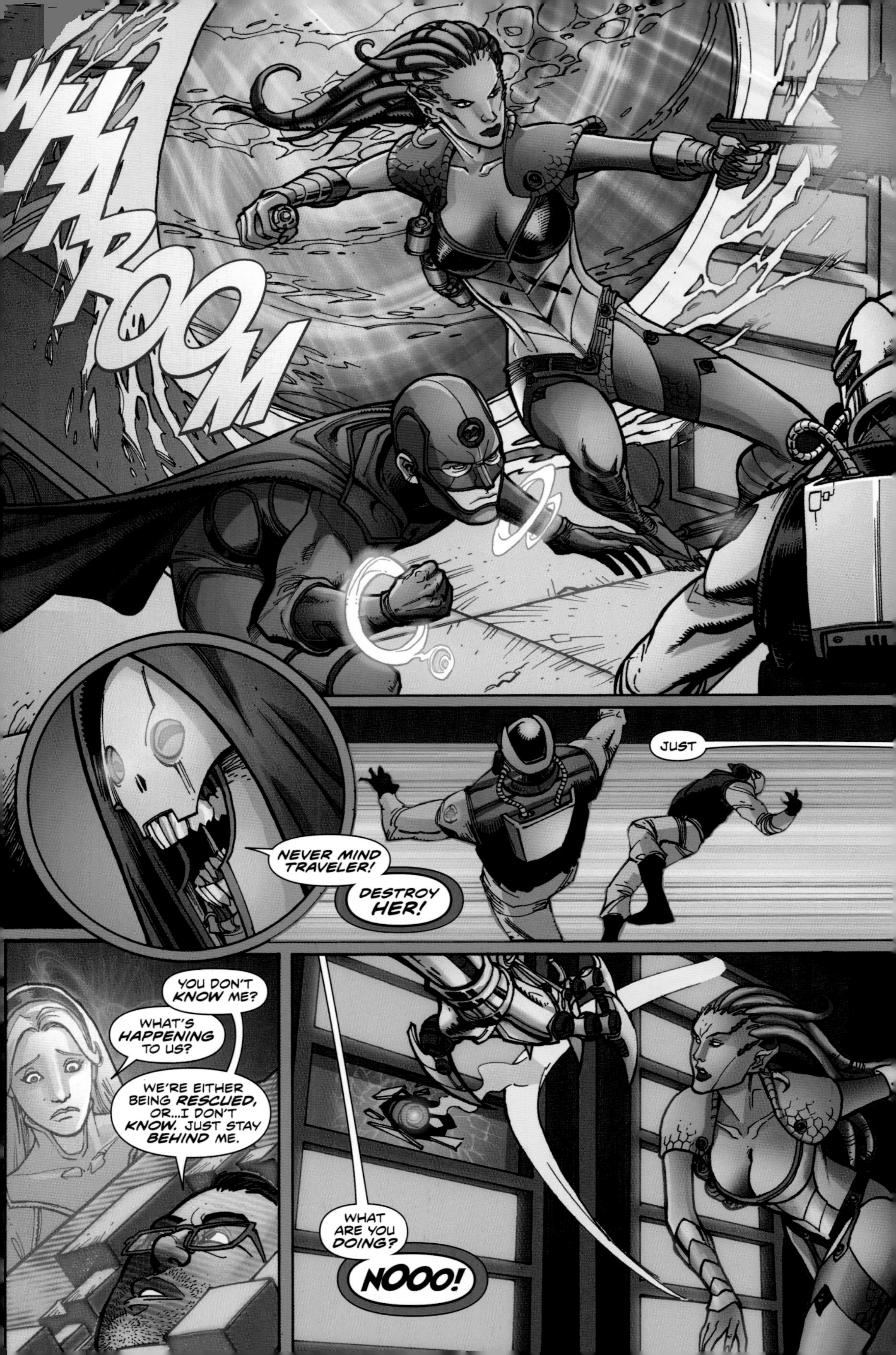
WHA-ROOM
JUST
NEVER MIND TRAVELER!
DESTROY HER!
YOU DON'T KNOW ME?
WHAT'S HAPPENING TO US?
WE'RE EITHER BEING RESCUED, OR...I DON'T KNOW. JUST STAY BEHIND ME.
WHAT ARE YOU DOING?
NOOO!

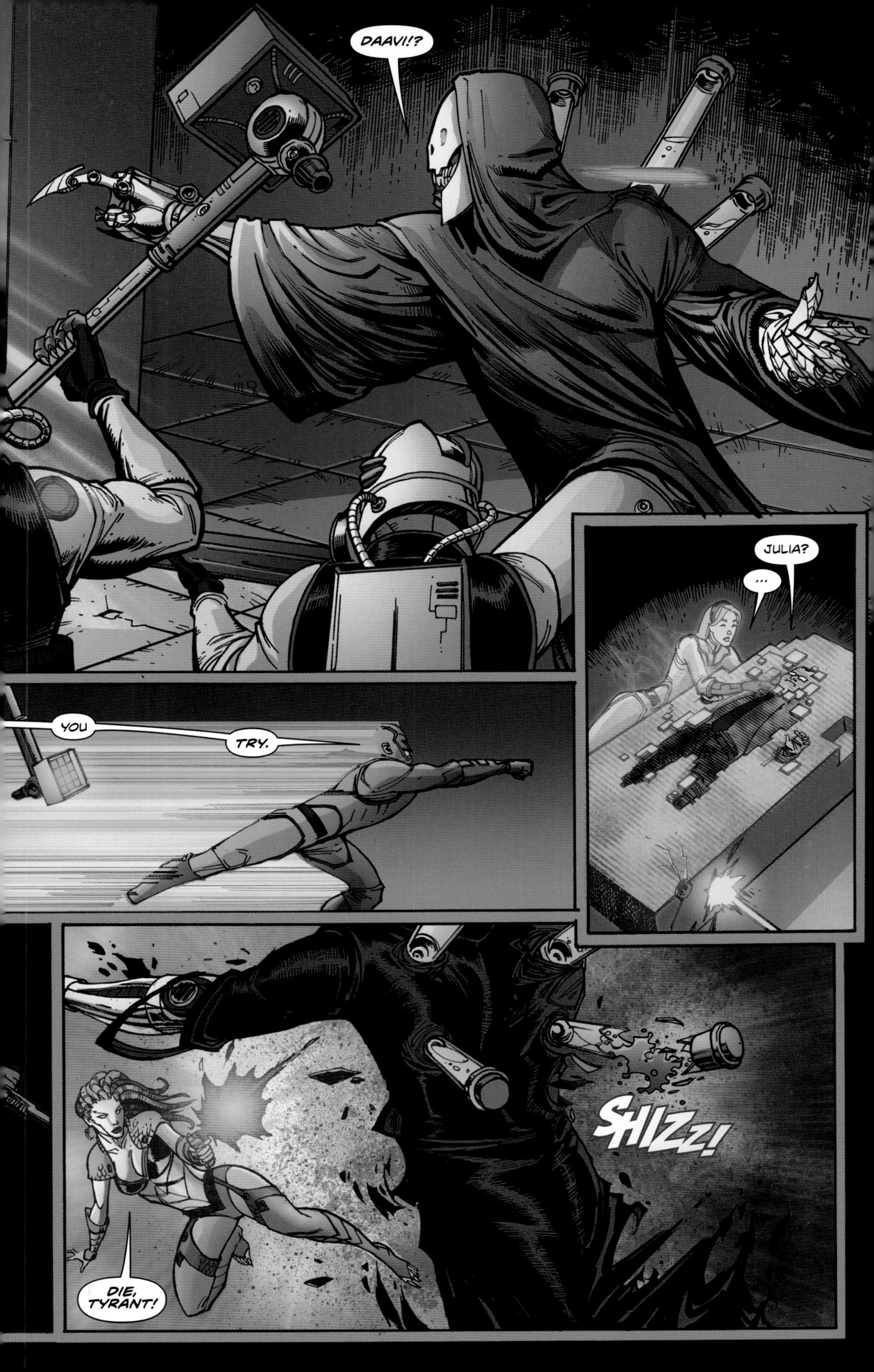
DAAVI!?
JULIA?
...
YOU
TRY.
SHIZZ!
DIE, TYRANT!

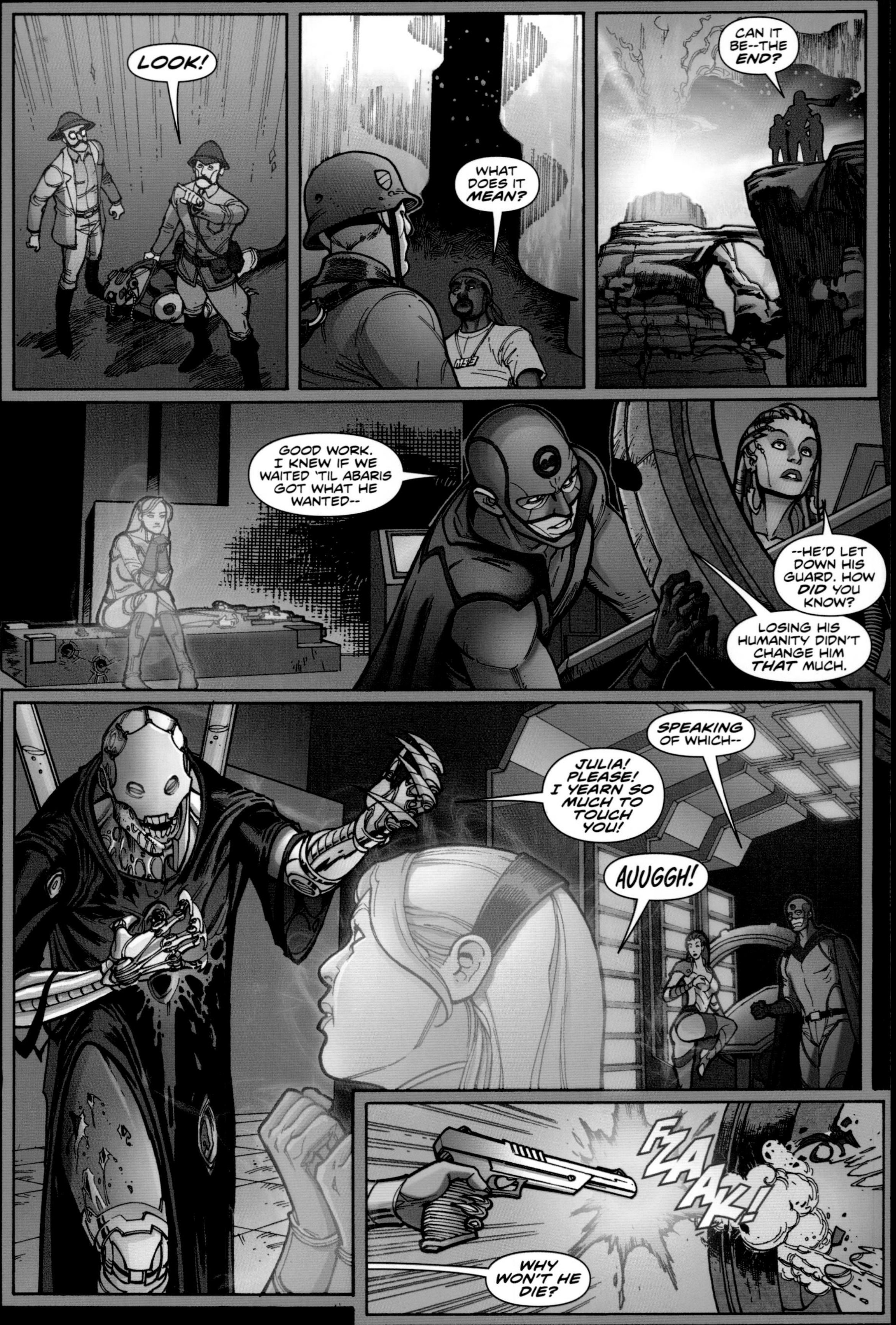
LOOK!
WHAT DOES IT MEAN?
CAN IT BE--THE END?
GOOD WORK. I KNEW IF WE WAITED 'TIL ABARIS GOT WHAT HE WANTED--
--HE'D LET DOWN HIS GUARD. HOW DID YOU KNOW?
LOSING HIS HUMANITY DIDN'T CHANGE HIM THAT MUCH.
SPEAKING OF WHICH--
JULIA! PLEASE! I YEARN SO MUCH TO TOUCH YOU!
AUUGGH!
FZZAAKK!
WHY WON'T HE DIE?

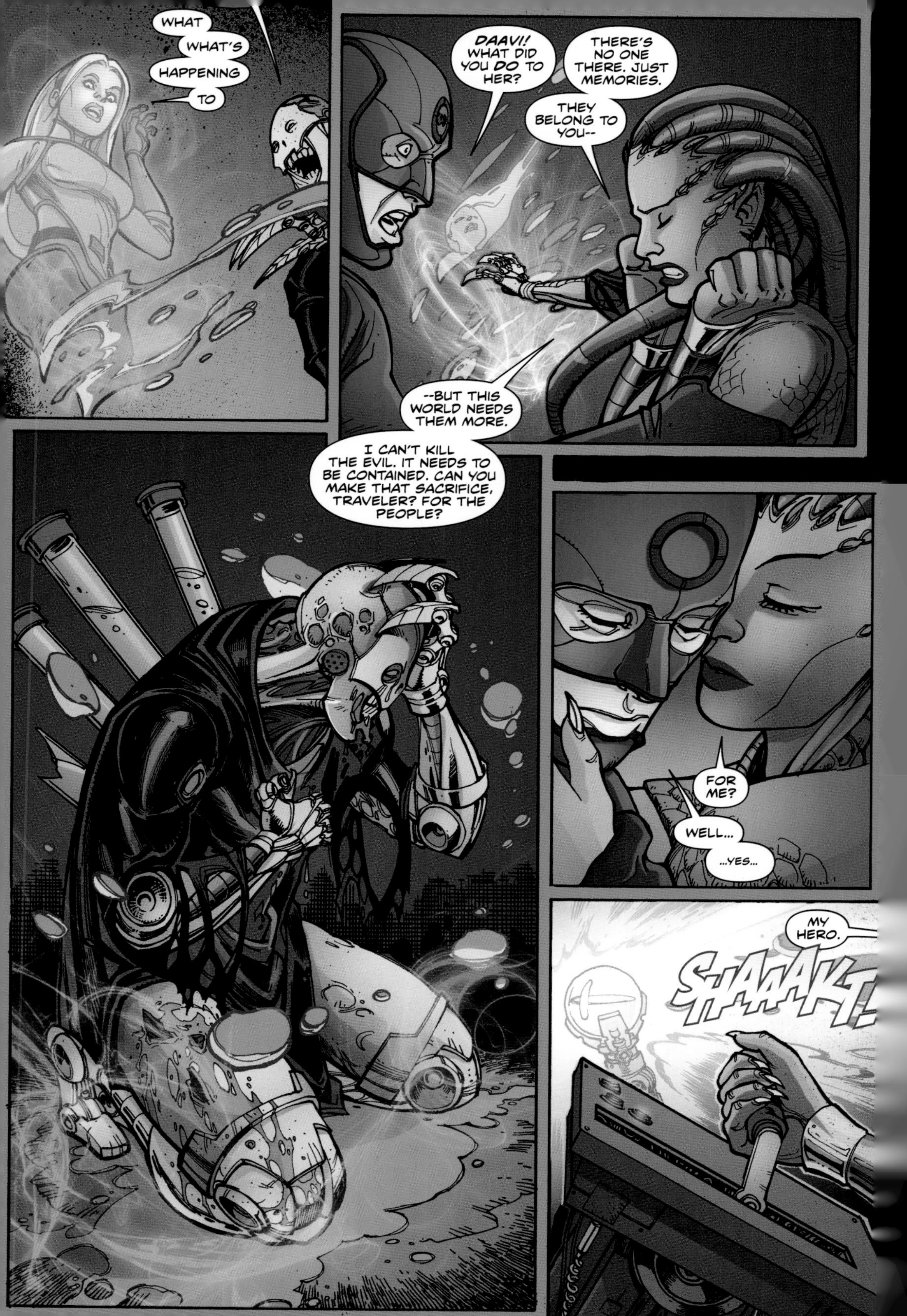
WHAT
WHAT'S
HAPPENING
TO
DAAVI! WHAT DID YOU DO TO HER?
THERE'S NO ONE THERE. JUST MEMORIES.
THEY BELONG TO YOU--
--BUT THIS WORLD NEEDS THEM MORE.
I CAN'T KILL THE EVIL. IT NEEDS TO BE CONTAINED. CAN YOU MAKE THAT SACRIFICE, TRAVELER? FOR THE PEOPLE?
FOR ME?
WELL...
...YES...
MY HERO.
SHAAAKT!

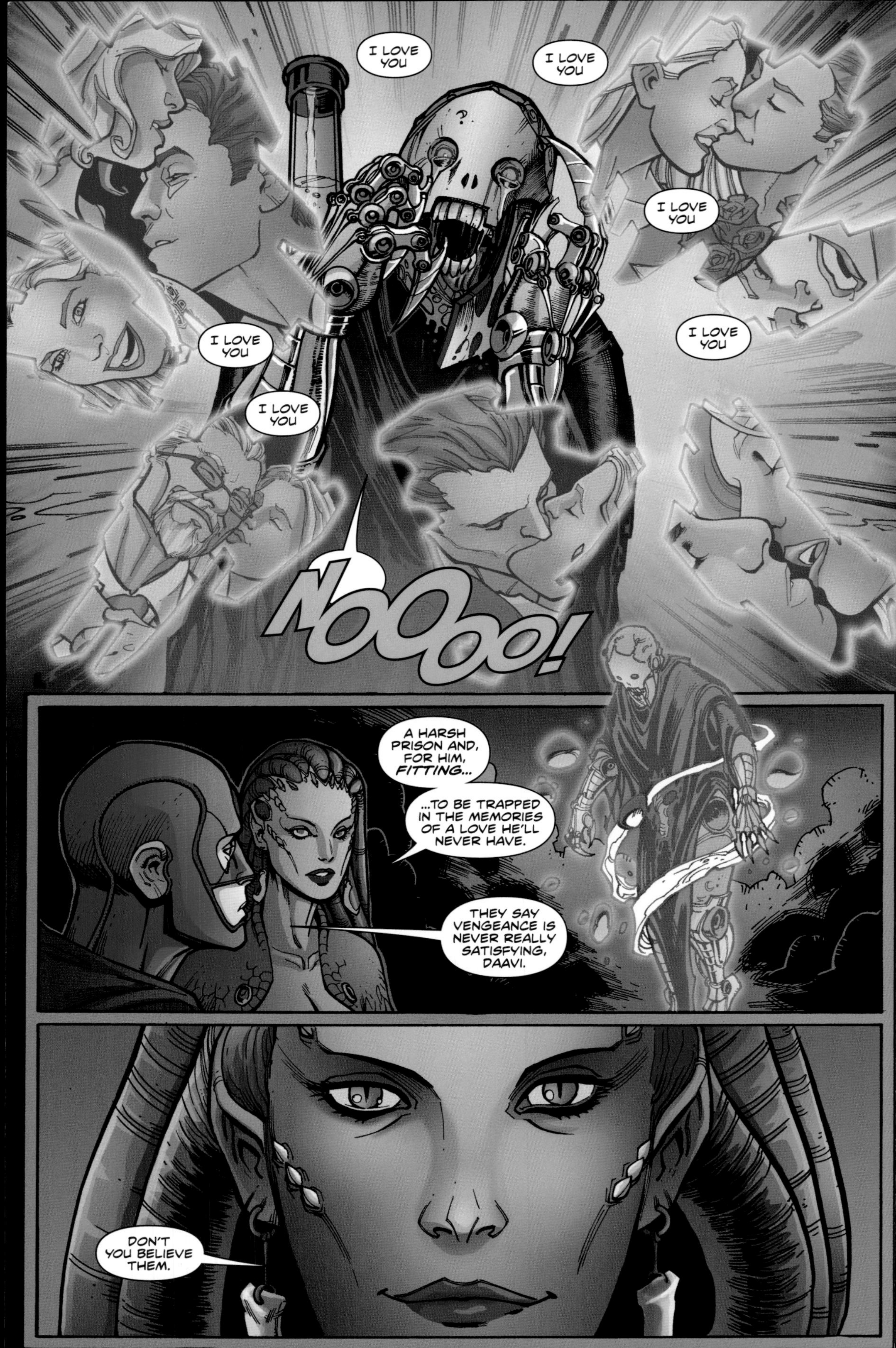
I LOVE YOU
I LOVE YOU
I LOVE YOU
I LOVE YOU
I LOVE YOU
I LOVE YOU
NOOOOO!
A HARSH PRISON AND, FOR HIM, FITTING...
...TO BE TRAPPED IN THE MEMORIES OF A LOVE HE'LL NEVER HAVE.
THEY SAY VENGEANCE IS NEVER REALLY SATISFYING, DAAVI.
DON'T YOU BELIEVE THEM.

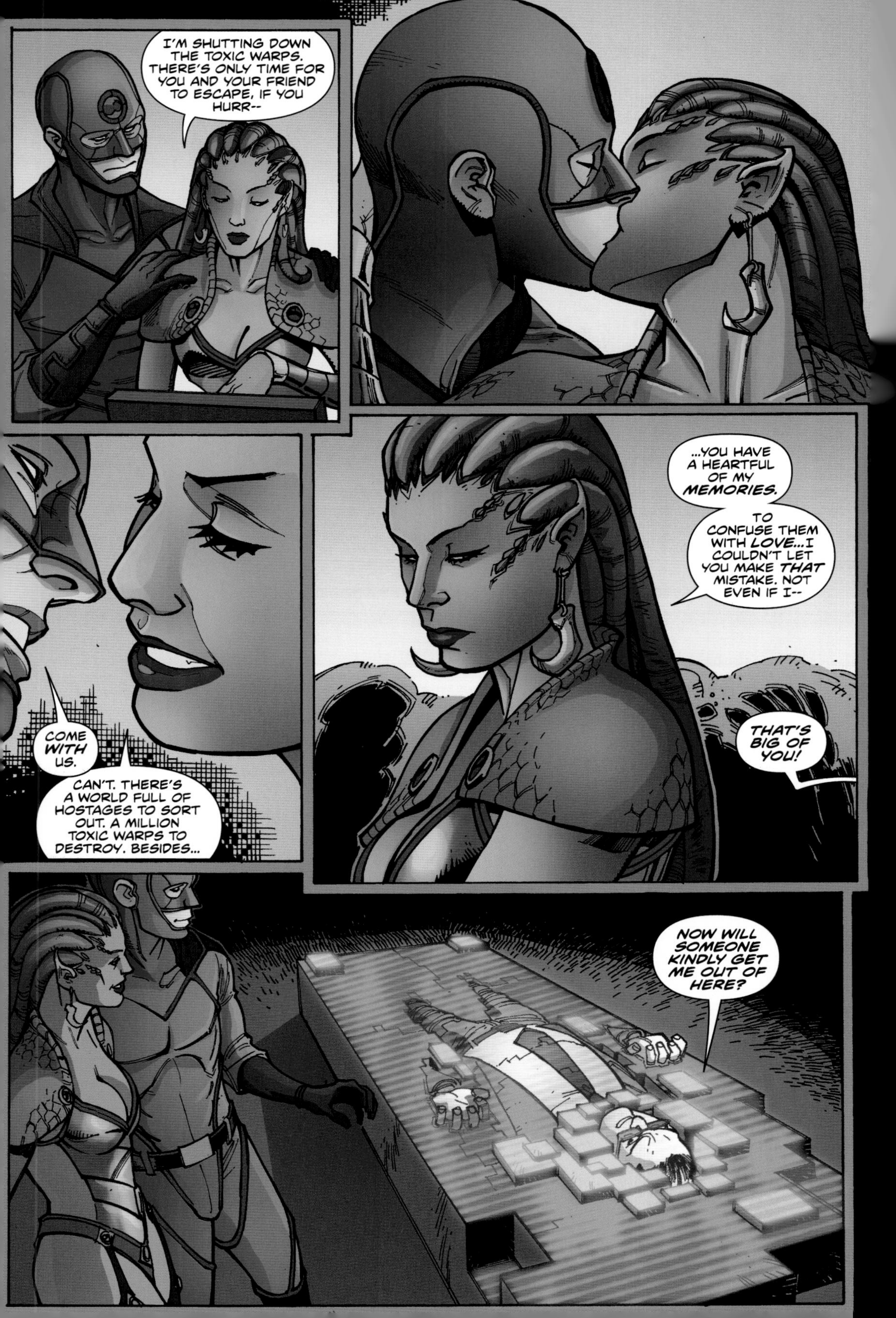

I'M SHUTTING DOWN THE TOXIC WARPS. THERE'S ONLY TIME FOR YOU AND YOUR FRIEND TO ESCAPE, IF YOU HURR--
COME WITH US.
CAN'T. THERE'S A WORLD FULL OF HOSTAGES TO SORT OUT. A MILLION TOXIC WARPS TO DESTROY. BESIDES...
...YOU HAVE A HEARTFUL OF MY MEMORIES.
TO CONFUSE THEM WITH LOVE...I COULDN'T LET YOU MAKE THAT MISTAKE. NOT EVEN IF I--
THAT'S BIG OF YOU!
NOW WILL SOMEONE KINDLY GET ME OUT OF HERE?

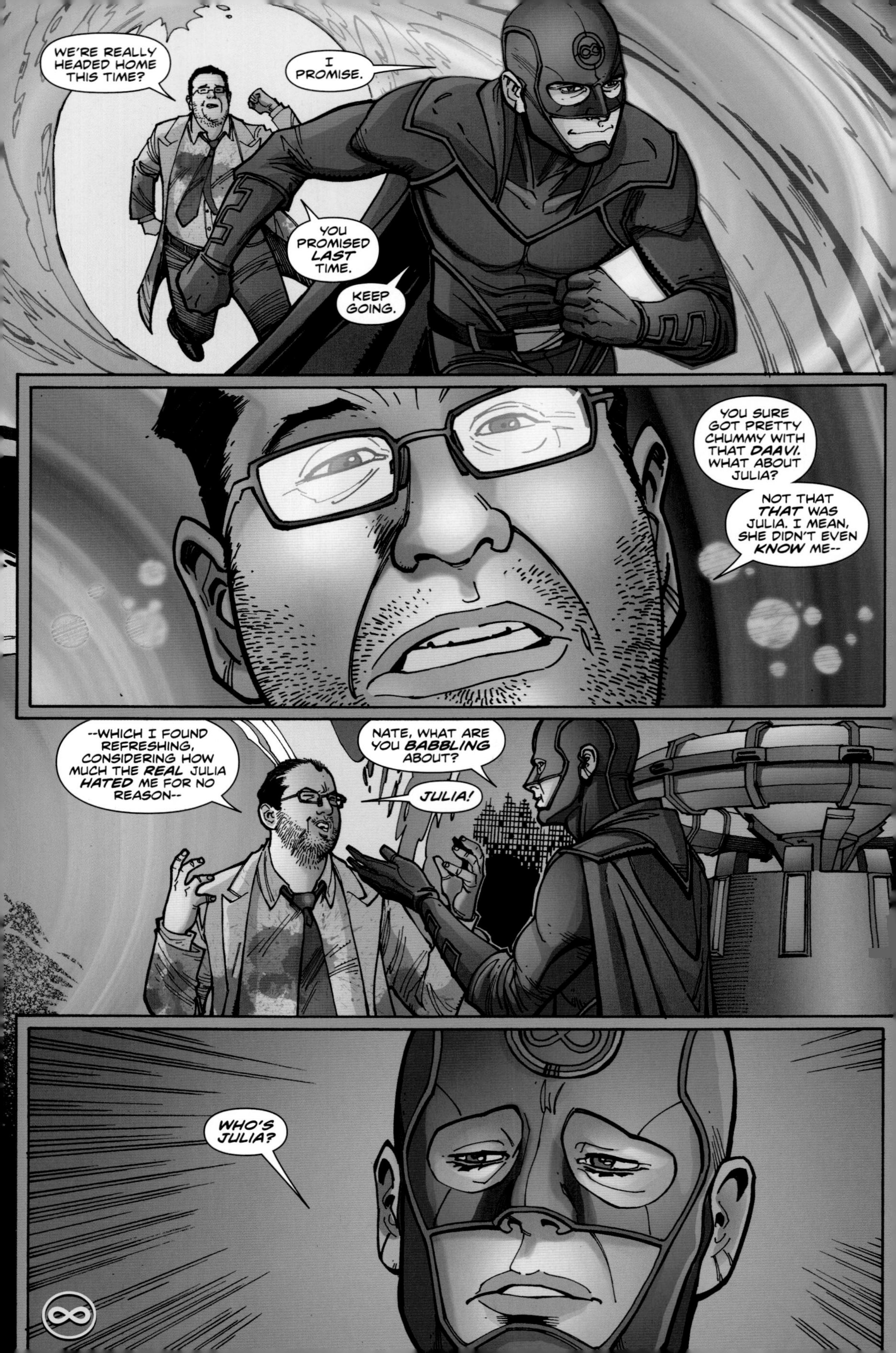
WE'RE REALLY HEADED HOME THIS TIME?
I PROMISE.
YOU PROMISED LAST TIME.
KEEP GOING.
YOU SURE GOT PRETTY CHUMMY WITH THAT DAAVI. WHAT ABOUT JULIA?
NOT THAT THAT WAS JULIA. I MEAN, SHE DIDN'T EVEN KNOW ME--
--WHICH I FOUND REFRESHING, CONSIDERING HOW MUCH THE REAL JULIA HATED ME FOR NO REASON--
NATE, WHAT ARE YOU BABBLING ABOUT?
JULIA!
WHO'S JULIA?

COMING SOON

∞ ATEMPORAL

THE TRAVELER

STAN LEE
MARK WAID
TOM PEYER
CHAD HARDIN

VOLUME THREE

COVER
GALLERY

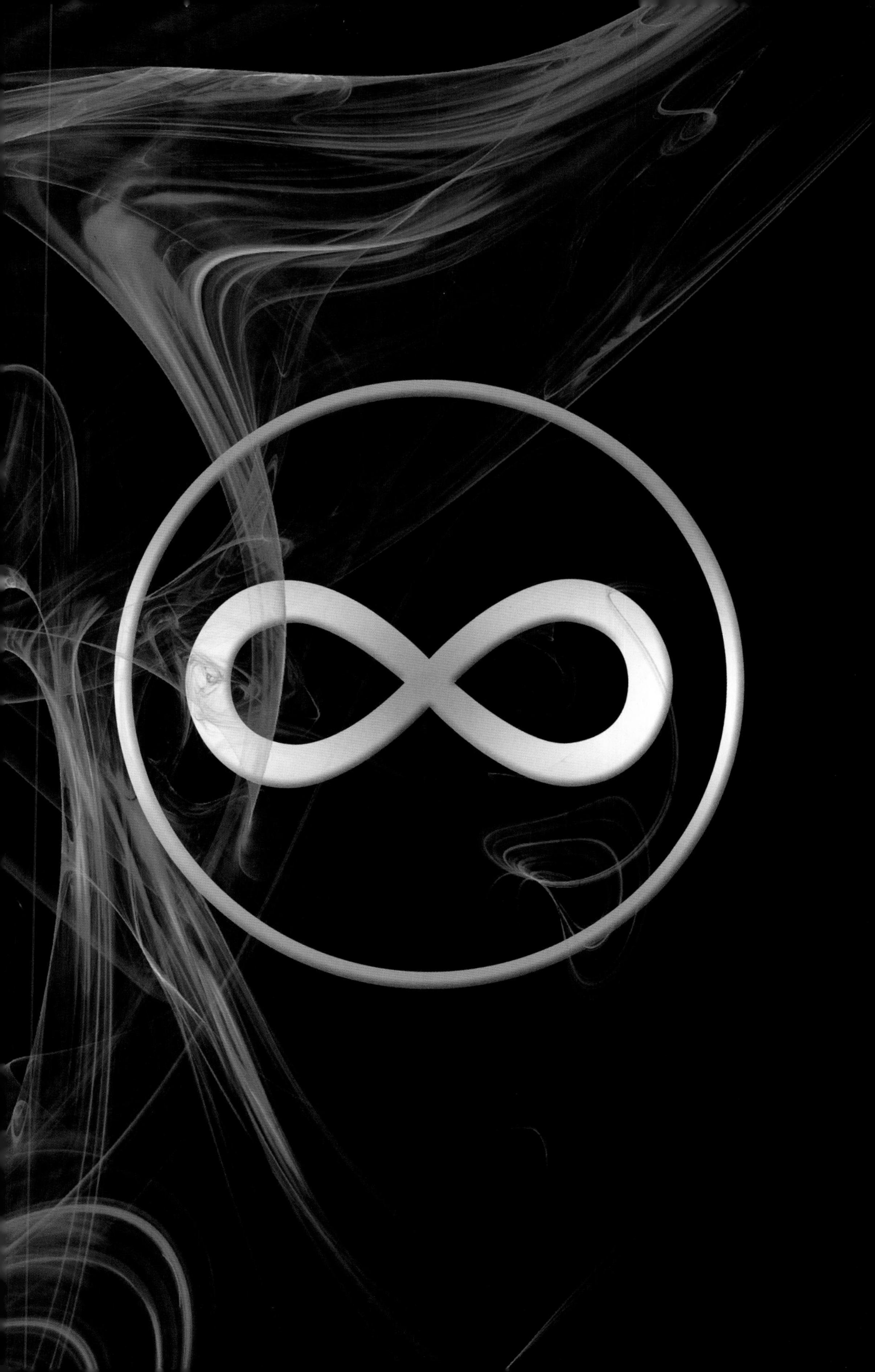

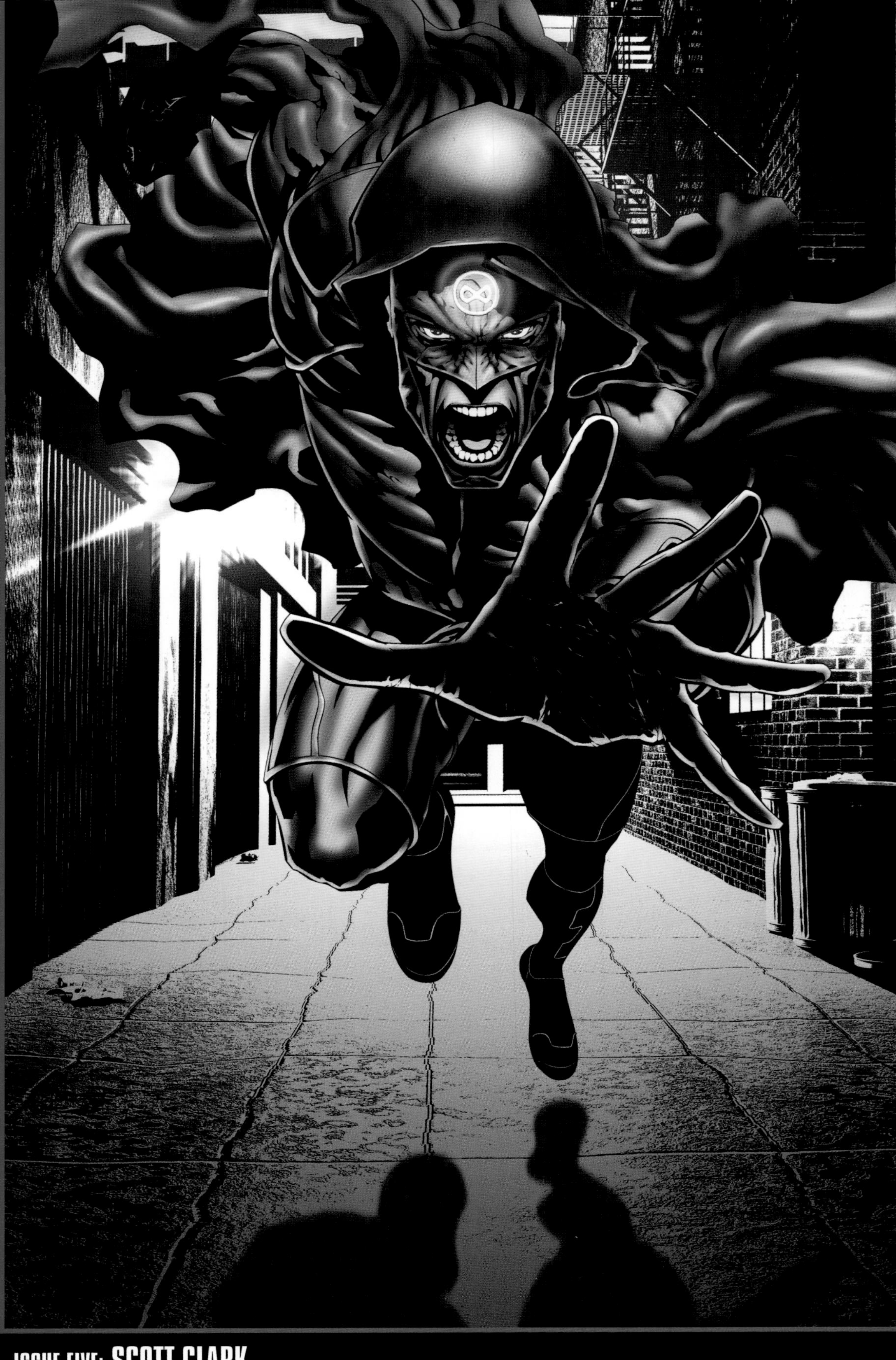

ISSUE FIVE: **SCOTT CLARK**

INKS: DAVE BEATY COLORS: JOE CESARIO

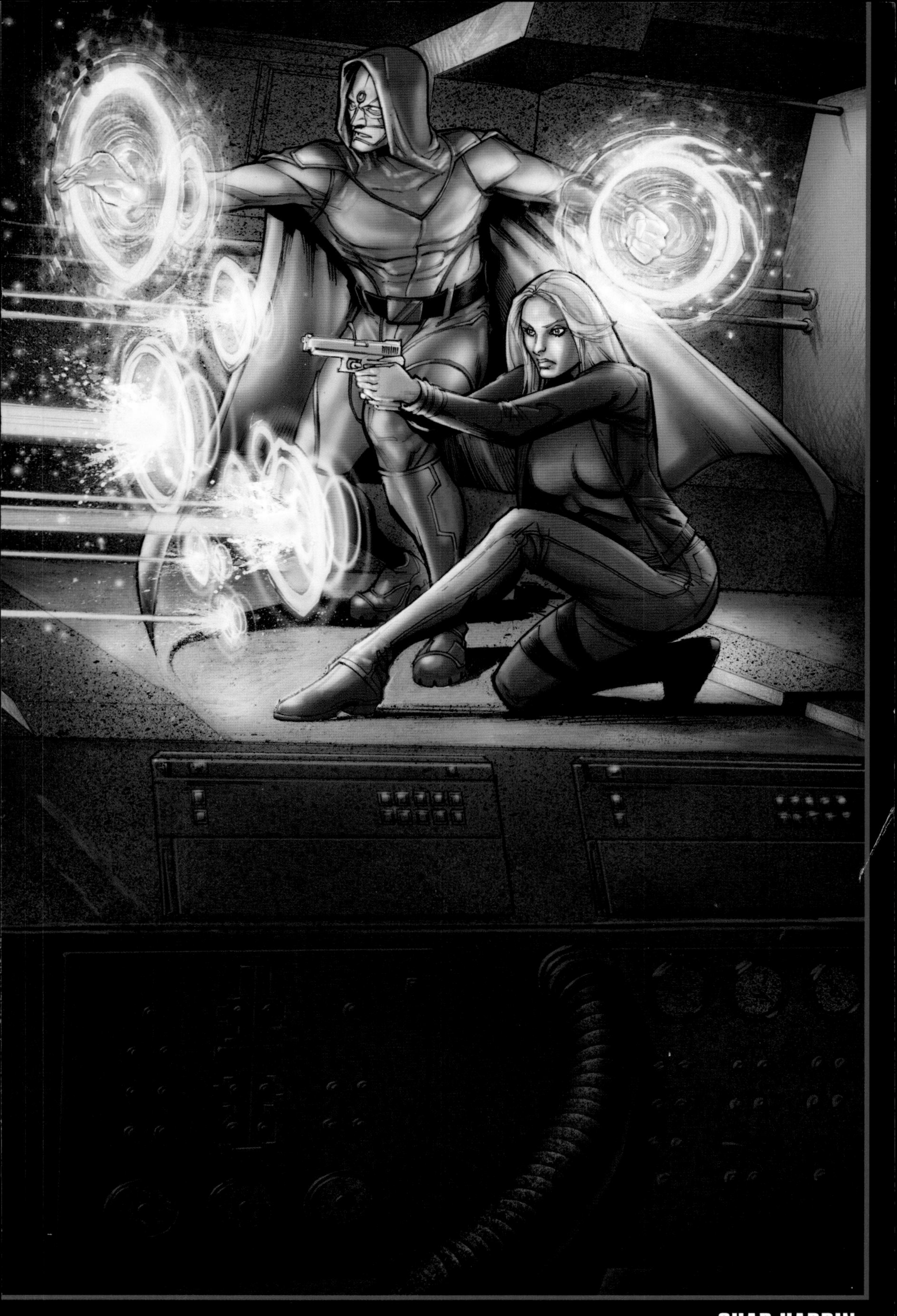

ISSUE FIVE: **CHAD HARDIN**
WITH ART LYON

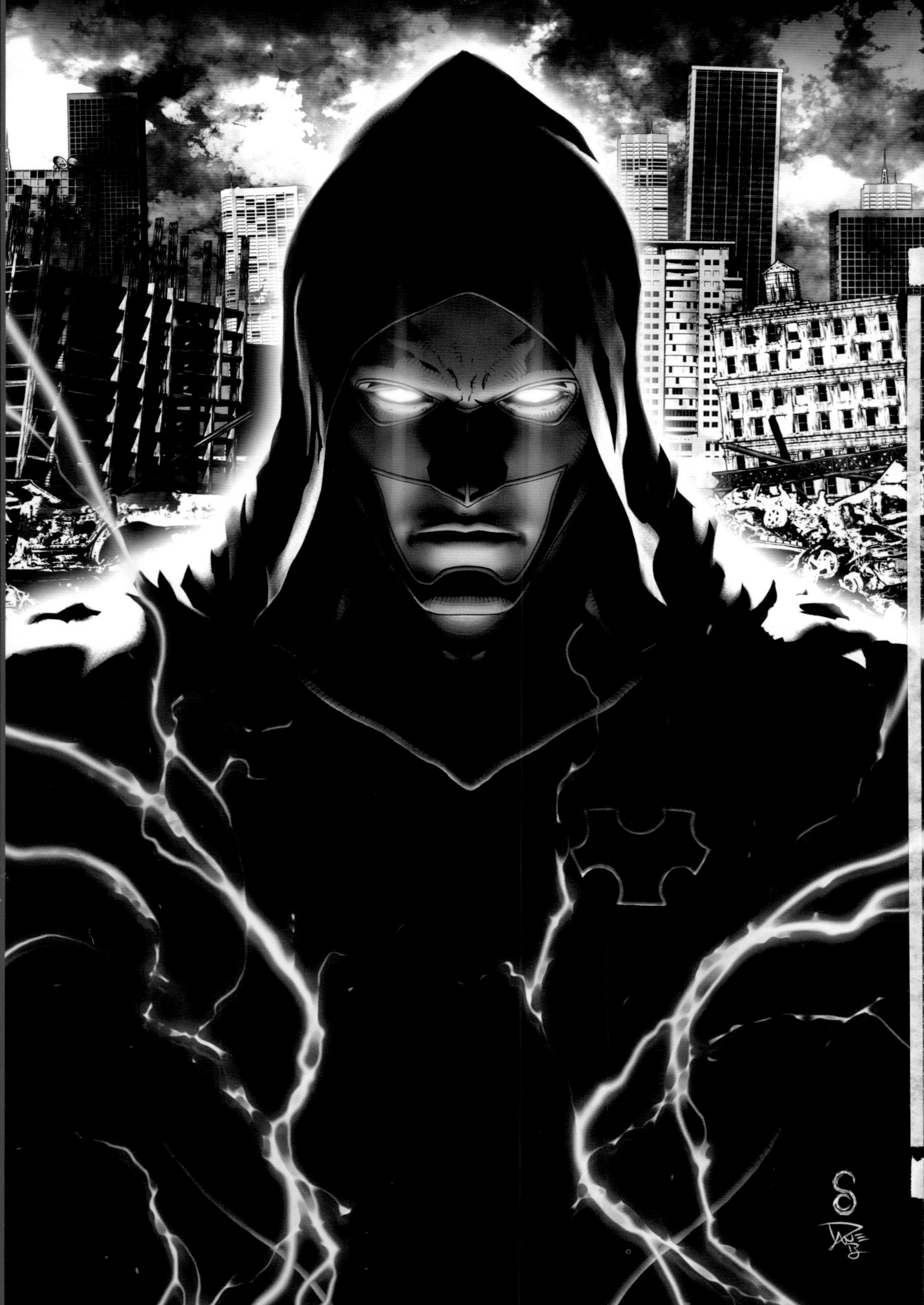

ISSUE SIX: SCOTT CLARK

INKS: DAVE BEATY COLORS: JOE CESARIO

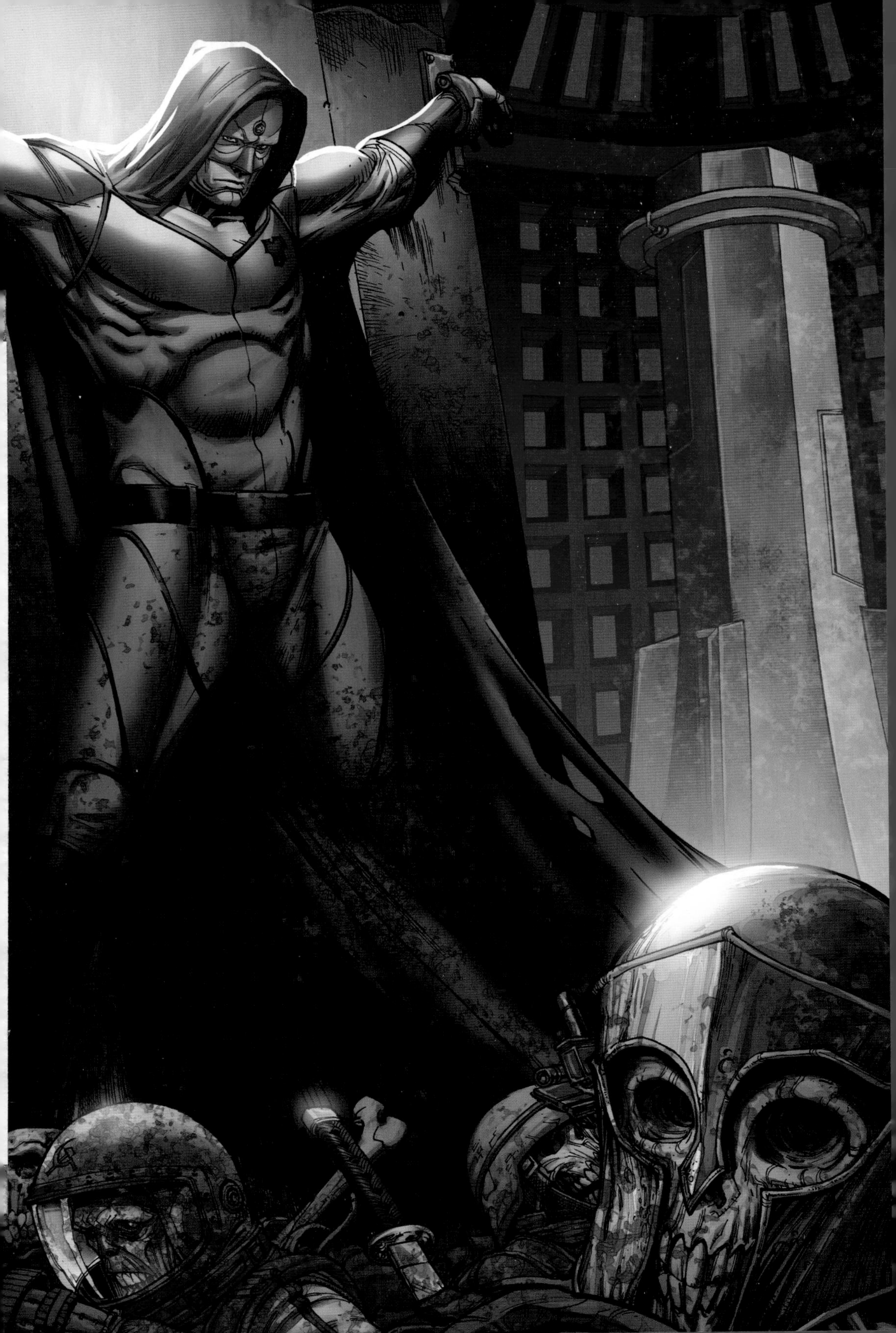

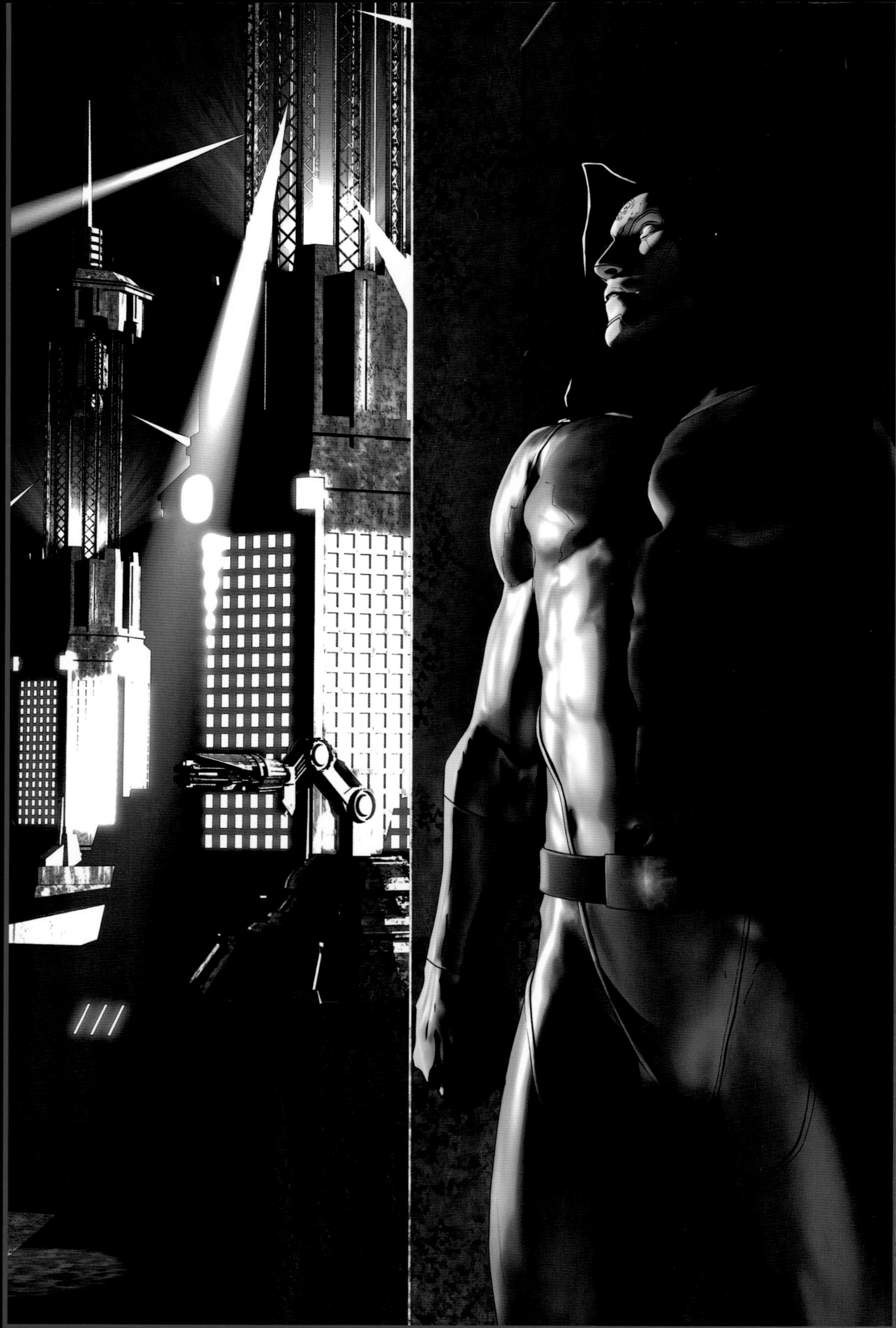

ISSUE SEVEN: SCOTT CLARK
WITH DAVE BEATY

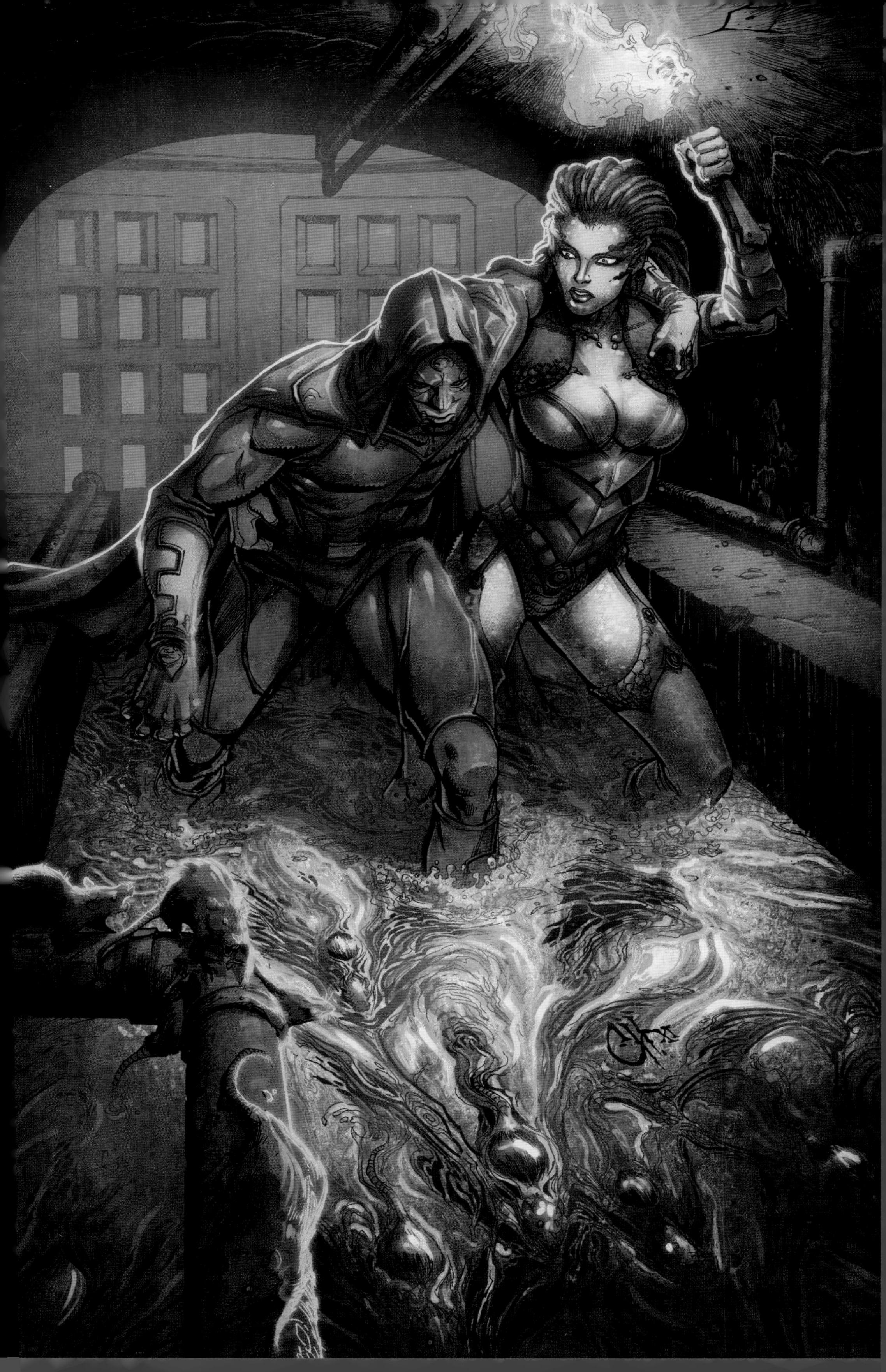

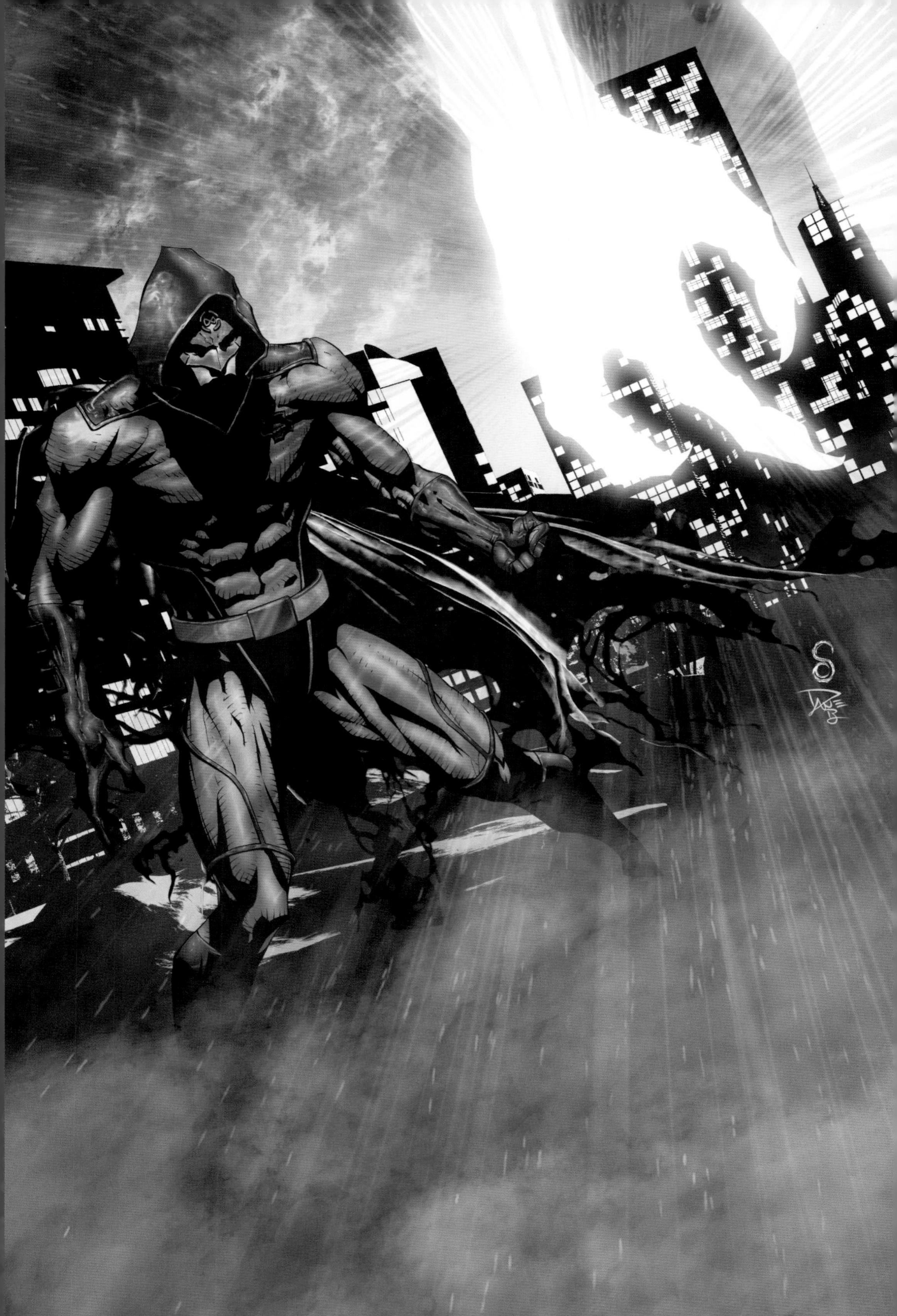

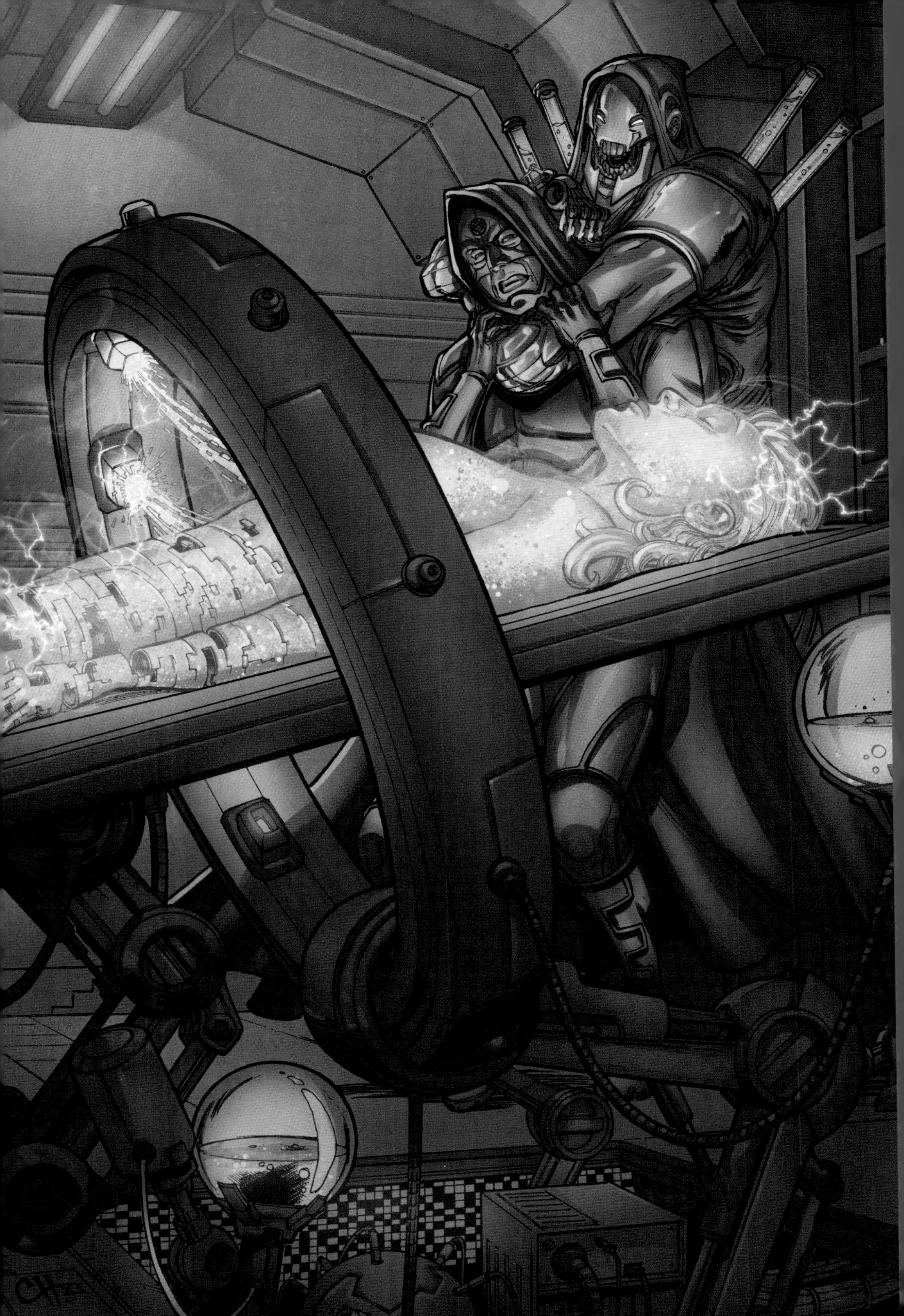

Stan Lee